EMPOWERING YOUR LIFE WITH DREAMS

Empowering Your Life with DREAMS

Sirona Knight

A member of Penguin Group (USA) Inc.

This book is dedicated to Skylor and Michael.

International Standard Book Number: 1-59257-092-5
Library of Congress Catalog Card Number: 2003111786

05 04 03 8 7 6 5 4 3 2 1

Interpretation of the printing code: The rightmost number of the first series of numbers is the year of the book's printing; the rightmost number of the second series of numbers is the number of the book's printing. For example, a printing code of 03-1 shows that the first printing occurred in 2003.

Printed in the United States of America

Publisher: Marie Butler-Knight
Product Manager: Phil Kitchel
Senior Managing Editor: Jennifer Chisholm
Senior Acquisitions Editor: Randy Ladenheim-Gil
Development Editor: Lynn Northrup
Copy Editor: Nancy Wagner
Cover Designer: Doug Wilkins
Book Designer: Trina Wurst
Creative Director: Robin Lasek
Indexer: Julie Bess
Layout: Becky Harmon

Contents

Introduction

The dream world is a mirrored image of the waking world and, as such, is a great place to practice life. It's a great place to discover what works and what doesn't work before you implement it into your life. This is what *Empowering Your Life with Dreams* is all about—finding the real you and living the life you've always dreamed of. The more you achieve with your dreams, the more empowering they become, and the more you become the person you want to be.

Dreams reflect the extraordinary experiences you have each time you go to sleep, as well as your hopes, desires, and expectations. *Empowering Your Life with Dreams* shows you how to integrate your dream reflections into a cohesive whole to empower your life. You will learn what dreams are, where they come from, and what your dreams are trying to tell you. You will also establish your dream goals for love, health, and abundance and determine how you can best attain them given enough effort and insight. Your dream goals reflect your full waking potential and what you can achieve given the chance. In this way, your sleeping dreams help you attain your waking dreams.

When establishing your dream goals, you need to get in touch with both the dreams you have each time you go to sleep and your hopes and desires for the future. They both reflect your dream self, which is a subtle extension of who you are, but without all of the social conditioning and ego associated with your waking self. The main benefit from setting dreams goals is that it gives you and your dreams a clear focus and direction.

Once you establish your dream goals, *Empowering Your Life with Dreams* shows you how to make functional dream plans that help you move forward toward your goals. Your sleeping dreams can help in this respect because of their inherent ability to provide useful information. Many famous people have applied their dreams to their work. These include scientists such as physicist Albert Einstein and inventor Thomas Edison, as well as creative artists such as author Robert Louis Stevenson and singer, composer, and musician Billy Joel. Dreams become a source of inspiration.

Dream empowerment tools can help you in your process. There are a variety of techniques, foods, and other tools that can affect the types of dreams you have. As you begin your empowerment quest, these dream tools become more important. If you were learning to play a musical instrument, the two tools you would most want would be a well-crafted instrument on which to learn and a superb teacher to teach you everything you need to know to be successful in your desire to play music. You can sometimes overcome not having the needed tools, but overall, having the needed tools for the job makes attaining your dream goals for love, health, and abundance a lot easier in the long run.

Often the biggest obstacle for most of us is remembering our dreams when we wake up. When we are lucky enough to remember our dream, trying to figure out its meaning becomes a jumbled puzzle. To help you overcome these obstacles, I've included several easy-to-follow techniques for remembering and interpreting your dreams.

When interpreting your dreams, always remember your dreams are best understood in terms of your personal perceptions and what is happening in your life at the particular time of the dream. Sometimes it can be helpful to reference dream symbols and their meanings such as in the Dream Interpretation Symbols list in Appendix A. You can also talk with others and get their feedback as to what is happening in your dreams. At the same time, keep in mind that only you truly know what your dreams really mean, as they are a reflection of your inner self.

Also included in this book are straightforward methods for tapping into the power of the ancient art of dream incubation. It is a dream technique in which you incubate a question or request over a period of time. Then using meditation, ritual, prayer, and affirmation, you bring the information you require to the foreground within your dreams. By incubating your dream requests and questions, you essentially create an energetic dream egg, incubate it, and eventually hatch it. As it hatches, so, too, does the answer or information you required.

In addition to incubation, another intriguing avenue of dreaming is communicating with your animal helpers. Most of us have pets and animals we resonate with energetically. Within the waking world, our pet companions are our friends and like members of our family. Within the dream world, animals and pets can act as powerful dream helpers who provide valuable knowledge and skills. By forging a positive dream relationship with your animal helpers, it becomes easier to attain your dream empowerment goals. With a little help from your animal friends, your chances for success greatly increase.

As shown through dream research and personal experience, time moves much differently in dreams. Dreamtime is the time of the "eternal now," where there is no specific past, present, or future, but instead everything becomes One. In dream, you can move forward and backward in time at will and in less than an instant.

Just as time becomes fluid and flexible while dreaming, so, too, does space and matter. Shapes shift in odd and mysterious ways; worlds alter and melt before you; and images blend into one another like a surreal collage. The beauty of this fluidity is that you can use it to transform and shape shift your dream world and waking life.

By changing how you dream about yourself, you begin to change your overall perception of who you are. By becoming who you want to be in your dreams, you need then only to move that image over through the dream mirror into your waking reality. Self-confidence in dreams translates into self-confidence in waking. The two worlds are energetically related in ways that we are only now beginning to understand. Interestingly, shamans from many different indigenous cultures have been exploring and utilizing the connection between dreaming and waking for thousands of years.

One of the most powerful techniques for transforming your dreams into your waking reality is lucid dreaming. It coalesces your waking world with your dream world. In lucid dreaming you are aware when you are dreaming and you are aware when you are awake. In a practical sense this means that if you are having a nightmare, you suddenly realize that it is a dream. In that realization, your awareness shifts and you can then either wake yourself up or actively direct and change the dream just as a director directs a movie. It's a lot like "Windows" on a computer where with the press of a button, you can shift back and forth between the dream world and the waking world. The implications and applications are far-reaching, not to mention fascinating!

Above all, dreams are a stepping-stone for moving in the direction you want to move. When you finally attain your dream empowerment goals, you feel a sensation within yourself that is far beyond anything words could possibly hope to express. When the emotion wells up inside you and your spirit soars, you know you have experienced a true moment of empowerment. By using the powerful dream techniques in this book, you can experience these empowering moments each and every day of your life.

How to Use This Book

The 12 chapters of *Empowering Your Life with Dreams* provide you with a wide selection of practical New Age dream techniques. All of these hands-on techniques are easy to do and apply to your daily life. They are intended to empower you by helping you realize your deepest dreams for love, health, and abundance.

Chapters 1, 2, and 3 offer straightforward steps for setting your dream goals, creating a dream plan, and finding the best dream tools and focals. Chapters 4, 5, and 6 explain how you can better remember your dreams, interpret your dreams, enact your dream plan, and take the necessary steps to realize your goals for love, health, and abundance. Chapters 7 and 8 help you to expand your dream awareness, answer questions, and resolve problems using your dreams; while Chapter 9 explores the concept of directing your own dreams and becoming a lucid dreamer. Chapters 10, 11, and 12 offer methods for manifesting your dream goals, enjoying the rewards to dream empowerment, and ways for reviewing your dream goals for the future.

Above all, the empowering methods in this book provide practical ways for positively transforming your life using your dreams. So go ahead and step through the dream doorway, learn to direct the power of your dreams, and create the life you have always dreamed of!

Acknowledgments

I would like to gratefully acknowledge one of the most empowering and inspiring women I know, Randy Ladenheim-Gil, senior acquisitions editor at Alpha Books. Thank you, Randy, for your encouragement, support, and enthusiasm! Many heartfelt thanks to Lynn Northrup, my development editor, for her fine efforts, intuitive editing, and for being such a dream to work with! I would also like to respectfully thank my publisher, Marie Butler-Knight, for the opportunity to write this book.

And many sincere thanks to my senior production editor, Christy Wagner; my copy editor, Nancy Wagner; my senior managing editor, Jennifer Chisholm; product manager, Phil Kitchel; creative director, Robin Lasek; and everyone at Alpha Books for their time and excellent work. In addition, I would like to thank my family and friends, as well as each and every person who reads this book and uses the methods within it to empower her or his dreams in positive ways. May your dreams always be pleasant and lucid!

Chapter One

Setting Your Dream Goals

Some time ago a man dreamed that he should go to the bridge at Regensburg where he would become rich. He went there, and after spending some 14 days there, a wealthy merchant, who wondered why the man was spending so much time on the bridge, approached him and asked him what he was doing there.

"I dreamed that I was to go to the bridge at Regensburg, where I would become rich," answered the man.

"What?" said the merchant, "You came here because of a dream? Dreams are fantasies and lies. Why, I myself dreamed that there is a large pot of gold buried beneath that large tree over there." And he pointed to the tree. "But I paid no attention, for dreams are fantasies."

Afterward the visitor dug beneath the tree where he found a great treasure that made him rich, and thus his dream was confirmed.

This German folktale, titled "The Dream of the Treasure on the Bridge," by Jacob and Wilhelm Grimm, gives an interesting contrast on dreams. On one hand, we have the person who completely believes and follows her dreams. On the other, we have the skeptic, who sometimes has dreams but believes that they are fantasies and have no meaning in the so-called "real world." The problem with this idea is that there are multitudes of people who have used their dreams to enrich and empower themselves beyond belief. Basically, this is the essence of dream empowerment: using your dreams to their fullest potential.

This idea of skeptics reminds me of a dinner party I was invited to recently where one of the guests, a conservative businessman, began talking about how he didn't dream and that dreams had no significance in his life. He finished his whole dismissal by saying that no one really cared about dreams anyway, that dreams were just dreams and not real. He went on to talk about how life is about the practical world and not about a bunch of meaningless dreams.

Almost immediately, everyone at the table begin talking at once, all loudly disagreeing with the businessman. Several guests shared their dreams and explained that, on several occasions, their dreams had helped them in some real and practical way. One woman told of a dream she had had of her husband before she met and married him. A young athlete told about food dreams he often had when he needed certain nutrients and vitamins. A teenage girl told of a dream about trying on clothes just before she got a part-time job in a clothing boutique.

It was amazing how so many of us at the dinner table had used our dreams to enrich and empower our lives in some way. By the end of the evening over tea and coffee, even the businessman finally admitted that a couple of times he had remembered dreaming dreams that had helped him make more positive business decisions.

This made me realize that there is a realness to dreams that equals any other reality I have experienced. Dreams provide information that people can either use or ignore. "Empowering your life with dreams" provides ways for tapping into and utilizing the information that your dreams impart to you. With six or seven dreams occurring each time you go to sleep, the information quickly compiles into an enormous database that you need to learn to access.

Dreams give wings to your creative spirit and can help you discover your full potential. Dreaming is a physical, mental, and spiritual experience that often provides an open doorway to deeper levels of awareness. It is through this dream doorway that some of the best songs, books, works of art, and inventions have been inspired. They were first seen as images that appeared in dreams.

Music producer Quincy Jones has said that when inspiration comes to you when you're dreaming, if you don't get up and do something about it, then it just moves on to the next person's house. One person who did something about it was Sir Paul McCartney. He has often told the story of how the melody for his song "Yesterday" came in a dream, and initially, until he worked out the lyrics, he used the phrase "scrambled eggs" as the temporary title. In a recent survey "Yesterday" was voted the number-one song of all time. This just goes to show that dreams can be solid gold in more ways than one, but only as long as you're paying attention and willing to do something with the information they give you.

Everyone Is a Dreamer

Everyone is a dreamer in the sense that we all dream. In fact, scientific researchers estimate that out of a lifetime, five to six years are spent dreaming! Rather than waste or ignore this time, we need to acknowledge and work with our dreams so that they become invaluable tools for self-development. When people realize the full potential of dreams and how they can move them into reality, there will be more dreamers than history has ever encountered, trying to create an atmosphere of peace and love.

Dreams, by virtue, are portals into the inner self. The life-affirming techniques provided in this book will help you tap into the natural power of your dreams to discover who you are in terms of your goals, and from there, to help you integrate your inner and outer self and help you make your dreams come true.

Whether or not you remember your dreams, you do have dream experiences. These dream experiences have universal significance and can be used in real and practical ways. Beginning in the 1950s, scientific researchers began studying and documenting the human sleep cycle. Their results provided insights into the inner workings of the realm of dreams.

Researchers discovered that most people experienced certain patterns of sleep that moved from periods of slow eye movement to periods when there was what they termed "REM" or "Rapid Eye Movement." During these periods of REM sleep, a person's brain is more active in terms of neural impulses than when the person is awake. Most everyone, except extreme manic-depressives and psychotics, experiences periods of REM sleep during their normal sleep cycle.

In Western culture, many people are not encouraged to remember their dreams because it is not as socially accepted as it is in other cultures. Fortunately, with the growing interest in all things New Age, this concept is rapidly changing.

For thousands of years, Eastern spiritual traditions have been using dreams to evolve to higher states of awareness that lead to enlightenment. In Eastern culture, it is accepted that one's dream body has experiences separate from one's waking body, and when both the dream body and the waking body become integrated into one, empowering, even miraculous, things start happening.

The Nature of Dreams

As part of negotiations with Hera during the Trojan War, Hypnos, the Greek god of sleep, was wed to Aglia (Brightness). She was one of the three Graces, the others being the goddesses of loveliness and charm. The union of Hypnos and Aglia produced a thousand offspring known as the Oneiros, who attended to people's dreams. Of these, the main three were Morpheus, god of dreams about people who could shape shift into any person; Ikelos or Phobetor, god of dreams about animals who could shape shift into any animal; and Phantasos, god of dreams about inanimate objects who could shape shift into any inanimate object.

In particular, Morpheus's name means "the shaper," and as such, he could lead people through the "Gates of Horn," which was the origin of false dreams, or through the "Gates of Ivory," which was the origin of dreams that come true. Because of this belief, people going to sleep often asked for the blessings of Morpheus so their dreams would come true.

The ancient Greeks built dream temples dedicated to Aesculapius, the god of healing. Beds were placed in the temples, and people would come to seek healing help from the god through their dreams. Using prayer, meditation, and ritual, they would connect their dreams with the divine energy that would help them to move toward better health.

This Greek notion that dreams were gifts from the divine is an idea that permeated early perceptions of dreams, especially in the Western part of the world, where biblical references to divine dreams are numerous and include Joseph's dream where God tells him of the coming of his son, the Christ child.

Only later were dreams and their divine connection condemned as demonic by the Christian Inquisition and characterized as fantasies or delusions of the unconscious mind by the emerging scientific community. Today, both spirituality and science are investigating the deeper and empowering levels of dreams that connect not only with the divine but also with the multiple aspects of the individual. Because of this, dreams can be one of the most effective means for personal growth and for manifesting your goals.

Within the nature of dreams, each person is like two people—a waking self and a dream self. These two selves are often aware of each other but sometimes don't always communicate as much as they could. The dream self is not just a nighttime creature but also has a tendency to come around during the day, during daydreams, for example.

Like many altered states of being, the dream world moves beyond the defined boundaries of time and space. The dream self dwells in the dream world and experiences life each time you go to sleep and dream. Both the dream world and dream self are reflections of you, the dreamer. At the same time, the dream self seems to have a life of its own.

The dream self, rather than being one entity, is actually more like a combination of multiple selves. These many selves are all part of you, but only come out when you dream or have other altered state experiences such as alpha or trance states. These multiple selves represent the various aspects of you that exist beyond your physical body. Names given to describe some of these other bodies or selves include, but are not limited to, the etheric, the astral, the mental, the spiritual, the cosmic, and the nirvanic.

Scientific research suggests that dreams emanate from the central cortex of the brain, that part representing the inner reaches of who you are, were, and will be. In a basic sense dreams are your mind's way of working out the internal dilemmas that you encounter on a daily basis. In the process, you are moving through your multiple selves, trying to resolve the perceived separations between them all, moving your dream and waking selves toward a wholeness or oneness.

The dream techniques in this book are designed to help you, the reader, integrate your multiple selves into a workable whole, an empowered one, that will help you manifest your deepest dreams and experience your life to its fullest potential. That is what empowering your life with dreams is all about. Dare to dream your dearest dreams, create them, and experience them, right now!

How Dreams Affect Your Life

Albert Einstein had a dream in which he was sliding down a mountain on a sled, and as he moved faster, he looked up and saw that the stars appeared to move out of shape. After waking, he recognized the implications of the dream, which he interpreted to mean that the speed of light distorts matter. This idea formed the foundation for Einstein's famous "Theory of Relativity," a concept so profound that it revolutionized the way in which physicists perceived the space/time continuum and the universe as a whole.

Einstein's dream gave a focus to his life's mission that revolved around his scientific theories. It affected everyone else's life as well. Suddenly the idea that time was somehow fixed became obsolete, replaced by the idea that time is relative and, as such, can change. Space and time linear become curved and operate on simultaneous levels. Like dreams, there are places in the continuum where space and time seem almost suspended or standing still.

As shown with Einstein's experience, dreams come in many forms and, as such, influence life in a variety of ways. Dreams can be insightful, inspirational, healing, prophetic, out of body, otherworldly, amusing, enriching, disturbing, nightmarish, frightening, enlightening, questioning, and empowering, to name just a few. Your multiple selves experience multiple dreams in multiple ways, and in multiple worlds. This reflects the infinite possibilities in dreams.

Because dreams stem from the inner reaches of your brain, they tell you a lot about yourself. As powerful empowerment tools for self discovery, your dreams can help you access your dream goals, an essential part of the empowerment process. After all, when you know where you want to go, it makes getting there so much easier.

When determining your dream goals, your calling in terms of love, health, and abundance, take your time and be realistic. Use your dreams to gain insights into your inner self, a persona that you often keep hidden from the external world. Keep in mind that dreams are a personal experience that you may or may not want to share with the outside world. They sometimes reveal more about yourself than you care to expose, so be selective about with whom you share your dreams.

Dreams give you an inner look at yourself that may not be otherwise visible, and when determining your goals, this can be invaluable. Dreams are a personal tool you can use to empower yourself. Many of your own dreams reveal information that is for your eyes only, and relevant only to you. They tell you things about yourself that only you or extensions of yourself should know. Remember, when you become your dream, you become empowered, and the ideal sings in harmony with the real.

Determining Your Dream Goals

Your deepest dreams are like a constellation of goals that fit together into one. The idea is to manifest each of your goals, and in the process, make your dreams come true and empower your life physically, mentally, and spiritually.

Goals and dreams work hand in hand in that once you start attaining your goals, your dearest dreams also start manifesting. In this sense, goals help you achieve your dreams, and your dreams help you be who you truly want to be.

Attaining your goals builds a foundation for your deepest dreams to come to fruition. This is why it's important to have a clear vision of your dreams as well as the goals you need to manifest to make those dreams happen. They combine to empower your life and to make your ideal and real one and the same.

Every time you set a dream goal and then achieve it, the process empowers you. Empowerment comes through understanding and utilizing the personal power that is already part of you. Determining your dream goals is the beginning of the process where you become aware of your potential and start making choices as to who you are and what you want to do. As you make your choices and set your goals, go ahead and dare to aspire to great heights and be who you want and do what you want with respect to your dreams.

Your goals need to be specific, measurable, attainable, within reach, and timely.

There is an obvious practicality to almost everything, including dream goals. At the same time, don't let the practical box you in and decide your dream empowerment goals for you. This also applies to other people in your life. Listen and even possibly utilize their advice, but avoid letting them make your goal choices for you. Ultimately, you alone must determine your dream goals.

The word *goal* is defined in *Webster's Dictionary* as "the end toward which effort is directed." When you set your empowerment goals, you are setting your sights on the things that you are going to work toward to make your life the way you want it to be.

Dreams are a means for determining what your true goals are in life. Oftentimes people pursue opportunities because of circumstances rather than choice. Most people take jobs because they are available and convenient and not because that is their desire in life. It's important to color your world through your choices rather than let your world paint you into a corner because of your lack of choices. This is why it's important to select your own dream goals.

As you begin determining your dream goals, one of the first things you will need to get is a dream empowerment journal. Use a spiral notebook, a binder filled with blank paper, or, if you prefer, a decorative writing book to start recording your dreams as well as your empowerment goals as you dream about them. At this beginning stage, don't worry about writing everything down; one of things you are trying to do is to keep your dreams free of boundaries for the moment. The idea at this point in the dream empowerment process is to get in touch with your dreams and in turn with who you are. Your journal will become more important as you progress, but for now it's important to create it and start using it.

Another extremely useful tool for tapping into your dreams, one that I use every morning, is a small handheld tape recorder. You can keep it by your bed and record your dreams when you wake up and then transcribe them into your dream empowerment journal later in the day. I am able to get more details about my dreams by using a tape recorder. I don't have to focus as much as I do when I write down words. At first, I thought I wouldn't be able to understand my sleepy voice over the recorder, but I found that I could easily understand my voice. I also find that there are things about my dreams that I have completely forgotten in a few hours when I go back to the recording. I wholeheartedly suggest you use a small tape recorder to better understand your dreams and tap into their immense natural power. You can also use it to record the guided meditations in this book in your own voice to make them easier to use and more personal.

Dream Empowerment Techniques

Robert Louis Stevenson, author of such classics as *Treasure Island,* readily admitted using dreams for inspiration. In his autobiography, *Across the Plains,* he states that he called upon his "dream helpers," who often aided him in his story ideas. In particular, the story "Dr. Jekyll and Mr. Hyde" was the result of a dream.

The concept of the dream helper is universal. Helpers come in many forms, from goddesses and angels to spirit guides and ancestors. The dream techniques in this book are intended to help you connect with your dream helpers as well as your dream self. By integrating these aspects of dreaming with your waking self, you become whole again.

Dreams help you to recognize your many personalities, and the empowerment process helps you to integrate these personalities into one so that they create a powerful, unified whole. When you bring divine energy into the equation, for instance, dreaming with a dream helper, that's when miraculous things begin happening.

The dream empowerment process described in this book is expressed in terms of love, health, and abundance. Love deals with your relationships, health with your overall well-being, and abundance with the things that you value in life—physically, mentally, and spiritually. These areas overlap into one another, meaning that you can adapt many of the techniques for use in the other areas.

Each of the love, health, and abundance sections include suggestions for setting up a sacred dream space, a dream ritual, a dream meditation, a dream prayer, a dream oracle, and a dream affirmation. These techniques will help you tap into the power of your dreams and empower you, making it easier to get both what you need and want in life.

Your sacred *dream space* is an area, preferably near your bed, where you set the items you will need in the dream techniques to help you in your dreams. In a sense, it is your dream altar or sacred table. It becomes the place where your dreams connect with the divine, the place where dreams truly become magical.

With just a few dollars spent on candles, scented oils, and flowers, you can create a luxurious atmosphere and dreamy altar setting for manifesting your dream empowerment goals. I have also made suggestions as to ritual focals (such as essential oils, candles, and crystals) and power objects you may want to put in your sacred space or altar.

For the purpose of this book, you can create three separate dream empowerment spaces for love, health, and abundance. If you like, you can combine the three spaces and altars into one. I find this is usually more convenient and practical and doesn't deter from the intention of the techniques.

The *dream rituals* are intended to create environments and states of awareness conducive to dream empowerment. The rituals presented in this book include everything from a ritual bath, a romantic midnight picnic, and the use of a dream catcher, to making dream pillows, dream aromatherapy, and positive dream invocations. In rituals, you work in rapport with the elements, the divine, and create a magical circle to work in that joins the ordinary world with the sacred. Rituals make your dream empowerment goals more accessible.

Followers of Eastern spiritual traditions such as Buddhism and Hinduism have for centuries practiced meditation as a means for becoming one with the divine. Because of its health benefits, such as lowering blood pressure and lessening anxiety and depression, meditation has been rapidly gaining in practice throughout the world.

In his book *The Best Guide to Meditation,* Victor N. Davich defines meditation as the art of opening to each moment of life with calm awareness. The effects of meditation include a state of deep relaxation. Your heartbeat rate, oxygen consumption, perspiration, muscle tension, and blood pressure all decrease. You feel calm and peaceful, yet your mind remains alert. This sensation of being relaxed yet alert is one that meditation and dreams share, which is why they work so well together.

The *dream meditations* in this book are guided meditations. They take you on journeys to the world of dreams and beyond. They are intended to give you a better understanding of both your waking self and your dream self, and in the process, integrate the two. Once this happens, you can set and align yourself with your dream empowerment goals, as well as gain the focus and direction you need to attain them.

The *dream prayer* is a suggestion you give yourself, while at the same time a request for divine help. Repeated, the prayer meaning penetrates your psyche, setting the stage for dreams that help in your empowerment process. No matter what divine energy you invoke when you pray, prayer positively influences your empowerment process.

When you pray, a prayer field is created. When you pray before you go to sleep, this prayer field carries over into the dream world. When this happens, divine help and guidance more readily appear in your dreams.

Because the dream meditation and dream prayer are to be done just before you go to sleep, you may want to record them in your own voice to make them more powerful and for convenience. If you prefer, you can have your partner, friend, or family member slowly read the meditation to you. When opting for this method, I suggest you put on some pleasing New Age or instrumental music to enhance the experience. Another easy way to do the meditations in this book is to read the meditation to yourself, sentence by sentence, closing your eyes after each sentence or paragraph and imagining the actions and images in the meditation as you read along.

Before meditating, be sure to turn off your cell phone if you have one, turn on your answering machine, volume down all the way and the ringer off, or if you prefer, just unplug your phone for a while. Let any other people in the house know that you will be meditating and don't want to be interrupted. Also, put your pets out of the room as they can be distracting.

Relax but keep your mind alert during the meditation, and then as you go to sleep, repeat the prayer to yourself. The meditation and prayer essentially set up your expectation as to what you want to dream about during your coming sleep period.

The *dream oracle* is performed after you awaken. After writing down everything you can remember from your dreams, consult the oracle. The oracles are everything from playing cards, to messages from nature, television programs, and Internet sites. The purpose of the dream oracle technique is to help you interpret and better understand the significance of your dreams.

An affirmation is a positive and empowering statement. By continually repeating this statement to yourself throughout the day, you gradually take the positive, empowering message of the affirmation and move it from your conscious to your subconscious mind. By doing so, you start to believe in yourself and your abilitiy to achieve your dream goals. Keep in mind, you can always adapt and personalize the *dream affirmations* provided to better suit your needs, preferences, and spiritual path.

Your sacred space, ritual, meditation, and prayer all help you with dreaming, whereas the dream oracle and affirmation are more for helping you with the interpretation and implementation of your dreams. In the dream world anything is possible, and when you move it over into the "real" world, that's when dreams come true.

When doing these dream techniques, use each group of exercises for three nights. First, do the love exercises for three nights, then the health ones, and lastly the abundance exercises. If after this you don't have a clear focus of your dream empowerment goals, repeat the process until you get a clear expectation of your goals.

Love

Your love goals have to do with the relationships in your life, especially with lovers, family, and friends. Use your dreams to determine what kind of relationships you want to have with these various people. Be clear on how you want your relationships with them to become in the future. Consider what makes you happy and the nature of your relationship with your primary partner. The beautiful thing about dreams is that you can play out an entire scenario in your dream, thus trying it on, so to speak, in real life. In this sense, dreams are like dressing rooms where you can try on the many costumes of life.

When determining your dream empowerment goals for love, begin by getting better acquainted with who you are as a person. In your dream empowerment journal, make a list of your needs. These are the things that you feel you absolutely have to have in terms of your relationships. Next, make a list of your desires, which are the things that you would like to have in your relationships. Each relationship in your life is different, and consequently your needs and desires are oftentimes different. The relationship you have with each of your parents contrasts with the relationship you have with your primary partner. Because of these differences, you might feel a need to create a separate list of your needs and desires for each of the significant relationships in your life.

As windows to your inner self, dreams offer an excellent view for understanding who you are and determining your needs and desires. Think back on dreams you have had, especially reoccurring ones, for insights on your true nature. How do you perceive yourself when dreaming?

What types of relationships do you have in your dreams? How do these compare or contrast to the relationships you have in waking life? The more you explore who your dream self is, the more you learn about your waking self.

Once you have a better understanding of who you are, the next step is to begin seeing yourself in relationships with people who fulfill your needs and desires. Again, you can use your dreams to experience different types of relationships with different people, transporting yourself ahead in time and seeing how a particular situation might unfold. In this way, you can use your dreams to try things on and get a sense of how they fit. Often, it is wise to act and feel things out in your dreams first, then to act them out in waking reality.

For best results, follow the dream techniques as they are presented as a seamless whole. First set up your sacred space, then do the ritual, media-tion, and dream prayer just before going to sleep. Upon waking, record and/or write down everything you recall from your dreams, and then use the oracle to clarify your dreams and personal goals as well as to guide you onward. To complete the process, repeat the affirmation at least nine times a day while you are determining your dream empowerment goals for love. You can repeat the process as many times as you like.

Sacred Love Dream Space

Your sacred love space is an area by your bedside. It includes a sacred love altar, which can be a nightstand, table, bureau top, or bookshelf by your bed where you can set tools and focals to be used with the dream-ing techniques. Also keep your dream empowerment journal in your sacred love space so that it is handy for recording your dreams, impres-sions, and dream empowerment goals for love. As you continue to progress through the techniques in each of the chapters, you will use and add to the items in your sacred love space.

Begin by collecting three red roses in a vase of water, rose-scented oil, a red votive candle in a holder, your dream empowerment journal, and a pen. Empower these items by holding them in your hands, one at time, and saying three times:

I empower this item with divine and sacred light.

Dream Ritual for Love

The purpose of this ritual is to help you clarify and determine your dream empowerment goals for love. You will need the three red roses, a red votive candle and holder, rose-scented oil, and dream empowerment journal from your sacred love altar, and some dreamy New Age or instrumental love music (without lyrics).

Put the roses in a vase on your love altar in your bedroom. Then go into the bathroom and fill your bathtub with warm water, adding nine drops of rose oil. Dim the lights and turn on a recording of your favorite love songs. Imagine a bright sphere of white light completely encircling you and your bath area. Then invite the elements into your ritual space by simply saying:

I respectfully invite the elements of earth, air, fire, water, and spirit into my sacred ritual space.

Before entering the bath, light the red candle, and as you do so say three times:

I ask for divine help in clarifying and determining my dream empowerment goals for love.

Next, put the candle in a place that is both safe and easily visible from the bathtub.

Immerse yourself in the bath. Take several slow, deep breaths to relax even more, and allow the fragrant, relaxing qualities of the warm water to fill your senses. As you breathe in, imagine breathing in pure energy. As you breathe out, let go of all the unwanted energies, worries, and tension that you may be feeling. Feel the stress of the day being washed away, flowing out of your body, and being neutralized in the warm water.

Now breathe normally and sit back comfortably in the bathtub. Focus on the candle flame, and repeat over and over:

I am clarifying and determining my dearest dream empowerment goals for love.

After doing this for at least five minutes, let your mind flow freely. Give yourself the suggestion that the dream techniques and your dreams will help you clarify and determine your dream empowerment goals for love.

When you are done, get out of the tub and towel off. As you do this, chant:

I am clarifying and determining my love goals.

Thank the divine and the elements by saying:

I thank the divine and the elements for their helpful presence and blessings.

Then visualize stepping out of the sphere of white light you imagined at the beginning of the ritual, and imagine the sphere diffusing into the air around you. Make a note of any dream empowerment goals for love that came to mind during the ritual bath in your dream empowerment journal. Be sure to date your entry.

You can either leave the music on or turn it off for the love meditation. If you leave the music on, realize that unless it has an automatic shutoff, it may be on the entire time you are sleeping.

Snuff out the candle and relight it the next day and safely burn it down. (Never leave a lit candle unattended!)

Dream Meditation for Love

The purpose of this meditation is to encourage dreams that will significantly help you clarify and determine your dream empowerment goals for love. After your ritual bath, sit or recline comfortably in bed. Hold the roses in your hands and breathe in their heady fragrance for a few minutes. Then set the roses back on your love altar. Settle back again and get a little more comfortable.

Begin to breathe deeply and completely. Breathe in for three heartbeats, still your breath for three heartbeats, and then breathe out for three heartbeats. Repeat this three times. As you breathe in, imagine breathing in the color rose. As you breathe out, imagine any residue tension flowing out of you.

Now close your eyes, and in your mind's eye, imagine a clear mountain stream. Breathe in deeply through your mouth, then pulse your breath sharply out through your nose and plant that image of the clear mountain stream in your mind. Repeat this pulse-breath method three times. Imagine the stream as clearly as you can, and imagine being next to the clear, pure water. Notice how the flowing water spills into a steaming pool formed naturally in the large granite boulders surrounding you. You step slowly into the pool and feel the clear, warm water soothing your body, mind, and spirit completely. You float on the surface of the pool, softly supported by the warm water. As you float, you gently move toward the mouth of a cave in surrounding granite boulders.

You find yourself at the mouth of the cave. The area around the cave entrance is lit up but the rest of the cave seems shrouded in darkness. After checking it out as much as you can from the outside, you begin slowly moving into the cave. After an initial period of blindness, your eyes become accustomed to the darkness of the cave. As you move about, you see shadows that loom around you. Gradually you sense a path that leads you farther into the cave.

At a certain point in your journey through the cave, you begin to experience a metamorphosis within yourself. At first you sense your entire being slowing down and moving as if in slow motion. You feel a lightness, as if a burden has been lifted from your shoulders. Without the heaviness, your spirit seems to float, and you feel different from how you felt when you entered the cave. You suddenly feel alive with expectations and possibilities. You can be anyone and do anything!

Soon after your metamorphosis, you sense a second opening to the cave. As you move toward it, the cave becomes more light-filled. Standing before the second opening, you look out into a world that seems surreal. You look at this world as a child who has just discovered the ultimate fantasy world. It is a world where anything and everything is possible, a world where dreams come true!

Now imagine soaring out of the cave into the sky. You fly high, floating on the wind currents. As you soar, your dream empowerment goals for love start coming into focus, giving your life direction. Like stars lighting up the night sky, your dream goals give off a brilliant light of their own and act as homing beacons. Setting your controls for the heart of the Sun, you move toward those goals that shine the brightest. These are ultimately your dearest love dream goals. When you achieve one of them, you bring your ideal and real closer together as One. There's no degree of separation from having everything you ever wanted. In a flicker of thought, you realize the nature of dreams as they fit neatly in the whole of Oneness, where all things come together into One energetic whole. For a brief moment, everything makes sense, and you are perfect love.

Take another deep breath, and begin to come back to your body, moving your hands and feet and slowly opening your eyes.

When you are done meditating, make an effort to remain in a relaxed state of mind. In your dream empowerment journal, write down your impressions of the meditation. Also note any dream empowerment goals for love that came to mind during the meditation. Writing these things down helps you focus on them even more and encourages helpful dreams with regard to your love goals. In a sense, it programs your mind to more likely dream about the designated matter—in this case, your dream empowerment goals for love.

Dream Prayer for Love

Just before going to sleep, make sure your tape recorder and/or journal are next to your bed so you can easily access them when you wake up. Then slip into bed and say the following love prayer:

Dear God and Goddess, please bless and inspire my dreams tonight, so that I can clearly know and determine my dream empowerment goals for love. In our Lord and Lady's name, blessed be.

As you drift to sleep, chant silently to yourself:

I am dreaming of my dream empowerment goals for love, and I will remember my dreams when I wake up.

Leave the roses on your love altar. As you sleep, the fragrance of the roses will fill your bedroom, giving your love dreams an added dimension. (Note: When the roses wilt, return them respectfully to the earth.)

When you wake up, be sure to record everything you remember from your dreams and/or write down what you recall in your dream empowerment journal.

Oracle of Dreams for Love

The idea of the oracle is to help you understand the meanings behind your dreams. Sometimes you can interpret your dreams clearly, and at other times they seem like they're transmitted in an alien language that seems vaguely familiar. When this happens, oracles can help clarify what your dreams are telling you about yourself, your goals, and the world around you.

Go over your entries in your dream empowerment journal. Then select a recording of your favorite love songs and do one of the following: If it's a CD with a remote, there's an option called "shuffle," where the machine randomly selects a song from the CD; if it's another form of recording such as tape or album, then write down the numbers of the songs on separate pieces of paper and fold them so you can't see the numbers. Toss the pieces of paper into a bowl or basket or onto flat surface, and select one.

Play the song you have selected or shuffled to at least three times in a row. While you listen to the song, reflect on the many ways it relates to your recent dreams about love as well as your dream empowerment goals for love. By choosing a selection of music that you are already connected to in terms of love, you provide added power to the process of accessing your dream empowerment goals that relate to love and your relationships with others. Write down the date, the song title, and the ways the song connects to your love goals, in your dream empowerment journal.

Dream Affirmation for Love

Before starting your day, write the following affirmation in your dream empowerment journal. Then repeat it at least 9 times during the day for 28 days:

Today and every day, my dream empowerment goals for love come more into focus, and I am closer to becoming the loving person I truly want to be.

Affirmations help you to move empowering thoughts from your subconscious or sleeping mind to your conscious or waking mind. As the idea moves into your waking mind, it becomes an integral part of who you are. This is why it's essential that your affirmation be a positive and empowering message.

Health

Everyone wants to be healthy. The obvious question is, what are you really willing to do to make this happen? What changes do you need to make in your diet, lifestyle, and environment? This needs to be calculated when determining your health goals. I suggest you set your dream empowerment goals for health a little higher than you might have thought possible. Take a few minutes to daydream about perfect health and a strong and flexible body.

Once again, perform the dream techniques as a seamless whole. Create your sacred healing space, do your ritual and meditation, and say the healing prayer before going to sleep. Then consult the oracle and say the affirmation after you wake up.

Sacred Healing Dream Space

Add a vial of lavender oil, five bay leaves, and a clear quartz crystal to your sacred healing altar. Also put an uplifting picture or photograph of nature in your sacred healing space. Consecrate and make these dream focals sacred by holding them in your hands and saying three times:

May these dream focals be filled with divine and empowering healing energy.

Dream Ritual for Health

The purpose of this ritual is to help bring your dream empowerment goals for health into focus. It will help you clarify and hone them. You will need your dream empowerment journal, some healing New Age or instrumental music, and the lavender oil, bay leaves, and clear quartz crystal from your sacred healing altar.

Run a bath and dim the lights. Turn on the healing music, and invite the Goddess and God, or whatever divine energies or beings you prefer, by slowly dripping a few drops of lavender oil into the bathwater. As you do, say:

I respectfully invite divine light into my ritual.

Next, imagine a bright sphere of white light completely encircling you and your bath area. Then invite the elements into your ritual space by saying:

I respectfully invite the healing elements of earth, air, fire, water, and spirit into my sacred space.

Put the bay leaves and quartz crystal where you can easily reach them once you are in the tub. Step into the bath and get comfortable. Hold the quartz crystal in your receiving or dream hand. (This is your left hand if you are right-handed and your right hand if you are left-handed—usually the hand you don't eat with.)

With your power hand (the hand you do eat with), begin putting each bay leaf individually into the tub with you. As you submerse the leaf in the water, imagine its natural healing qualities flowing into the water and into you. Allow the bay water to soothe you.

Take several deep, complete breaths, and as you do imagine breathing in the fragrant healing power of the bathwater into your being. As you breathe, breathe in healing energy and white light. Let go of any tension you may be feeling with your exhale, just allowing it to be absorbed and neutralized in the warm water.

Now breathe normally and sit back comfortably in the bathtub. Repeat to yourself several times:

My dream empowerment goals for healing and good health are clearly in focus.

Continue doing this for a few minutes. Then close your eyes and imagine a blank sheet of paper in front of you. Imagine each of your dream empowerment goals for healing and good health magically appearing on the sheet of paper. Each goal represents a healing quality that you truly want to integrate into your life. Imagine being vibrant and healthy as you bathe in the healing lavender and bay ritual bath.

When you are done, towel off and anoint yourself with a few drops of the lavender oil. Gather the bay leaves together and return them to the earth tomorrow when you have an opportunity.

Then visualize stepping out of the sphere of white light you imagined at the beginning of the ritual, and imagine the sphere diffusing into the air around you. Make a note of any dream empowerment goals for healing and good health that came to mind during the ritual bath in your dream empowerment journal. Be sure to date your entry.

Thank the divine and also thank the elements by saying:

I thank the divine and the elements for their helpful presence and blessings.

Put the stone next to your bedside for use during the meditation. Again, you can either leave the music on or turn it off as you get ready for the healing meditation.

Dream Meditation for Health

Recline or sit comfortably in bed, and hold the clear quartz crystal in your left hand. Begin by taking a few deep breaths to relax and center your awareness. Gently rock your body back and forth several times while continuing to breath deeply. Clear your mind of all thoughts, and feel your spirit start to move upward and outward.

Now breathe normally, and in your mind's eye imagine your spirit flowing on the back a swift pony that rides like the breeze across a vast expanse of grassland that stretches out before you. You feel free, at ease, and without boundaries. Up ahead, you see a rock outcropping. Following a path through the giant rocks, you find yourself at a safe distance from the edge of a cliff that drops down to a river canyon far below. From this vantage point, you can see forever as if catching a glimpse of Oneness itself.

A fertile green plateau stands at a distance. Looking across the divide that separates you from the plateau, you see all the things that you dreamed possible, including an image of yourself in optimum health.

Sitting atop your spirit steed, you take a moment to say a prayer to the divine before riding like the wind toward the edge of the cliff and the plateau beyond it. As you reach the edge, the pony transforms into a magical winged steed, and you ride in slow motion into the air and over the divide. While in flight across the great divide, you magically transform into the healthy person you truly dream of being. You delight in the transformation as you ride on.

In an instant of what seems to be an eternity, you sense the hooves of your magical pony touch down on the plateau. As you ride like the wind across the fertile, green plateau, your dream empowerment goals for healing and good health come into clear focus. You realize what you need to do to attain your goals for healing and health and can see yourself easily and successfully taking the steps necessary toward optimum health.

Your magical pony slowly comes to a stop at the edge of a wooded glen. You get off the pony and walk over to the nearest tree. At the tree base you spot a small, clear quartz crystal, much like the one you hold in your hand. As you pick up the crystal, you can feel its healing energy flow through you.

Now take a deep complete breath, feeling the crystal energy energizing you. Slowly begin moving your toes and fingers and then open your eyes, bringing your awareness back to the present time and place, yet remaining peacefully relaxed during prayer.

Dream Prayer for Health

Just before you drift to sleep, say the following prayer:

God and Goddess of healing, I pray you,
Help me to dream about my health goals,
So that I shall be clear and focused
On healing and good health.
I thank you for your blessings and guidance
As I sleep and dream. Blessed be. Amen.

As you drift to sleep, repeat over and over to yourself:

I am dreaming about healing and good health, and I will remember my dreams when I wake up.

When you wake up, record everything you remember from your dreams and/or write down what you recall in your dream empowerment journal.

Oracle of Dreams for Health

Review the entries in your dream empowerment journal. Then pick a recording that makes you feel happy and healthy and do one of the following: If it's a CD with a remote, use the shuffle option to select a song. If it's another form of recording, write down the numbers of the songs on separate pieces of paper and fold them so you can't see the numbers. Put the pieces of paper into a bowl or basket, or toss them onto the surface in front of you, and then select one.

Play the song you have selected or shuffled to at least three times in a row. While you listen to the song, reflect on the many ways it relates to your recent dreams about healing and good health as well as your dream empowerment goals for optimum health. Write down in your dream empowerment journal the date and song title, as well as the ways the song relates to your healing and health goals.

Dream Affirmation for Health

Gaze at the picture or photo of nature you put in your sacred healing space for a few minutes. Then write down the following affirmation and repeat it at least 9 times throughout the day for 28 days:

My dream empowerment goals for health come clearly into focus, and I naturally choose to be healthy and happy today and every day.

Abundance

Historical and famous figures such as Albert Einstein, Sir Paul McCartney, and Robert Louis Stevenson, whom I mentioned previously, as well as

René Descartes and Gandhi, all used dreams to enhance their professional lives. Their dreams gave them messages that called them into political, scientific, and artistic action. This indicates that there is a connecting link between dreaming and the energies that call to you in the form of dream messages. These energies, in whatever form they take, can help you more readily attain your dream empowerment goals for abundance within your given calling.

Keep in mind that abundance can mean everything from monetary wealth to spiritual enlightenment. It is the physical, mental, and spiritual things in your life that you value, with regard to your present perception. As your perception changes with experience, you will find that some of the things you value also change. For example, Sally is a good friend who used to travel to Hawaii every year. She saved up her money all year just to go on the two-week trip. Three years ago, Sally got married and now has a baby daughter. She no longer saves her money for traveling to Hawaii, but now is saving for a new home. Her values have changed; thus her prosperity dreams have also changed.

Your dreams of abundance are those things you dearly wish for, things you come back to again and again over the months or years. They are things you want with all of your heart. When thinking about your prosperity dream empowerment goals, consider your present needs and dreams as well as your future needs and dreams.

Again, the techniques presented produce the most powerful dreams and results when done as a whole over the period of a night and morning. As with the dream techniques for love and health, they can be repeated as often as you like.

Sacred Abundance Dream Space

Add five chamomile tea bags, rosemary oil, a white tea candle and holder, and a key to your sacred abundance altar. Empower these dream focals for prosperity by holding them in your hands and saying three times:

May these dream focals be empowered with divine abundance and prosperity.

Dream Ritual for Abundance

The purpose of this ritual is to bring your prosperity and abundance dream empowerment goals clearly into focus. It can also help you connect with your dream self. You will need the tea bags, rosemary oil, a white tea candle, and the key from your sacred abundance space and some New Age or instrumental music that uplifts and inspires you.

Draw a warm bath. Put eight drops of rosemary oil and the chamomile tea bags into the bathwater. Then turn on the uplifting music and dim the light. Imagine a bright sphere of white light completely encircling you and your bath area. Then invite the elements into your ritual space by simply saying:

I respectfully invite the elements of earth, air, fire, water, and spirit into my sacred ritual space.

Before entering the bath, light the tea candle, dedicating it to the divine. Simply say:

I dedicate this candle to the divine.

Put the candle in a place that is both safe and easily visible from the bathtub, and put the key next to the candle. Then get into the tub. Take a few deep breaths to center your awareness. Allow the warm water to soothe your body. As you breathe in, imagine breathing in the uplifting energy of the music. As you breathe out, let go of any tension you may be feeling. Just let the stress of the day flow out of you.

Now breathe quietly and sit back comfortably in the tub. Focus on the candle flame and chant:

I am now able to easily focus on my dream empowerment goals for prosperity and abundance.

After doing this for a couple of minutes, stop chanting and turn your mind toward your dearest dreams for prosperity and abundance. Take the key in your power hand, and imagine opening the doorway to your dream world of abundance. Tap the key softly on the tub nine times, in a series of three sets of three, and then chant:

My dreams are the key to abundance and prosperity.

Continue chanting a few minutes. When you are done, get out of the tub and towel off. As you do, chant:

My dreams are the key to abundance and prosperity.

Thank the divine and the elements by saying:

I thank the divine and the elements for their helpful presence and blessings.

Then visualize stepping out of the sphere of white light you imagined at the beginning of the ritual, and imagine the sphere diffusing into the air around you. Make a note in your dream empowerment journal of any dream empowerment goals for abundance that came to mind during the ritual bath. Be sure to date your entry. You can either leave the music on or turn it off.

Snuff out the candle for now. The next day, relight it and let it safely burn down.

Dream Meditation for Abundance

Anoint your pillowcase with a couple of drops of rosemary oil. Then recline or sit comfortably in bed, holding the key in your receiving hand. Breathe in deeply and hold it for the count of three, and as you exhale, sound a tone using the word *OM*. Do this several times, each time focusing on sounding the "OM" tone for as long as you can. After the last "OM," you will feel centered and more in tune with yourself.

In your mind's eye, imagine being at the beach, in the surf and sand. Sense the sand in your fingers as you begin building a giant, magnificent sand castle. After completing it, you sit back and revel in your accomplishment. Suddenly you see a faint glimmer coming from one of the walls of your sand castle. Looking closer, you see a small golden key partially embedded on one side of your castle. You gently pull the key from the castle wall, and almost instantly, a small doorway appears in the castle wall. You put the key in the keyhole of the doorway, and it opens. Through the doorway, you glimpse the image of a person much like yourself, living a prosperous and abundant life. You see the world of your dreams. You open the doorway far enough to slip through it into your dream world. You also remember to pull the key from the keyhole and take it with you.

As you move through the doorway, you feel a transformation within yourself. You sense that anything and everything is possible. Reality and dream fold together into one, and you realize that your deepest dreams are possible. To attain them, you need clarity, focus, intelligent determination, and action, as well as all the dream help from divine sources that you can muster.

You sense a metamorphosis of everything and everyone around you and begin to recognize the influence your intentions, expectations, and perceptions have on your immediate environment. You focus your intentions and expectations on your prosperity dream goals, and as you do so, your goals for abundance become more clear. A warm, empowering sensation flows through you as you start to better understand your deepest dreams for abundance and prosperity.

Now take a deep breath, breathing in the clarity and delight of your dream world, a place of prosperity and abundance. Take another deep breath and tone an "OM" as you exhale. Begin moving your hands and feet. Slowly open your eyes, and come back to the present time and place.

Dream Prayer for Abundance

Say the following prayer just before you go to sleep:

Tonight as I sleep and dream, I ask for divine guidance and blessings in my quest. I ask for clarity to help me bring my dream empowerment goals for abundance into full focus. Blessed be. Amen.

As you drift to sleep, chant silently to yourself:

I am dreaming of my dream empowerment goals for abundance, and I will remember my dreams when I wake up.

When you wake up, record everything you remember from your dreams and/or write down what you recall in your dream empowerment journal.

Oracle of Dreams for Abundance

Review the entries regarding your dream empowerment goals for prosperity in your dream empowerment journal. Then select a CD, tape, or album that uplifts and motivates you and do one of the following: If it's a CD with a remote, use the shuffle option to select a song. If it's another form of recording, write down the numbers of the songs on separate pieces of paper and fold them so you can't see the numbers. Put the pieces of paper into a bowl or basket, or toss them onto the surface in front of you, and pick one.

Play the song you have selected or shuffled to at least three times in a row. As you listen to the song, think about how it relates to your dreams of prosperity and your dream goals for abundance and wealth. Write the date, song title, and how the song relates to your dream empowerment goals for abundance, in your dream empowerment journal.

Dream Affirmation for Abundance

Write the following abundance affirmation down in your dream empowerment journal. Then repeat it at least 9 times a day for 28 days:

Today and every day, my dream empowerment goals for abundance come into clear focus, and I move one step closer to living the prosperous life I truly desire and dream of.

Chapter Two

Creating Your Dream Plan

In an interview I did for *Magical Blend* magazine, psychiatrist and author Dr. Judith Orloff told of a dream she had about one of her patients, who was in reality at that moment attempting suicide. It was that dream that showed her the power of dreams, a power that she utilizes to take positive action. Dr. Orloff feels that dreams are the purest psychic conduit we have, because our egos aren't involved. When writing her book, *Second Sight,* Dr. Orloff would have dreams at night that would tell her what to write. The voice she hears frequently comes to her in dreams. When describing the dream voice, she said, "It's a totally neutral voice with a quality different from anything on Earth. It tells me things, and it's very clear and specific. I listen and write down everything it says because whenever the voice comes through this way, it's always quite accurate."

Dr. Orloff's dream voice, her inner voice, has helped her in many positive ways. For instance, her inner voice once gave her a phone number in a dream. Not knowing whose it was, she called the number, left a message introducing herself, and also left a contact number. A woman returned Dr. Orloff's call. The woman was a healer who was having tremendous problems and crying out for help. She had just rented an apartment, and Dr. Orloff's call was the first she had received at her new phone number. It was Dr. Orloff's inner voice, her dream voice, that had picked up on and relayed the woman's call for help.

Judith Orloff's experience and use of dreams in her work is not that unusual in that dreams have long been used for problem-solving and overall personal evolvement, especially on a spiritual level. Thomas Edison, inventor of the light bulb and the phonograph, always kept a cot in his work area so that if a problem arose, he would go and take a short nap. Upon awaking, he would often find that his dreams had helped in giving him the answer he had been seeking. Edison realized that there was something within the sleep cycle that was good for solving problems.

Eastern spiritual masters and traditional shamans use the problem-solving aspect of dreams in a personal quest for spiritual evolvement. In his book *The Lucid Dreamer,* Malcolm Godwin states, "Lucid or conscious dreaming allows shamans or "travelers between worlds" to visit the realms of the spirits in order to gain healing power and insight for both themselves and their peoples." In addition, the Tibetan Bonpo school uses dreaming as a form of spiritual meditation, the Hindu Upanishads allude to "a conscious dream world," and Buddhism states we are dreaming all the time and when we realize and become aware of this, we awaken within the dream and become enlightened.

Using Dreams for Problem-Solving

The idea that problem-solving is the major purpose of dreams has been proposed by several renowned persons. Sigmund Freud, who believed dreams were a product of unconscious and preconscious activity of the spirit, wrote that dreams seek to "solve the problems that our psychic life is faced with." Famous psychic Edgar Cayce felt that dreams work to solve the problems of the dreamer's conscious, waking life and they work to quicken in the dreamer new potentials and ideas.

Realizing and using these potentials is the key to *Empowering Your Life with Dreams*. Oftentimes this potential needs to be both prodded and understood. With your expectation and the dreaming techniques in this book, you can guide and shape your dreams in such a way so they will help you in your empowerment process.

Dreams are invaluable for establishing your goals and designing ingenious ways to make these dream goals happen. In a way, you establish a link between your dream world and your waking world, and when they become connected, miraculous things begin happening in your life.

Dream researchers say you have between five to seven dreams every sleep cycle. Your waking life carries over into your dream life, and as such, you are continually working out solutions for the things that come into your life. With a little direction, your dreams can become a means for solving your problems. This is particularly helpful when working on your dream empowerment plans.

Dreams often speak through metaphor, which sometimes obscures their meaning. Because of this, there is an emphasis on dream interpretation. Beyond this, once you have put the expectation out to Oneness, then help starts coming from many sources. As Wilda Tanner writes in her book *The Mystical, Magical, Marvelous World of Dreams,* "Occasionally our questions are not specifically answered in a dream, but are answered by means of a book. a television program, a conversation we just 'happened' to hear, a 'chance' meeting, a magazine article, and so forth." These are often oracles that allude to prevailing potentials, an essential part of the problem-solving process using your dreams.

This means you always have to be aware of the signs that are happening all around you. Sometimes they are subtle and sometimes they hit you where it hurts. Anything you can dream can and will come true. This is a power of divine proportions. Exercise it accordingly. There is humor in what I say, but the truth is what you seek. That is what gives you forward movement and propels you forward in terms of evolution.

Once you learn to walk, step by step, the process is a cakewalk, a dance of life, and you are the dream walker, moving between worlds while enabling your dreams to come true. You are One with the dream maker. You *are* the dream maker. At that point, everything is possible as long as you're willing to dream, something that happens naturally every time you go to sleep. It's the perfect form of self-help—inexpensive yet very effective.

As long as you're willing to apply yourself and follow through, your intentions and expectations will become real in one form or another. This is why it's important to be clear with your expectations. Don't wish for something unless you really want it to become true. If you really want it, wish with all your heart and might until it becomes reality.

Staging Your Dreams

In the 1941 movie *Tom, Dick, and Harry,* the main female character, played by Ginger Rogers, is pursued by three suitors, all of whom she is equally attracted to and becomes engaged to. At a point of indecision, she has a night of dreams in which she envisions her life with each one of her suitors. Her dreams show her what life would be like with each man. Her dream where she is married to Tom, the businessman, shows him to be a workaholic who is never home; her dream with Dick, the millionaire, is one with lots of money but not necessarily any genuine caring and love; and her dream of Harry, the philanthropist, is one where she is poor and happy, with lots of children.

The idea behind this movie sequence offers an interesting aspect to dreams in the sense that you can try things out in the dream world to see how they might work in the "real" world. In a way it is a staging area for making your dreams come true. Within the empowerment process, it is the perfect place for enacting your plans to see if they work. You can play out different scenarios in your dreams to see if they work with who you are and who you want to be.

When determining your dream empowerment goals and creating your dream plans, you can stage your dreams in a way that can give you insights into the various selections available to you. Determining your goals and creating your plans require that you make choices, something that doesn't always come easy, especially when there are a lot of promising possibilities.

If you are looking for a new job, you have to make some choices when determining your goals. If you have or had a job, do you want to stay in the same profession or try something new? If you want to change your profession, then what do you like to do? What are you good at? What do you want to spend your life doing?

Once you have decided which profession you would like to work in, then you need to create a plan for securing that perfect job. This is where the problem-solving ability of your dreams becomes very useful because you can stage and work through the many possible plans available, using your dreams to choose the plan with the best possibilities for success.

As you begin creating your dream plans, you may find that you need to go back and adapt your dream empowerment goals a little bit.

Because you are continually changing as a person, your dreams and goals also change to reflect who you are at that juncture in time. Also, when creating your plans, you may come to the conclusion that in order to make your plans work, you have to modify your goals. Understand that this is a normal part of the dream empowerment process. It's an essential part of your personal growth and evolvement.

Feng Shui for Dreams

Your home and work environments can empower or disempower you. They greatly affect your relationships, prosperity, and well-being. For thousands of years the art of Feng Shui has been used to promote success, good health, and happiness in the home, workplace, and garden.

Feng Shui means "wind and water." It is the ancient Chinese art of sacred placement while maximizing good chi to bring good fortune and luck. Chi is the invisible, vital energy of the cosmos. *Chi* translates as "cosmic breath." Good chi energy empowers, enriches, and helps you realize your dreams. Bad chi does just the opposite. By balancing the chi, you can create a harmonious environment in tune with nature and the five Chinese elements of water, fire, wood, earth, and metal.

Applying basic Feng Shui, you can learn how to arrange your environment to fully support your goals. Your dreaming room, most likely your bedroom, can be enhanced to create a romantic, peaceful place of dream empowerment.

It's important to create a soft chi flow (more yin or feminine than yang or masculine) in your sleeping and dreaming area to renew, regenerate, and strengthen your body, mind, and spirit. By changing your outer environment and making it more harmonious, you can likewise change your inner environment.

The ideal location for your master bedroom should be in the west area of your home, as this is the chi position that encourages dreaming, romance, relaxation, intimacy, and improves your general well-being. Ideally, position your bed along an axis that passes through the center of your home.

Refer to the following list to help select the optimum dreaming directions for your bed and head:

- **Head pointing north**—Enhances feelings of quiet dreams, calm, peace, and spiritual harmony. Considered the quiet direction, this position is beneficial for elderly people and insomniacs.
- **Head pointing northeast**—A sharp and piercing direction not recommended for sleep. This position may increase nightmares, insomnia, and depression.
- **Head pointing east**—Good career-building and motivation position. Ideal for dreaming of growth and the future. Good lucid dreaming position.
- **Head pointing southeast**—A position for increased dream activity, lucid dreaming, increased creativity, and short, informative dreams. Encourages subtle growth.
- **Head pointing south**—Not a direction recommended for sound sleep because of its fiery nature. Use this position for short periods to enhance the passion and romance in your life.
- **Head pointing southwest**—This direction encourages peaceful relationships and dreams as well as lucid dreaming.
- **Head pointing west**—This is the direction of contentment and peaceful and lucid dreams. It also encourages romance and prosperity.
- **Head pointing northwest**—This is the "parent" direction of leadership, lucid dreaming, dreams of people and pets that have passed on, and deep sleep.

The following Feng Shui guidelines can be applied to further enhance the chi energy in your bedroom. I suggest you keep it simple to begin with and make adjustments and changes that feel right for you. These guidelines are based on personal experience as well as the information gathered from resource books such as Steven Skinner's *Feng Shui: Before and After,* Simon Brown's *Practical Feng Shui*, and Jami Lin's *Earth Design.*

- You should be able to easily see the door and windows of the room from your bed, so no one can surprise you when entering.
- Avoid positioning your bed with your feet directly in line with the door. This is called the "coffin" position.

- Make sure you cannot see your reflection from any mirror in the bedroom when you are in bed.
- Table and floor lamps with lamp shades or wall sconces are the best choices for lighting the bedroom. Candles also add romantic and natural glow. Avoid a hanging chandelier, lighting fixture, or ceiling fan over the bed.
- Round-leaved living or silk plants enhance the mental energy of the room when placed in the west or northwest.
- Select bedroom furniture with round edges when possible. Make sure no sharp furniture or wall corners cut or point into the bed.
- Avoid sleeping directly under an exposed beam, overhanging cabinets, or ledges.
- Use a draped four poster bed to soften the bad chi effects of open-beamed ceilings, or wrap the beams in fabric.
- Use soft carpet or rugs as well as soft draperies to slow the chi energy through the room.
- If possible, avoid putting mirrors in the bedroom. If you do have them in the room, cover them while you sleep. Mirrors contain the spirits of everyone and everything that have been reflected in them. These spirits are not necessarily conducive to sound sleep.
- Use natural bed linens made from cotton or silk to create a soft, natural flow of chi next to your skin when sleeping and dreaming.
- Hang a red and gold "double happiness" calligraphy print to enhance your relationship with your spouse or primary partner. (These are available from any Feng Shui supply store or catalog, New Age shops, or online.)
- Avoid putting the headboard of your bed in front of a window or backing it up to a closed fireplace. Wood headboards have a neutral or calming effect on chi energy.
- Close any connecting bathroom door to your bedroom, and keep it closed to keep bad chi from flowing into your bedroom.
- Drape or cover all open shelves to soften their edges.
- Avoid putting computers, televisions, and other electronic devices in the bedroom. When these devices are necessary, use fabric screens, drapes, or covers to reduce any sha (bad) chi when not in use.

- Avoid putting water features or fish tanks in the bedroom. These are better placed in the living room or at your home's entrance. The entryway represents prosperity and abundance that comes into the home.
- Keep clutter to a minimum; clutter traps the flow of chi.

Creating Your Dream Plans

Now that you have set the stage for empowering dreams by applying the principles of Feng Shui, it's time to create your dream plans. These are the plans that will propel you toward attaining your dream empowerment goals for love, healing and well-being, and abundance. Plans have the same relationship with goals that recipes have with cooking. If you don't follow the steps, your goals won't turn out the way you expect. Sometimes the results may be surprising, but usually not what you want.

To actualize your dream empowerment goals, you need to find or draw up a recipe or plan for success that you will stick to until your plan is completed and you are enjoying the banquet of life you have dreamed of. Your dream plan is a sequence of steps patterned toward a particular end. In this sense, your dream empowerment goals are the ends, and your dream plans are your means for getting there.

The first thing you need to do is to take each of your dream empowerment goals and work out the steps needed to achieve that goal. Go through the steps in your mind and in your dreams, and then write down the steps in your dream empowerment journal. Make the steps basic and easy to follow. After you have worked out the basic plan, then you can work out the details. As you start out, keep it direct—"A" to "B" to "C."

The dream techniques presented in this chapter are intended to help you create your dream plans. The idea is to pattern your dreams so that they help you create the best possible plans for achieving your dream empowerment goals. Because dreams move beyond the tethers of your waking self and ego, they often give you a clearer perspective for seeing things for what they are. This perspective is important when making your dream plans because the steps that you create have to be anchored in reality if your goals are going to become real within the scope of your life.

Dreams are the mirrors of the spirit. They reflect in some ways who we truly are, without the exterior facades that we exhibit. Because of this quality, dreams are a clear channel for determining your goals and creating your plans. When you dream about something you have always desired, set a plan for attaining it, and achieve it, there is a burst of energy that I call empowerment.

Empowerment is about that feeling you get when you've done what you planned to do and it turned out exactly, or at least pretty much, the way you wanted it to. You get a euphoric natural high that is incredible and, depending on its intensity, may last for long periods of time.

In terms of life, one empowering experience sustains the next, so that you are empowered again. It becomes a continual, circular process that is dynamic by nature, propelling you into today, tomorrow, and the future.

Love

Your dream empowerment goals for love relate to your relationships in life, and as a result, these relationships impact the nature of your plans. Because people are individuals and as such unique, each relationship is different from every other, even though at times there are similarities. The idea when creating your dream plans for love is to treat each of your relationships separately and to appreciate and account for their individual qualities.

Learn to appreciate the relationships that you have. If you can't find anything positive or empowering about certain relationships, it may be time to get rid of them or at least minimize your interaction. When you interact with more positive people, it helps you to be more positive. When you are feeling more positive, your dreams are also often more positive.

Use the following dream techniques to help you create your dream plans for love. Do them at least three nights in a row before moving on to the next section. Keep in mind you can repeat the techniques as many times as you like. Most likely, each time you do repeat the process your experience will be different.

Sacred Love Dream Space

To develop a deeper awareness of your surroundings and enhance the chi energy of the room, slowly walk around your bedroom. Then stand in the center of the room and close your eyes. Take a few deep, complete breaths, and with your eyes still closed, make a mental note of how the room feels to you.

Now open your eyes and look around the room. Make a mental note about how the room feels now. Which furniture, items, colors, and pictures feel as though they belong? Which don't? Go ahead and rearrange the room to feel more comfortable and inviting. (You can repeat this process in all the rooms of your home and in your office to create more pleasant and empowering surroundings.)

Next, place pink or red flowers in the west direction of your bedroom to promote romance, pleasure, and passion. Also put a vial of vanilla oil on your dream altar. Bless the oil by holding the vial in your hands until it warms up. Then say:

Bless this oil. May it bring divine dreams of love.

Dream Ritual for Love

The purpose of this ritual is to create your list of dream empowerment goals for love and a three-step plan for attaining them. You will need a pen, a clean sheet of paper, your dream empowerment journal, and the vanilla oil from your dream altar.

Begin by anointing yourself at the ankles, wrists, and throat with the vanilla oil. Imagine a bright sphere of white light completely encircling you and your sacred space. Then invite the elements into your ritual space by saying:

I respectfully invite the elements of earth, air, fire, water, and spirit into my sacred ritual space.

If you like, you can invite any helpful Goddesses and Gods or other divine energies of choice by asking them into your ritual space now. This helps connect your personal plan with that of the divine.

Write down three of your most important dream empowerment goals for love on the piece of paper, one goal at a time. Leave room under each goal to write a simple three-step plan. When you are done writing your goals on the sheet of paper, write them down in your dream empowerment journal and date your entry. Once again, leave room to write a three-step plan under each of the three dream empowerment goals. When you write down your dream goals, it reinforces them in your mind.

Now review your dream empowerment goals, and ask that you be given the plan for achieving your goals in your dreams, tonight, tomorrow night, and so on until you receive a clear plan. Anoint the edges of the paper with the vanilla oil. Put the paper on your dream altar, and then thank the divine and the elements by saying:

I thank the divine and the elements for their helpful presence and blessings.

Then visualize stepping out of the sphere of white light you imagined at the beginning of the ritual, and imagine the sphere diffusing into the air around you.

Dream Meditation for Love

Sit back, relax, and begin breathing deeply. This is the essence of meditation—to get in a relaxed, calm state of mind where you view everything in terms of what's happening to you "right now." As the "right now" changes, so does your view or perception. You realize that every thought you have is you, and you are every thought. When you change your perception of who you are, you change who you are.

In your mind you sense a curtain rising, and suddenly life looks much different than it did before. You see many more possibilities that linger within your mind's eye. You rejoice within at the potential that lies before you. You realize your greater potential and that you have the ability to achieve this dream. The idea empowers you beyond belief as you begin to map out the plan for making your dream a reality.

Within the dream play, you begin imagining the steps you would need to take to make your dream love life real. Imagine everything in your dream sequence coming true, and you have the love life you have always desired. Try it on and look at yourself in the mirror, asking yourself, "Is it everything I want?" Depending on the answer to the question, you adapt the dream play accordingly. You realize this is an ongoing process that continues until your dreams come true.

Take another deep breath, and begin to come back to your body, moving your hands and feet and slowly opening your eyes.

When you are done meditating, make an effort to remain in a relaxed state of mind. In your dream empowerment journal, write down your impressions of the meditation. Also note any dream empowerment goals for love that came to mind during the meditation. Writing these things down helps you focus on them even more, and encourages helpful dreams with regard to your love goals.

Dream Prayer for Love

Just before you go to sleep, say this dream prayer:

Divine ones of light, please guide me.
Reveal the steps I need to take
In order to make my dream goals for love
Blossom and come to fruition.

As you drift to sleep, repeat softly to yourself:

My dreams guide me to love, and I will remember my dreams when I wake up.

When you wake up, record or write down everything you remember from your dreams.

Oracle of Dreams for Love

One of the most popular divination practices throughout the world is consulting mirrors. The Naskapis of Labrador call gazing into a mirror "waponatca kwoma'u" or "he sees his soul."

The mirror can be used to see your inner self. It provides a doorway to your dreams when used as an oracle. Start by standing or sitting in front of a mirror. Look at yourself for a few minutes. Smile, grin, frown, and make faces. Just let your feelings, thoughts, images, and sensations flow through you.

After a few minutes, look at yourself and imagine seeing yourself for the very first time. Now close your eyes and inhale for three heartbeats, hold your breath for three heartbeats, and then exhale for three heartbeats.

In your mind's eye, review your dream last night, or review a recent dream that you recall. Go over as much of the dream as you remember, like a movie in your mind. Be sure to make a mental note of the parts of the dream that seem most important, strange, or vivid to you. Now open your eyes and look at yourself in the mirror for a few minutes again.

Write down your impressions in your dream empowerment journal. Note how you felt looking in the mirror at the beginning of the oracle process and also after you opened your eyes and saw yourself for the first time. Also write down any insights you received about your dream and dream empowerment goals for love while consulting the mirror.

Dream Affirmation for Love

As you begin your day, write the following affirmation in your dream empowerment journal. Then repeat it several times during the day and evening for 28 days:

My dream empowerment goals and plans for attaining them are clearly revealed to me in waking and dreams. I am taking the steps to make my dreams come true.

Health

Be realistic when determining your dream empowerment goals and creating your dream plans for health. Deep down within yourself, you know what you are capable of in terms of your full potential. At the same time, leave some room for giving wings to your dreams and experiencing miracles!

Start with simple goals and plans, and move up from there, until you actually achieve your dreams. You have to be realistic at first, but in the end, anything and everything is possible as long as you have the expectation and determination to make it happen.

If your goals are to lose weight, strengthen your body, or heal yourself from a disease, start outlining the action steps to take. You may need to exercise more, take healing baths, change your diet to include more healthy foods, go for a daily walk, make an appointment with an acupuncturist or massage therapist, or make other positive changes in your living or working environment and lifestyle.

Whatever the steps you need to take to attain your dream goals for health, be sure to include them in your plans. The Dream Ritual for Health and the other dream techniques in this section can help you determine your dream empowerment goals for healing and well-being, as well as set a basic three-point plan for attaining them.

Sacred Healing Dream Space

Sea salt is found in your blood stream in the form of sodium. Sea salt pulls chi energy to it and has a purifying and stabilizing influence. Put 2 tablespoons sea salt in a shallow white bowl. Put the bowl on the floor, shelf, or table, away from children and pets, in the southwest or northeast area of your sacred healing dream space. Bless the bowl of salt by holding it in your hands and saying:

Bless this bowl of salt.

Dream Ritual for Health

The purpose of this ritual is to create your list of dream empowerment goals for healing and well-being and a three-step plan for attaining them. You will need a pen, a clean sheet of paper, your dream empowerment journal, and the bowl of sea salt from your sacred healing dream space.

Clear any unwanted energies from your sacred dream space with the sea salt and your intention. Face north, sprinkle a bit of the salt from the bowl toward the north, and say:

Divine guardians of the north,
May your blessings and wisdom guide my dreams.

Then face east, sprinkle a bit of the salt toward the east, and say:

Divine guardians of the east,
May your blessings and wisdom guide my dreams.

Face south and sprinkle a bit of the salt toward the south and say:

Divine guardians of the south,
May your blessings and wisdom guide my dreams.

Then face west and sprinkle a bit of the salt toward the west and say:

Divine guardians of the west,
May your blessings and wisdom guide my dreams.

Put the bowl of salt down on your dream altar. Then imagine a bright sphere of white light completely encircling you and your sacred space, and invite the elements into your ritual space by saying:

I respectfully invite the elements of earth, air, fire, water, and spirit into my sacred ritual space.

Invite helpful Goddesses and Gods of healing and other divine energies by asking them into your ritual space now. This connects your personal plan with the divine.

Write down three of your most important dream empowerment goals for health on the sheet of paper, one goal at a time. Leave room under each goal to write a three-point plan. When you have finished writing your goals on the paper, write them in your dream empowerment journal and date the entry. Once again, leave room to write a three-point plan under each of the three dream empowerment goals. Writing down your dream empowerment goals for health sets them in place in your mind.

Now review your goals, and imagine the best possible plan for attaining dream goals for healing being revealed in your dreams tonight, tomorrow night, and so on until you receive a clear and concise plan for making your dreams come true. Put the paper on your dream altar, and then thank the divine and the elements by saying:

I thank the divine and the elements for their helpful presence and blessings.

Visualize stepping out of the sphere of white light you imagined at the beginning of the ritual, and imagine the sphere diffusing into the air around you. Sprinkle a bit of the sea salt under or next to your bed and put the bowl of salt back in its place in your sacred healing dream space.

Dream Meditation for Health

Lie back and take a few deep breaths. Deep breathing provides you with life-giving oxygen, and it expels toxins in your body. As you breathe, feel your body beginning to relax. As you inhale, imagine a single point of white light where everything comes together, and then when you exhale, imagine the white light diffusing into Oneness, and as you do so, you sense the weights and burdens of the day being lifted from your shoulders. Keep doing this until you feel completely relaxed and in tune with the universe within you and around you.

After several more deep breaths, you feel a wave of relaxing energy envelop your being, and with it you feel a peaceful, calm awareness that spreads everywhere within you. Within your spirit, you sense a divine smile that gives you a warm, glowing feeling.

The relaxing energy spreads its glowing light around you like an embryo surrounding your body. You feel completely protected and at ease within the embryo, and as such, you begin moving toward better health. In your mind's eye, you set the parameters and effects of the embryo. If you so desire, you can achieve perfect health. All you have to do is imagine it, and it comes true.

Within the embryo, you imagine yourself in perfect health, exactly the way you want to be. You sense your body strong and vital, your mind full of wonder and cohesion, and your spirit linking you to your higher self and the divine in whatever form you perceive it. Perfect health means balancing your body, mind, and spirit together into one cohesive whole. In this way you can realize your full healing potential and make your dreams come true.

The embryo is the place where dreams happen, a world that mirrors the waking world. In the embryo or dream world, you become your perfect health. You can perceive yourself in terms of your ideal. You are strong, healthy, and without pain. Within the embryo, it's all real. You begin moving the dream world into the real world with your intention and imagination.

In your mind's eye, you perceive the steps you need to take to achieve your dream goals for health. Once you know what you want, the question then becomes how to get it. Within the embryo, the answer to all this becomes clear. You clearly see what you need to do to make your health dream goals come true. These are your health plans.

Feel any doubts begin to fade as you realize you have the power to make your life the life of your dreams. You sense yourself moving toward optimum health as you take the steps to get there. Like walking up stairs, each one leads you a little higher up until you reach the top, which in this case are your dream goals for health.

Take a deep and complete breath, and let the faith you have in yourself, your spirituality, and your dream empowerment goals flow through your body, mind, and spirit. Take another deep breath and breathe the faith in and exhale all your doubts. Repeat this a few times and begin to come back to your body, moving your hands and feet and slowly opening your eyes.

When you are done meditating, remain in a relaxed state of mind. In your dream empowerment journal, write down your impressions of the meditation.

Dream Prayer for Health

Just before you go to sleep, repeat the following prayer:

Blessed and divine ones, please light the path
To help me attain my dream goals for health.

I pray you, guide and bless my dreams tonight
And help me to remember my dreams when I wake.
Thank you blessed and divine ones. Amen.

As you drift to sleep, softly repeat to yourself:

Please guide and bless my dreams, and I will remember when I wake up.

When you wake up, be sure to record or write down everything you recall from your dreams in your dream empowerment journal and date your entry.

Oracle of Dreams for Health

Stand or sit comfortably in front of the mirror and look at yourself. Smile, giggle, grin, grimace, frown, and make faces. After a few minutes, look at yourself and imagine seeing yourself for the very first time. Now close your eyes and inhale for three heartbeats, hold your breath for three heartbeats, and then exhale for three heartbeats.

In your mind's eye, review your dream last night or recall a recent dream about health and well-being. Go over as much of the dream as you remember, like a movie in your mind. Make sure to make a mental note of the parts of the dream that seem most important to you. Now open your eyes and look at yourself in the mirror.

Write down your impressions in your dream empowerment journal. Also make a note of any insights about your dream empowerment goals for health and the plans for attaining them that came to you while consulting the mirror.

Dream Affirmation for Health

Write the following affirmation in your dream empowerment journal. Then repeat it several times during the day and evening for 28 days and nights:

Today and every day, my dream empowerment goals for health and well-being and the plans for attaining them are clearly revealed to me in waking and dreams. I am taking the steps to make my dreams come true.

Abundance

When mapping out the steps of your dream plans for abundance, be as simple and direct as you can be. If you desire that new job, you need to plan out the steps to ensure that you eventually find yourself in that position. Your plans are again your recipe for success.

When making decisions regarding work, use your dreams to help you make better choices. Successful planning is planning to be a success. Plans need to be methodical, creative, and even a little magical!

Keep a balanced and positive attitude. If you expect to be successful, you increase your chances for success. When creating your dream plan for abundance, become the dream weaver and weave your dreams for abundance into the fabric of your waking life. You can do this by focusing your mind on your dream empowerment goals, making a plan to attain your goals, taking the necessary steps, and using your dreams to guide and empower you.

Sacred Abundance Dream Space

Add a small bell with a harmonious sound to your dream altar. The bell is a traditional Feng Shui cure. Ringing a bell clears and refreshes the chi energy in a room. Empower the bell by holding it in your hands and saying:

I empower this dream bell with divine energy.

Then ring the bell three times.

Dream Ritual for Abundance

The purpose of this ritual is to create a short list of dream empowerment goals for abundance and a three-step plan for attaining them. You will need a pen, a clean sheet of paper, your dream empowerment journal, and the bell from your dream altar.

Ring the bell three times and in your mind's eye imagine a bright sphere of white light completely encircling you and your sacred space. Then invite the elements into your ritual space by ringing the bell three more times and saying:

I respectfully invite the elements of earth, air, fire, water, and spirit into my sacred ritual space.

Invite any helpful Goddesses and Gods or other divine energies of your choice by ringing the bell three times and asking them into your ritual space now. This helps connect your personal plan with the divine and adds tremendous power to your efforts.

Ring the bell three more times, and write down your dream empowerment goals for love on the sheet of paper, one goal at a time, leaving space for a simple three-point plan beneath each goal. Before writing down each goal, ring the bell three times.

Write the same thing in your dream empowerment journal and date your entry, once again, ringing the bell three times before each goal entry. When you write your dream goals down, it reinforces them in your mind. Ringing the bell creates a double reinforcement which, by its nature, merges the ordinary and divine into one.

Next, write down three simple steps you can take to make your dream goals for abundance come closer to fruition. Again, ring the bell before writing down the three steps under each goal. Copy your notes into your journal under each specific goal.

Review your dream empowerment goals and the steps you need to take by reading over your notes. Then ring the bell three times and say:

I ask for divine guidance and help
In attaining my dream goals for abundance.
As I dream it, so it will be!

Ring the bell three times. Put the sheet of paper on your dream altar, and then thank the divine and the elements by ringing the bell three times and saying:

I thank the divine and the elements for their helpful presence and blessings.

Then visualize stepping out of the sphere of white light you imagined at the beginning of the ritual, and imagine the sphere diffusing into the air around you. When you are done, ring the bell three times.

Dream Meditation for Abundance

You will need the bell from your dream altar. Relax comfortably. Ring the bell three times. Then breathe in through your nose for three heartbeats, still your breath for three heartbeats, and breathe out completely through your mouth.

Ring the bell again three times and breathe in through your nose for three heartbeats. As you breathe in, fill your abdomen and then your chest with air. Breathe out through your mouth, from the top of your chest to the bottom of your abdomen. Ring the bell three times before you take each deep, refreshing breath. Repeat this process, breathing in through your nose and out through your mouth, for a few minutes to quiet and center your mind.

Now put the bell down and close your eyes. In your mind's eye imagine you have already attained your dream goals. Your dream and waking worlds merge into one as your dream empowerment goals for abundance move from your dream world into waking reality. Envision exactly what it is like to attain your dream goals, what it would be like in reality. See it, taste and smell it, hear it, be it, and feel what it feels like when your dream goals are actualized.

Now that you know what your dream empowerment goals are, begin envisioning the steps you need to take to get there. Take a few more deep breaths, and begin imagining a few of the main steps involved in making your dream goals for abundance come true. Know that you will be divinely guided and blessed as you work toward attaining your dream goals.

Be realistic, but at the same time, remain open to all your options as you move your mind toward figuring the best course to navigate. Check in with your inner self, and determine what's best for you and, from that perspective, how you should proceed.

Like an explorer of new worlds, map out your course to make your dream empowerment goals for abundance come true. Within your inner self, you know where to go to be who you want to be. Through the valleys, deserts, and oceans and over the mountains and hills of your body, mind, and spirit, you chart a course and make a plan for attaining your goals. For a few moments, imagine you are a savvy and experienced explorer who naturally selects the best course to take in order to reach your destination and attain your dream goals for abundance.

Take another deep breath, feeling refreshed and relaxed, confident that if you have the ability to dream it, you can create it! Breathe in deeply through your nose and out through your mouth, and begin to come back to the present time and place. Breathe in through your nose and move your toes, and breathe out through your mouth, moving your fingers. Open your eyes slowly, stretch your body, and get even more comfortable.

When you are done meditating, remain in a relaxed but aware state of mind. In your dream empowerment journal, write down your impressions of the meditation. Include a description of your dream map and the course you charted to attain your dream empowerment goals for abundance.

Dream Prayer for Abundance

Just before you go to sleep, ring the bell three times and say this prayer (you can substitute specific divine names from your personal spiritual tradition for "divine and wise Ones"):

Divine and wise Ones, I pray you
Please reveal the best plan
For attaining my goals for abundance
To me in my dreams.
Please help me to remember my dreams
So that I will know how to proceed.
Thank you divine and wise ones.
Blessed be! Amen.

As you drift to sleep, repeat softly to yourself:

Reveal the best plan, and I will remember my dreams when I wake up.

When you wake up, be sure to record everything you remember from your dreams on your handheld tape recorder and then transcribe your notes into your dream empowerment journal, or if you prefer, write down what you recall in your journal.

Oracle of Dreams for Abundance

Stand or sit comfortably in front of a mirror. Look at yourself for several minutes. Smile, grin, frown, and make faces. Just let your feelings, thoughts, images, and sensations flow through you.

After a few minutes, close your eyes; then open them suddenly, look at yourself, and imagine seeing yourself for the very first time.

Now close your eyes and inhale for three heartbeats, hold your breath for three heartbeats, and then exhale for three heartbeats.

In your mind's eye, review your dream last night or review a recent dream about abundance that you recall. Go over as much of the dream as you remember, like a movie in your mind. Make sure to make a mental note of the parts of the dream that seem most important, strange, or vivid to you. Now open your eyes and look at yourself in the mirror for a few minutes again. In what ways do you seem different?

Write down your impressions in your dream empowerment journal. Note how you felt looking in the mirror at the beginning of the oracle process and also after you opened your eyes and saw yourself for the first time. Also write down any insights about your dream and dream empowerment goals for abundance while consulting the mirror. Did any words, past experiences, or images come to mind? Did you see any other faces in the mirror? Did you see, feel, or think about your goals and yourself differently at the beginning and the end of the oracle process? If so, in what ways?

Dream Affirmation for Abundance

Write the following affirmation in your dream empowerment journal and date your entry. Then ring the bell three times and repeat the affirmation in the morning and several times during the day. At night just before going to sleep, ring the bell three times and repeat the affirmation again. Do this for 28 days and nights:

My dream empowerment goals for abundance and the plans for attaining them are clearly revealed to me in waking and dreams. I now know what my dreams are, and I am taking the steps to make them come true.

Chapter Three

Dream Tools and Focals

Most likely, you have one or more dreams—sort of fantasies that you wish would come true. You can actualize these dreams by setting, planning, enacting, and attaining certain dream empowerment goals.

Whether you choose to acknowledge and follow your dreams is up to you. Dreams are sometimes overwhelming so you try to ignore them, but that seldom works as they keep tapping at your psyche. Just as you are what you eat, you are also what you dream. It's vital that you hold on strongly to that ideal and joyous image, that sensation, that dream in your mind's eye. Your dreams are to your spirit what food is to your physical body. This is why it is important to keep your dream alive, nourishing your spirit and moving the events of your life forward.

Within the realm of dreams, tools and focals are relevant in two ways: Dreams themselves are tools and focals to be used in your empowerment process, and different tools and focals can be used with your dreams to make them even more effective in terms of problem-solving and reaching into the great beyond.

What is this great beyond that you tap into when you dream? And what tools and focals can you use to get an even clearer channel than you are presently? In other words, how can you better utilize your dreams to give you the specific information you need to help you attain your dream goals?

Where Do You Go When You Dream?

When creating the sewing machine, Elias Howe ran into a problem. Traditional needles with their holes in the back end for the thread did not work with his concept of the bobbin. One night he had a dream that he was being chased by African natives, and when they came close to him, he saw that their spears had holes in the front or sharp end. The dream gave Howe the answer to his dilemma, and he went on to finish the sewing machine, a machine which has completely changed the clothing industry. This is an example of the wondrous and far-reaching power of dreams.

Where are you going when you enter the realm of dreams? As with Elias Howe, inventors, creative artists, and problem-solvers use the information they receive in dreams in many useful and positive ways. Two basic things seem to happen when you enter the dream world: Your mind relaxes and when doing so, starts viewing the events of your life in different ways; and you tap into what could be termed the "universal dream" or "collective dream," where everyone's personal dreams come together into one central database that represents the whole of everything.

Imminent psychologist Carl Jung called this whole the "collective unconsciousness." Edgar Cayce called it the "Akashic Records," a place where everything that ever was, is, or will be resides in an immense cosmic library. Like a holistic Internet, all the information is there. It's just a matter of accessing it.

For his part, Cayce would consult the Akashic Records for everything from the illnesses of his patients to making predictions about the future. The important thing about Cayce is that he was extremely accurate and helpful in the things he said, giving validity to his information source.

This collective whole is called "Oneness." It is the place where God (masculine yang) and Goddess (feminine yin) meet and in their union become One—Yin and Yang. The dualities and polarities are created by our perceptions as a means for understanding our world. As you evolve, these definitions cease to be useful, and you begin seeing things more as a whole, as one. You begin perceiving your world as a circular whole. This divine whole is Oneness.

Well-known singer and songwriter Billy Joel, composer of such classics as "Piano Man" and "River of Dreams," in past interviews has talked about how the songs he writes come from dreams. Rather than dreams where he is doing something like riding down the street, he says his dreams come more in the form of abstractions, such as colors, shapes, and music. He described waking up out of a dream at 4:30 in the morning with a whole symphony in his head. The notes in the dream were so vivid and the music so good that he figured he didn't have to get up and write it down because he would remember it when he woke up. Unfortunately, when morning came and he woke up, the music was gone, but then again not really. It's still there somewhere, residing in his dreams. And then sometime in the future—maybe weeks, months, years later—he will be writing a song and it will occur to him that the song he has just written is from a past dream. He recognizes that the music is from a dream when the writing of the song flows out fast and easily.

Everyone taps into the dream database in their own way. If you are an artist like Billy Joel, you might tap into it in a more abstract or artistic way. Whereas, if you're a scientist or business person, you might have different types of dreams.

Within each of us is our personal dream and beyond that is the collective dream. The personal is important in terms of individual development and your personal life, and the collective is important because it taps into a database that has everything you have ever wanted and more. It is the database of your dreams; you just have to know how to access it, and you can create everything from great scientific achievements to great works of art. Dreams are the key to attaining these goals and to your empowerment. In this sense they are the ultimate tool. They can give you secret messages, reveal hidden messages, and help you learn, know, and attain your dream goals.

Oracles are ways of tapping into the meanings behind your dreams. Often times your dreams are veiled attempts by your dream mind to communicate with your conscious mind. As a whole, your dream mind has a tendency to communicate in terms of symbolism that has deeper meaning when put within the context of your life. Oracles are tools meant to help you decipher the symbols so that your dreams make better sense to you and so you can benefit from their insights.

Using Dream Tools and Focals

The purpose of tools is to make the tasks of life easier and pleasures more enjoyable. Your dream empowerment journal and/or tape recorder are your most important dream tools. Always keep them on your sacred dream space next to where you sleep. That way, if you wake up at 4 o'clock in the morning with a symphony, best-selling novel, or the answer to world peace buzzing around in your head, you have the tools to write it down or record it as it's happening. Then when you wake up again later, it won't matter if you remember the dream or not because it's written down in your journal or recorded on tape which can later be transcribed into your journal.

Your journal also acts as a powerful dream empowerment focal because when you write down your goals in it and then the plans to achieve these goals, you establish a focus point that you can frequently refer to that keeps you on course. Oftentimes this is the edge you need to be successful and to attain your dream goals.

Use your dream empowerment journal to keep track of your goals, plans, and tools for love, healing and well-being, and abundance. Organize your energies so that you can get the most amount done with the least amount of effort. Keep lists, and learn to set your priorities with regard to your goals so that you work from the most important on down to the least important. Organization is probably the most important tool you have at your disposal.

Other dream focals include your sacred space, meditation, prayer, and affirmation. Once again, these dream methods give direction and focus to the path that your life follows, including your dreams. Every time you look at your sacred space, you are reminded of your goals. Every time you say the prayer before you go to sleep at night, you are giving the suggestion that your dreams be positive and fulfilling. Each time you repeat your dream affirmation during the day, you are reminded of your overall purpose, something that usually supersedes everything else you do, the element that links everything else in your life together into one cohesive whole. You can be that person, who as Rudyard Kipling writes in his poem

"If," can keep your head about you when all about you are losing theirs. This is the true nature of focals and the focus they bring with them. They help you focus your awareness on the task at hand.

As the Rolling Stones sing in the song "Ruby Tuesday," "Lose your dreams and you will lose your mind." In reverse, this would say, "Keep your dreams, and you will gain your empowerment and mental harmony." The deciding factor here is your dreams.

Friedrich Kekule receives the distinction of being listed in Leslie Alan Horvitz's book, *Eureka: Scientific Breakthroughs That Changed the World,* because of Kekule's discovery of carbon compounds, something that at the time was totally alien to anything else in chemistry but quickly came to revolutionize the way chemists perceived the structure of atoms. One of the things that makes Friedrich Kekule's breakthrough interesting is because the idea came to him while he was dreaming.

The overall concept came to Kekule in two different dreams. The first was while he was on a trolley car; he dozed off and had a dream where atoms seemed to bond together to form chains. This dream became the basis for the "structural theory" of atoms. From this first dream, he had a second dream when he dozed off in front of a fireplace. This time he saw these chains intertwining one another like serpents. Suddenly in the dream, the snakes swallowed their tails, thus forming a circle, and from this symbolism, Kekule saw what he was looking for—the carbon atoms formed an hexagonal ring with alternating single and double bonds. Each one held its own hydrogen atom, like charms on a bracelet.

Friedrich Kekule's dreams changed the world and, as a result, again show the effect that dreams can have on your waking world. The dream mind is just a blink of an eye beyond the waking mind and as such are mirrored reflections of one another. Within this scenario you are not only the dreamer, but the dream maker, the one who ensures that your dreams become reality. Your spirit is a horse that rides on the wind; your reality is a world that also needs earth, fire, and water in order to survive. Empowerment is about balancing the elements in your life so that they all work together to make your life what you want it to be.

Working within these elements is what the dream tools and focals are all about in terms of empowerment. The many forms of tools and focals work within both your waking and dream worlds, and oftentimes they help to bridge the gap between the two worlds.

Aromatherapy for Dream Empowerment

Smell is the most primal of your senses, and scents invoke forgotten memories, feelings, and altered states of awareness. The natural fragrances of plant oils used in aromatherapy stimulate your sense of smell and affect your body, mind, and spirit in positive ways. Because of this, aromatherapy can be applied to dream empowerment as a way to encourage helpful and vivid dreams.

The crafting of aromatic oils dates back to before the rise of the Egyptian dynasty. Essential oils used in aromatherapy today are concentrated essences from aromatic herbs, resins, and plants made by extracting their fragrances through steam distillation. Most of them have a watery consistency and evaporate quickly when exposed to air. They are also somewhat costly, but remember, a small bottle of essential oil can go a long way when it is diluted in a carrier oil. Unless you're using lavender essential oil, which doesn't need to be diluted, it's important to always dilute essential oils with a carrier or base oil before applying it to your skin. Examples of carrier oils include apricot, olive, and jojoba.

The easiest way to use aromatherapy for dream empowerment is by putting a few drops of essential oil in your evening bath just before you go to sleep. Lavender is an excellent choice for this purpose. You can also use an oil burner for aromatherapy. Fill the bowl of the burner with water and then add a few drops of essential oil. Light the candle at the base of the burner. As the water and oil warm up, the fragrance of the oil slowly permeates the room. Or you can mix a few drops of essential oil with a carrier oil such as sweet apricot and use it as massage oil. When using aromatherapy massage oil, be sure to rub it in for at least 30 minutes for best results. Other aromatherapy applications include aroma lamps, misting sprays, dream pillows, body creams or powders, diffusers, specially crafted jewelry and aromatic pouches, and inhalers.

If you use aromatic oils on your skin, remember they are potent and care must be taken. Do not get them in your eyes. Do a skin patch text first, and if you have an adverse reaction, apply pure lavender essential oil or jojoba oil to the area to soothe it. Pregnant women should use only safe oils that are especially made for expectant mothers and labeled as such. Remember to always store your oils in a cool, dark place out of children's reach and sight.

Crystals and Gemstones for Dream Empowerment

Crystals and gemstones are powerful tools that have been worn for luck, protection, and well-being for thousands of years by the ancient Sumerians, Native Americans, Egyptians, Chinese, and Celts. They are minerals consisting of either organic or inorganic materials. There are more than 3,000 minerals, but only about 50 crystals and gemstones are valued for their beauty.

Quartz crystals and gemstones have naturally balanced, solid state energy fields. That is why they are used so often in watches, radios, credit cards, and so forth. Every crystal and gemstone has energetic properties and exhibits extremely high and exact rates of vibration. These vibrational rates can be augmented, amplified, transformed, and focused on other rates of vibration, such as the energy of your body, mind, and spirit. Because of their energetic properties, they can be used to amplify thought energy, intensify your focus and concentration, and invoke vivid dreams. Please refer to my book *The Pocket Guide to Crystals and Gemstones* (see Appendix B) for the specific spiritual and dreaming properties of crystals and gemstones.

Dream Empowerment with Exercise and Body Work

Body, mind, and spirit work together. When you develop your physical fitness, you also enhance your mental and spiritual fitness. Your dreams can benefit from this enhanced fitness. When you exercise regularly you sleep better, and your dreams are generally more vivid and colorful. I urge you to enhance your dreams with some form of regular exercise at least three times a week. It can be a walk around the block, a short swim, a bike ride through the park, a jaunt with the family dog, or dancing joyously with your children in the living room for a few minutes. (Don't do any strenuous exercise right before bedtime, though. It can make it harder for you to fall asleep.)

Martial arts such as Chi Kung, Tai Chi, Aikido, and Karate are also excellent forms of exercise that can help you develop inner resolve, improve concentration, and expand your self-awareness. The martial arts help you become more aware of your breathing and how you move and hold your body.

Yoga originated in India more than 6,000 years ago by Tibetan monks, and many of the martial arts are offshoots of it. The word *yoga* stems from the Sanskrit word that means "to unite" or "to join." It refers to the union of your conscious mind with the collective unconscious, with Oneness. Practicing yoga helps you to be more in balance and harmony with your life and everything around you.

Beneficial for women, men, and children of all ages, yoga employs breathing techniques, body postures, and meditation techniques to promote well-being. These benefits include, but are not limited to, improved concentration, more vivid dreams, relief from insomnia, improved health, weight loss, and decreased stress. With the advent of the New Age, the many paths or schools of yoga have found tremendous popularity in modern culture.

Acupuncture is an ancient Chinese medical practice based on the traditional oriental principle that chi, or natural energy, flows through the body's meridians or channels. These channels can become blocked by tension, stress, and illness. Acupuncture treatments use very thin needles that are inserted into the acupuncture points along the body's meridians and then twirled slightly to restore energy flow to that specific area. In my experience, treatments to the ear especially promote restful and creative dreams. For me, the effect lasts at least three nights after the treatment. I have found that the best way to find a good acupuncturist is by word of mouth.

Acupressure is a catch-all word that describes pressure-point massage. Similar to acupuncture, acupressure uses firm pressure on the acupressure point with your thumbs and fingertips instead of needles. You can do this at home on yourself, but proceed with caution and common sense. For example, pregnant women and people with high blood pressure should avoid acupressure treatments unless prescribed by a doctor.

Less technical than acupuncture, acupressure is more holistic and not as intrusive. I have found it to be of great value for general toning, relieving stress, and promoting relaxation and vivid dreams.

Therapeutic massage has been popular for thousands of years. It was used by the ancient Greeks to promote relaxation and peacefulness. In massage, scented oil or creme is rubbed on your body, and your muscles and tissues are kneaded, pounded, stretched, and stroked. This releases blockages in your body, relaxes your muscles, and promotes your body's natural healing abilities. Massage is especially helpful for insomnia and nightmares.

Other powerful alternative body work therapies and other New Age modalities that can be used to encourage helpful dreams include but are not limited to Feldenkrais, Alexander Technique, Bach Flower Essences, homeopathy, naturopathy, bioenergetics, therapeutic touch, hypnosis, reiki, magnetic therapy, kinesiology, ayurvedic healing, shiatsu, and chiropractic adjustment. There are several good books on these specific therapies available from bookstores, the library, and the Internet.

Dream-Empowering Music

Most of us are deeply moved—body, mind, and spirit—by music. Empowering music can instantly change your mood, uplift you, and improve your vitality and emotional well-being. New Age and instrumental music are especially effective when used in meditation and applied to dreams.

New Age music combines the musical traditions of many cultures and can be relaxing and conducive to dream empowerment. Often natural sounds, such as rain, ocean waves, wind, and bird song, are layered into the music and add a natural dimension that helps to relax you.

One effective way to use music to enhance your dreams is to listen to music as you go to sleep and give yourself a dream suggestion. Then listening to the same piece of music when you wake up helps you better remember the details of your dreams. The music acts as a triggering device.

Dream Foods

What you eat can have an effect on what you dream. Certain foods such as bananas and pasta release chemicals in the brain such as serotonin (a hormone) and tryptophan (an amino acid), that influence dreaming and aid sound sleep. Taking vitamins and supplements such as B_6, B_{12}, bee pollen, Choline, and Inositol help you remember your dreams and increase their vividness. Melatonin, a neurotransmitter hormone, promotes vivid, frequent, and lucid dreams. Foods such as soy products, dairy products, avocados, pears, and eggs (and eggnog) also stimulate your dreams. Herbs such as nutmeg, rosemary, marjoram, lavender, mint, chamomile, gota kola, and ginkgo biloba influence both the clarity and frequency of your dreams, as do nuts such as almonds and cashews. Kava Kava root is used to promote intense and lucid dreams. For best results eat dream foods a couple hours before you go to sleep.

Love

Within your heart, you most likely have dreams of love that transcend your present situation. These dreams are in a sense the accumulation of the dreams you have when you sleep. Oftentimes you don't recall what you dream, but then the dream filters back into your life in unforeseen ways, reminding you that you first encountered this situation in a dream.

You can use tools and focals for love both as a way to enhance your dreams and as a way to enhance your overall life. An example is using an aromatic dream bag or pillow to enhance your dreams of love and buying your loved one a special gift and surprising him or her with it. Tools and focals are ways to build and solidify relationships and help them become more long term.

It's important to make every effort to be more positive in your interactions with people as a whole. Practice your communication skills until they become assets for you. At this point, these skills are tools to help you have better relationships from your primary relationship, your family, relatives, friends, and working relationships. Good communication is also a primary key for opening the dream door to love empowerment.

Sacred Love Dream Space

Add a misting bottle, ½ cup spring water, lavender essential oil or other favorite, calming essential oil such as marjoram, lemon grass, or rose to your dream space. Also add ½ cup dried lavender flowers, ½ cup dried rose petals, ⅛ cup dried rosemary, 1 tablespoon dried mint leaves, 1 tablespoon dried marjoram, a cloth drawstring bag or small fabric pillow. Empower these items with dream power by holding your hands, palms down, over the items on your altar and saying three times:

May these helpful dream tools and focals be blessed with divine, loving dream power.

Dream Ritual for Love

The purpose of this ritual is to create a dream mist to promote helpful dreams, as well as make a dream bag to encourage dream insights regarding your dream empowerment goals for love. You will need the misting bottle, water, lavender essential oil (or other favorite, calming oil), ½ cup dried lavender flowers, ½ cup dried rose petals, ⅛ cup dried rosemary, 1 tablespoon dried mint leaves, 1 tablespoon dried marjoram, and cloth drawstring bag from your sacred love dream altar. You will also need a large bowl in which to mix the herbs.

The natural, fragrant qualities of herbs and flowers have a positive effect on dreaming and can be used to produce vivid dreams. Begin by gathering everything together. Imagine a bright sphere of white light completely encircling you and your sacred space. Then invite the elements into your ritual space by saying:

I respectfully invite the elements of earth, air, fire, water, and spirit into my sacred ritual space.

Invite any favorite, helpful love Goddesses and Gods or other divine energies into your ritual space by respectfully calling them by name and asking them to be present.

Next, put the spring water in the misting bottle and add six drops of lavender essential oil. Cap the bottle and shake it. As you shake the bottle chant:

Divine dream mist empower my dreams.

Spray the dream mist on your pillowcase and bed linens. Then close your eyes and spray the mist upward above your face. It's important that the mist fall in front of your face. Breathe in deeply, and then continue with the ritual and make your dream bag. Remember to spray the mist, close your eyes, and breathe it in, just before doing all the dream techniques in this chapter to enhance their effectiveness.

For your dream bag, use a small drawstring cloth bag (or square pillow you sew). If you sew the bag yourself, be sure to leave one end open to put the herbs in. Select a bag color that appeals to you.

Put the herbs and flowers in the large bowl. Then rub your hands together briskly for a minute to warm them up and get the energy flowing in them. Now begin slowly mixing the flowers and herbs together with the fingers of your power hand. As you do this, imagine filling the pieces of herbs and flowers with divine and loving dream power and chant:

Divine and loving dreams, come to me.

Put the mixture into the bag, and draw it tightly shut with the drawstring (or sew it shut). Then hold the filled bag in your hands and empower it by merging with the divine and repeating three times:

Divine and loving dreams, come to me.

Then put the bag close to your face and breathe in its fragrance for a few minutes. When you are done, thank the divine and the elements by saying:

I thank the divine and the elements for their helpful presence and blessings.

Visualize stepping out of the sphere of white light you imagined at the beginning of the ritual, and imagine the sphere diffusing into the air around you.

Put the dream bag inside your pillowcase and leave it there for 10 consecutive nights for best results. As you sleep, the movement of your head crushes the herbs, releasing their dream-enhancing properties.

Dream Meditation for Love

Begin the meditation by spraying the dream mist above your head, closing your eyes, and breathing it in. Then use a basic yoga breathing exercise called "The Waterfall" to relax. First breathe in deeply; then still your breath briefly and exhale through slightly parted lips for as long as you can. Continue breathing in this manner for a few minutes.

Now close your eyes and imagine being inside a crystal dream castle. Like a knight of King Arthur's Round Table, you are about to begin a quest for your dream goal of love. In preparation for this event, you are gathering up your best tools to take with you to help make your adventure a success.

Imagine entering a room in the dream castle where you are greeted by the aroma of roses. The room itself is made out of rose quartz, and as you enter it, you are filled with an immense feeling of love that extends from yourself out into Oneness. On the table in front of you sits a heart-shape piece of rose quartz, and as you pick it up and put it in your pocket, you understand that it is the power of love and that you will carry it with you at all times, wherever you go.

As you enter the next room in the dream castle, you are greeted by the soothing sounds of celestial instruments that seem to surround you in every way. Made of emerald, the whole room reverberates with webs of communication that generate from the cellular to the spiritual. On the table in front of you sits an emerald amulet, and as you pick it up, it gives you the power to dream any dream you desire. You put the amulet in your other pocket to help you on your forthcoming dream quest for love.

The third room you enter is made of clear quartz crystals. The sensation you get when you enter the room is one of clarity, where all the masks and facades have been removed and everyone is just who they are in life. On the table in front of you sits a clear quartz crystal carved in the shape of a small eye. When you touch it, you have the power to see everything for what it truly is. It enables you to see the true love within people and to discard everything that is false. You carry the eye with you and step out the door that leads you on your quest to a more loving way of life. You venture out into the world, using your tools to help you in your dream quest to make your love goals come true.

Now take a deep waterfall breath, feeling peaceful and refreshed. Take another waterfall breath and slowly open your eyes. Move your feet and hands, and come back to the present time and place. Take another waterfall breath and stretch your body, yet remain in a relaxed and calm state of mind.

Dream Prayer for Love

Prayer opens the door for divine power to flow through you and help you in your quest for love. Breathe in the dream mist for a few moments, and then say this prayer just before you go to sleep. If you like, you can alter this prayer, or any of the other prayers in this book, to match your spiritual preferences:

Dear God and Goddess, please bless my dreams
With your divine knowledge and wisdom.
Show me the best tools to use
To attain my dreams for love.
Thank you, dear Lord and Lady
Blessed dreams, blessed be.

As you drift to sleep, repeat softly:

Blessed dreams, blessed be, and I will clearly remember my dreams when I wake up.

When you wake up, be sure to record and/or write everything you remember from your dreams in your dream empowerment journal.

In addition to writing or recording your dreams, you can create a sort of dream time capsule in many unusual ways. For example, if you have an artistic flair, you can draw, sculpt, paint, sew, or quilt your dreams, or if you are an avid gardener, you can plant flowers and create gardens that represent your dreams. All of these ways of expressing your dreams help to reinforce the power of your dreams and propel you toward the successful attainment of your dream goals.

Oracle of Dreams for Love

Once you have misted yourself with the dream mist, consult this oracle that was perfected by the "baru," the psychics of ancient Babylon, to better understand your dreams. Based on a scrying method presented in Sarvananda Bluestone's book *How to Read Signs and Omens in Everyday Life* (see Appendix B), it shows you how to use household items as handy, readily available divination tools.

Gather together a bowl, a half cup of olive or other salad oil, and water. Thoroughly wash the bowl in warm water and then fill the bowl with cool water. Leave a couple of inches room at the top of the bowl. Then pour a small amount of olive oil on the water's surface. Be careful not to cover the entire surface. Leave some room for shapes to evolve.

Take a deep breath to center yourself. Hold your hands over the bowl of water and oil and say:

I empower this scrying bowl as a dream divination tool for love.

Now close your eyes. As you breathe in through your nose, roll your eyes upward, and as you exhale out through your mouth, roll your eyes downward. As you breathe in and roll your closed eyes upward, in your mind's eye imagine a rainbow flowing into the top of your head and filling you completely. Then imagine the rainbow flowing out of the top of your head. Take a few more quiet breaths and think about a question regarding your dream empowerment goals for love, or if you prefer, think of a question regarding your dream last night.

Now open your eyes and slowly run the index finger of your receiving or dream hand (your left hand if you are right-handed, and your right hand if you are left-handed) in the bowl of water and oil for a moment or two. Gaze at the oil and water for a few minutes. Do any insights come to you regarding your question about love? Are there any recognizable shapes, signs, or patterns in the oil and water? Write down your question and observations in your dream empowerment journal and date your entry.

Dream Affirmation for Love

Spray yourself with the dream mist each time you say this dream affirmation for love. For most powerful results, repeat the love affirmation several times a day for 28 days:

Today and every day, I discover and successfully use dream tools for attaining my empowerment goals for love. I believe in love! I believe in my goals! I believe in my plans! I believe in myself and those I love!

Health

Go ahead and be the healthy person you want to be. Give yourself permission and then set your goals, make your plans, and take the steps, using the appropriate dream tools and focals to do just that! Above all, it's important to stay focused and motivated toward making your dream goals come true.

At all times, whether you are asleep or awake, there is an interplay between the waking mind and dream mind. As such they are both reflections of each other and, by virtue, have an effect on each other. If you have healthy and happy dreams, then they affect the overall temperament of your waking life. If your life or dreams aren't what you want them to be, then it's time to stop and start making different choices. Set your mind on what you want, then outline the steps you need to take to make it happen and the tools that would make the job easier. Use the following dream techniques to help you realize your dream goals for healing and well-being.

Sacred Healing Dream Space

Add a finger-size, clear quartz crystal point to your sacred healing dream altar. Also add carrier oil, lavender oil, sandalwood oil, chamomile oil, and a small cup. Empower these items by holding your hands over them, palms down, and saying:

May the divine healing power of the universe fill these dream tools and focals. So be it!

Dream Ritual for Health

The purpose of this ritual is to make a dream oil to promote helpful dreams, insights, and messages regarding your dream empowerment goals for health. You will need 2 teaspoons carrier oil (such as apricot or extra-light olive), lavender oil, sandalwood oil, chamomile oil, and a small cup.

Put the oils and cup on your altar. Then imagine a bright sphere of white light completely encircling you and your sacred space. Invite the elements into your ritual space by saying:

I respectfully invite the elements of earth, air, fire, water, and spirit into my sacred ritual space.

Next, ask helpful divine energies into your ritual by saying:

I ask the divine energies of (state the name of Goddess, God, guardian angel, spirit guide, and so forth) into my ritual space now.

Put 2 teaspoons carrier oil into the cup. Add 4 drops lavender oil and say:

May the healing power and wisdom
Of the universe fill this dream oil.

Add two drops of sandalwood oil and repeat:

May the healing power and wisdom
Of the universe fill this dream oil.

Then add four drops of chamomile oil and repeat:

May the healing power and wisdom
Of the universe fill this dream oil.

Blend the oil with the fingers of your power hand (usually the hand you eat with) for a minute. As you do, imagine filling the oil with divine healing dream power and wisdom. Anoint your wrists, ankles, third eye, and the back of your head with a couple of drops of dream oil. Then rub the remainder of the oil on your upper chest and neck for 30 minutes. As you rub the oil in, repeat:

May the healing power and wisdom
Of this dream oil guide my dreams tonight.

When you are done, thank the divine and the elements by saying:

I thank the divine and the elements for their helpful presence and blessings.

Visualize stepping out of the sphere of white light you imagined at the beginning of the ritual, and imagine the sphere diffusing into the air around you. Remain in a peaceful state of mind for the meditation.

Dream Meditation for Health

In this meditation, you will actually be placing the crystal from your healing altar on your acupressure points and chakras to activate your body's natural healing energy. Crystals are natural energy amplifiers.

First, clean the crystal by rinsing it in cool water for at least a minute with its point downward. Then, mist yourself with the dream mist and also mist the crystal. Hold the crystal between your hands and use a pulse-breath method to charge it. Breathe in and imagine a single point of brilliant white light in your mind's eye. As you exhale, imagine planting that image, that point of white light, into the crystal body itself. Use your breath as a carrier wave for your intention. Repeat this process three times to fully charge the stone.

When you have finished charging the crystal with white light, hold the crystal in your right hand. Put the crystal on the point about one hand's width below your right knee joint on your outer calf along your leg bone. This acupressure point, known as the three-mile point, is used for general toning, increasing energy, and enhancing endurance. Take a deep breath and imagine breathing healing energy and white light into this point for about 30 seconds.

Hold the crystal in your left hand and put it about one hand's width below your left knee joint on your outer calf along your leg bone. Take a deep breath and imagine breathing healing energy and light into this point for about 30 seconds as well.

Hold the crystal in your power hand and put it on your first chakra. This is the area at the base of your spine. It is called the root or survival chakra. Very slowly imagine a beautiful red rose resting in that chakra. Imagine the perfect rosebud, and with your breath, open that red rose. As you breathe in, slowly unfold the petals, noticing the texture, scent, exquisite pattern, and beauty of the rose. Breathe in and open the rose a little more. You can almost feel the soft velvety texture of the red petals. After you get the rose open to a perfect blossom, begin closing the rose with your breath, closing it again, and then opening it just to where it feels comfortable.

Breathe in and hold the crystal on your second chakra, also called your sacral chakra. This is the point just below your navel. It is where your emotions reside, your feelings toward yourself and others in your world. Imagine a beautiful orange-colored rosebud in your second chakra. With your breath begin to open the rose, slowly and completely. Imagine every aspect of the orange-colored rose as you do this. Take a deep breath to see even more details of the rose. Now slowly begin to close the orange-colored rose back into a bud form. Then open it back up just to where it's comfortable, balancing your emotions and feelings as you do so.

Place the crystal on your third chakra, above your navel and just under your breastbone. This is your solar plexus or power chakra where you generate light and love. In your mind's eye, imagine a beautiful golden yellow rosebud, and begin to open it into a perfect rose. Become one with the rose and see the energy radiating from it. Use your breath to open the golden yellow rose completely, then close it back down just to where it feels comfortable. As you do this, tune in to your inner strength and inner healing energies.

Slowly put the crystal on your fourth chakra, your heart chakra. With your intention and breath, open a beautiful rose-colored rosebud in your heart space, slowly and completely. As you do this, open yourself to Oneness, to the healing energy all around you. All that is you is reflected in the rose. Open yourself to the light and love of the universe. Now begin to close the rose-colored rose, opening it again just to where it feels comfortable.

Place the crystal on your fifth chakra, your throat chakra. This is where you communicate with the world, with yourself, and with others. This is where your sense of smell and taste reside, and also where your telepathic abilities dwell. Slowly begin to imagine a lavender-blue rosebud in your throat area. The rose is full of fragrant vitality and healing energy. Open yourself to communication from helpful healing energies while you sleep and dream. Allow them to help you feel better and be healthier. Slowly begin to close the lavender-blue rose and then open it just to where it feels comfortable.

Put the crystal on your sixth chakra, your third eye, at the center of your forehead. Knowing and observation reside in your third eye. Imagine a beautiful deep magenta rosebud in your third eye. Use your breath and intention to open the magenta rosebud completely. As you do this, you open yourself to realms of healing dreams. Step through the healing dream doorway of well-being as you become one with the magenta rose. Take a deep breath to open it a little more, and then use your breath to close the rose back down. Breathe in again, and open the magenta rose just to where it feels comfortable.

Put the crystal on your seventh chakra, your crown chakra, at the top of your head. This chakra connects you with the divine, with oneness. Slowly use your breath to completely unfold a beautiful white rosebud in your crown chakra. Become one with the white rose. Connect with the divine healing energies of the universe and within yourself. Know that all things are one. Slowly begin to close the white rose, closing it and then opening it just to where it feels comfortable.

Take another deep breath, holding the crystal between your hands for a few moments. Feel its details, facets, warmth, or coolness. Breathe in the healing, balancing energy of the crystal for a minute or two. Fill yourself completely with its natural healing light. Breathe in again and move your toes. Then slowly open your eyes without really focusing on anything in particular and come back to the present time and place, bringing the healing light and energy from the meditation with you.

Dream Prayer for Health

Mist yourself and the crystal. Then hold the crystal between your hands as you say this prayer:

I pray that the divine healing energies of the universe empower my dream tools and guide my dreams tonight. Divine Ones, please share your wisdom and light and bless my dreams with helpful messages. May we dream as one, in harmony and health. Amen.

As you drift to sleep, hold the crystal in your receiving, dream hand, and repeat softly to yourself:

May we dream as one, and I will remember my dreams clearly when I wake up.

When you wake up, hold the crystal in your receiving hand as you write down everything you recall from your dreams in your dream empowerment journal. If you prefer, tape record your dreams and then transcribe them into your journal. Hold the crystal in your receiving hand as you record them.

Oracle of Dreams for Health

Once you have sprayed yourself with the dream mist, consult this oracle. Use a bowl, ½ cup salad oil, and water. Wash the bowl in warm water and fill it with cool water. Leave a couple of inches of space at the top. Pour a thin film of oil on the water's surface. Don't cover the entire surface. Leave some room for shapes to evolve.

Take a deep breath to center yourself. Then hold your hands over the bowl of water and oil and say:

I empower this scrying bowl as a dream divination tool for health.

Close your eyes. As you breathe in through your nose, roll your eyes upward. As you exhale out through your mouth, roll your eyes downward. As you breathe in and roll your closed eyes upward, in your mind's eye imagine a rainbow flowing into the top of your head and filling you completely. As you breathe out, imagine the rainbow flowing out of the top of your head. Take a few more deep, quiet rainbow breaths and think about a single question regarding your dream empowerment goals for health, or if you prefer, think of a single question regarding your dream last night.

Open your eyes. Run your index finger of your dream hand in the bowl of water and oil for a moment or two. Gaze at the oil and water for a few minutes. Do any insights come to you regarding your question? Are there any recognizable shapes, signs, or patterns in the oil and water? In your dream empowerment journal, write your question, insights, and so forth, and date your entry.

Dream Affirmation for Health

Mist yourself with the dream mist and say this affirmation several times during the day for the next 28 days for the best results:

Today and every day, I discover and successfully use dream tools for healing and well-being. I believe in my goals! I believe in my plans! I believe in myself and in my dreams for well-being!

Abundance

As your perception of abundance changes, so, too, do your goals, plans, and tools. The empowerment process is dynamic, meaning that the only thing that is constant is change, and because it is dynamic, the idea is to move it in a forward direction so that you evolve as a human being in this lifetime and all other lifetimes.

Your dream tools and focals for abundance help you in your plans to actualize your goals. If your goal is to build your dream home, then you need to draw up the plans to make it a reality. The third step is to assemble all the tools you need to make it happen, such as good house plans, a reliable contractor, and the funds to pay for it all. Overall, your tools are as important as your goals and plans. They all need each other in order for your empowerment to truly work out.

Don't be afraid to ask questions when it comes to tools and focals because new ones are being invented and distributed every day, and sometimes the right question to the right person can give you just the tool you need when you need it. Oftentimes synchronicity starts to play in and that's when things usually get interesting, especially when this synchronicity begins alternating back and forth between your dream and waking worlds.

Tools such as the "Dream Interpretation Symbols" in Appendix A help you to understand the deeper meaning behind our dreams and how these can help you in your empowerment process. Tools such as dream interpretation are most effective when used within terms of who you are. Each person is different, and your experience with a tool or focal is not always going to be the same as another person's experience. After all, dreams are a very personal experience and reflective of your inner self.

Sacred Abundance Dream Space

Add a green candle, a sage and cedar smudge stick, 8 teaspoons barley, 8 teaspoons rice, 8 teaspoons flaxseed, 8 teaspoons rolled oats, a 4 by 4-inch green or gold pouch, and a clear quartz crystal to your sacred abundance dream altar. Empower these items by holding your hands palms down over them, merging with the divine, and saying:

May the divine abundance of the universe fill these dream tools and focals. So be it!

Dream Ritual for Abundance

The purpose of this ritual is to make a dream pouch to encourage dream insights and messages regarding your goals for abundance. You will need the green candle, a sage and cedar smudge stick, 8 teaspoons barley, 8 teaspoons rice, 8 teaspoons flaxseed, 8 teaspoons rolled oats, a 4 by 4-inch green or gold pouch, and the clear quartz crystal from your sacred abundance dream space. You will also need a bowl and matches.

Make this dream pouch on a night just before the full moon. Gather the items needed together. Then imagine a bright sphere of white light completely encircling you and your sacred space, and invite the elements into your ritual space by saying:

I respectfully invite the elements of earth, air, fire, water, and spirit into my sacred ritual space.

Light the green candle and invite helpful divine energies of abundance, prosperity, and wealth into your ritual space now. If you have rapport with favorite deities, dream helpers, and other divine beings, chant those names three times now.

Next, light the smudge stick from the candle flame. Use the bowl to catch any hot ash. Bathe the crystal and pouch in the smoke for a few minutes to cleanse them of any unwanted energies. Then open the pouch and put the barley, rice, flaxseed, and rolled oats inside. Also put the crystal inside. Hold the filled pouch in your hands and empower it by saying three times:

Dream pouch inspire dreams
Of abundance and prosperity.

Thank the divine and the elements by saying:

I thank the divine and the elements for their helpful presence and blessings.

Visualize stepping out of the sphere of white light you imagined at the beginning of the ritual, and imagine the sphere diffusing into the air around you.

When you are done with the ritual, allow the candle to continue burning as you do the meditation, or if you prefer, snuff it out for now, and then relight it when you are ready to meditate.

Put the pouch next to your bedside and leave it there for eight weeks to encourage insightful dreams and helpful dream messages regarding your dream empowerment goals for abundance. Then disassemble the pouch and return the herbs to the earth. You can clean and reuse both the pouch and crystal.

Dream Meditation for Abundance

Mist yourself and relight the green candle. Sit comfortably and gaze at the candle flame or, if you prefer, its reflection. Take a deep breath in and out to relax and calm your mind. Inhale again and as you exhale say the word *abundance.* Do this several times. Each time you breathe out and say the word *abundance,* focus your awareness completely on the word. Just empty your mind of all other thoughts and worries. You will feel more naturally relaxed and calm as you do this.

As your mind quiets, stop saying the word *abundance*. Take a few quiet breaths and imagine that your best friend has just invented a virtual dream room. The environment is created by a computer that takes your dreams and makes them virtually real within the room. You are excited because you get to be the first person to try it out. The idea is to gradually transform the virtual room, step by step, within your dreams, using any tools you might need in the process much like a dream version of the BBC television show *Ground Force,* where participants start with a drawing or vision of what they want. Then they map it all out and do the steps needed, using many tools and materials in the process. The end result is this beautiful garden that is a surprise for the owner.

In terms of your friend's virtual dream room, imagine telling the computer exactly what you would like the room to look like. You describe your dreams for abundance in detail; for yourself and your family, your community, country, and the world. After a few blinking lights and a series of calculations, the computer screen lights up and shows you each step you need to take to get there. Along with the directions is a listing of the tools and focals needed to make the whole process a lot easier to accomplish.

Imagine beginning to take the steps as outlined by the computer printout. Every night you dream the step, and the next morning you go to the virtual dream room to view and experience the effects of your dreams. Before your eyes on a nightly and daily basis, you transform your life into the abundant and prosperous one you have always dreamed of. Your dreams work hand in hand with reality to create an enriching and empowering life for you. Depending on your expectations and determination, you can accomplish most anything as long as you put your mind to it. As you realize this, you understand that you need to maintain your focus and motivation on your goals.

Take a few minutes to imagine your ultimate goals of abundance coming to fruition within both your dreams and the virtual dream room. Go ahead and dream it exactly how you would like it to be. Follow your dream path to abundance.

Now breathe deeply and completely. Inhale, and as you breathe out say the word *abundance*. Slowly open your eyes and softly gaze at the candle flame. Take another deep breath, and as you exhale repeat the word *abundance*. Begin to move your toes and fingers, coming back to the present time and place. Take a third deep breath, and as you exhale repeat the word *abundance*. When you are finished meditating, be sure to snuff out the candle.

Dream Prayer for Abundance

Use the dream mist and say this prayer just before going to sleep:

Bright and divine ones, I pray you
Please guide my dreams tonight.
Show me the best tools
To use to attain my goals for abundance.
Please light my path
Each night and every day.
May my dreams be blessed. Amen.

As you drift off to sleep, repeat softly to yourself:

May my dreams be blessed, and I will remember my dreams clearly when I wake up.

When you wake up, write down or record everything you remember from your dreams.

Oracle of Dreams for Abundance

Once you have used the dream mist, gather together a bowl, water, and oil. Wash the bowl and fill it to about two inches from the top with cool water. Pour a film of oil on the water, but don't cover the entire surface.

Take a deep breath to center your awareness. Hold your hands over the bowl of water and oil and say:

I empower this scrying bowl as a dream divination tool for abundance.

Close your eyes. As you breathe in through your nose, roll your eyes upward, and as you exhale out your mouth, roll your eyes downward. As you breathe in and roll your closed eyes upward, in your mind's eye imagine a rainbow flowing into the top of your head and filling you completely. As you breathe out, imagine the rainbow flowing out of the top of your head. Take a few more deep breaths and think about a question regarding your dream empowerment goals for abundance, or if you prefer, think of a question regarding your most recent dream regarding abundance.

Then open your eyes and run your index finger of your dream hand in the bowl of water and oil. Gaze at the oil and water for a few minutes. Do any insights come to you regarding your question? Are there any recognizable images or shapes, signs, or patterns in the oil and water? Write these impressions down in your dream empowerment journal along with your question, and date your entry.

Dream Affirmation for Abundance

Spray the dream mist above your face, close your eyes, and deeply inhale its fragrance. Then say this affirmation. Repeat the affirmation several times a day for at least 28 days for the most powerful results:

Today and every day, I discover and successfully use dream tools to attain my dream empowerment goals for abundance. I believe in my goals! I believe in my plans! I believe in myself and in my dreams for living an abundant life.

Chapter Four

Becoming One with Your Dreams

Arising out of the philosophical movement called Dadaism after World War I, Surrealism worked from the premise that dreams tap into the unconscious and your true self. Surrealist writers and painters accessed what they termed the "unconscious" mind as a link into that point of their mind where dualities such as life and death, past and future, awake and dream, and good and evil are no longer contradictory polarities, but instead are part of the overall fabric of Oneness. Surrealistic painter Salvador Dali described his paintings as hand-painted dream photographs. Indeed, Dali had a photographic sense about his paintings, which he insisted were inspired by dreams and other unconscious forces.

Surrealist painter Joan Miro described the first part of the creative process as free and unconscious, but, in contrast, the second stage was carefully calculated. He believed dreams were thoughts and creations in pure form, straight from the divine, universal mind.

One of the more striking aspects of surrealistic paintings is the way the artist realistically combines incongruent elements to create a scene that reminds you of dreams. An example of this dreamlike incongruence is Dali's famous painting *Persistence of Memory,* which depicts melting, misshapen clocks on a seashore. Another example is René Magritte's *Le Mal du Pays,* which depicts a man with wings on a bridge with a lion at his feet.

Because dreams move beyond ordinary reality, they are often incongruent with it. Strange, magical, and unusual happenings frequently occur in dreams—for instance, flying dreams or dreams of alien worlds. These happenings are what makes dreams fascinating to everyone. They are also one of the reasons dreams have fueled the imaginations of so many creative artists throughout the history of humankind.

Remembering Your Dreams

In the summer of 1797, poet Samuel Taylor Coleridge was feeling low. One night while reading Purchas's pilgrimage with Kubla Khan, he dozed off into three hours of intense dreaming that revealed a series of images to him. When he awoke, he envisioned the whole idea from the dream and began writing a most exquisite poem titled "Kubla Khan." While writing down the images from the dream, Coleridge was called away on business for about an hour, and when he returned, he discovered that the dream images had vanished from his mind, leaving only a vague memory. What he remembered and saved from his dream created a classic poem, but who knows what it would have been like if Coleridge had written down the whole poem without interruption as he first envisioned it in his dream.

Like Coleridge, most people experience an initial period of time when they first wake up from sleeping that they remember their dreams. After this initial period of time is over, the dream seems to vanish into a haze, leaving only a piecemeal recollection of the dream's particulars. Without these specifics, the dream remains elusive, and its meaning and insights are difficult to consciously ascertain.

This shows the need to record your dreams immediately upon waking from a dream sequence. Avoid beguiling yourself into thinking you will remember your dream later, because most times you won't. Also keep in mind you may need to get up at odd times in your sleep cycle to write down or record a dream, but the benefit in the long term as you connect with your dream self is enormous.

When you are better able to remember your dreams, you open up a whole new and fascinating world to yourself. The beauty of it is that this dream world can be deliberately accessed to help you determine and achieve your empowerment goals for love, well-being, and abundance.

As with most talents and skills, remembering your dreams becomes easier with practice. It also helps to learn a few basic techniques for developing better skills for dream recall. One of the best ways to remember your dreams is to lie as still as possible upon awakening, with your eyes closed. If you move or open your eyes, your brain rhythms and chemistry change, sensory information flows in, and it becomes more difficult to remember your dream. As you lie still, go over the particulars of your dream in your head for a minute before recording your dream or writing it down.

I invite you to apply the following 10 methods to help you better remember your dreams and increase your own dream recall:

- Give yourself the suggestion to take an active part in your dreaming experience, and right before you go to sleep and just as you awaken, repeat over and over the suggestion to remember your dreams when you wake up.
- Body positioning is a basic method for merging with the dreamscape. Be as still as you can and keep your eyes closed for a minute as you go over the dream in your head. Don't stretch or get up from bed. Also, resume your last sleeping position as well as other body positions to trigger dream recall and provide more dream details.
- Once you recall your dream and go over it in your mind for a minute or so, immediately tape record or jot down images and events from your dream. Don't worry about getting everything in order. Just record or write down all the details you can recall. Speak or write in the active, present tense as if the dream is happening right now. For example, "I am talking with a goddesslike woman with flowing red hair, and she guides me to a castle made of crystal. I enter the doorway to the castle and see a crowd of people. I know some of the people and the others seem familiar, too."

- Often there is one element of the dream that is most vivid. Decide on a simple metaphorical statement about your dream that describes that element. For instance, if you dreamed about finding your soul mate while swimming, you might call the dream "soul mate swimming." Metaphor is a way to move deeper into the elements of your dreaming experience.
- Check for body signals, scents, moods, feelings, and emotions, and make an effort to remember whether your dream took place in the day or at night. Note whether your dream was in color or black and white. Make a note of anything that seemed incongruent, odd, or intriguing. Also check for any precognitive content that may have appeared in the dream.
- Dialogue with your dream as if it were an interactive movie. Talk with the other characters and with your dream self about some of the events and situations. Ask what the parts of your dream mean. Ask people within your dream what they are trying to communicate. Logical parameters do not necessarily apply in dreams, so rather than think about it too much, get a feel for the dream and what it is saying to you.
- Check to see if anything in your dream coincides with your waking experience. Pay close attention to similarities in your dreams and waking life. For example, if you dream about rain, does it rain the next day or in the next week? Examine the pattern of your dream and what in your dreaming experience connects with your waking world. It's helpful to write down a few main things, events, or impressions about your waking day in your dream journal just before you go to sleep. Then check to see if your dreams correspond to or provide more information about these things.
- Use a personal dream symbol to access dream recall. Create or select an existing symbol that you like, and put it on the wall by your bed or on your bedside table where you will frequently look at it. Focus on the symbol just before you go to sleep and give yourself the suggestion to remember your dreams when you wake up. Then when you awaken, focus once again on the symbol to enhance your dream recall. Do this for at least 28 nights for best results.

- Use music as a triggering mechanism for dream recall by playing a specific piece of music as you go to sleep. Play the same piece of music when you awaken to enhance dream recall. Do this continuously until you derive the desired results. Make playing the music selection as easy as possible so you can just push a button without getting out of bed. Better yet, put the music on a timer that is set to play and awaken you instead of setting your alarm.
- Create something from your dream. Creative enactment of dreams includes, but is not limited to, drawing or painting your dreams, writing a poem, growing a garden, dancing, drumming, singing a song, making a dream cake, writing a letter or a story, crafting a piece of furniture, or quilting a dream quilt. All of these creative representations of your dreams are empowering ways of connecting with your dream self.

Interpreting Your Dreams

Starting with the early Egyptians and Greeks, the art of dream interpretation has evolved over the centuries and is a skill that has been extensively written about and practiced. The Greek philosopher Heraclitus said that each person's dream was unique to the person. In the "Phaedo" Plato describes how Socrates became a student of music and the arts because of instructions he received in a dream. The Greek philosopher Aristotle thought that the most skillful interpreter of dreams was a person who absorbed resemblances and understood that dream images were analogous to the forms reflected in water.

In this sense, dreams are a reflection or mirror of the waking world, but with unusual or incongruent aspects. Dreams often speak in terms of metaphor and symbols. In order to understand the deeper meaning of your dreams, you need to interpret the incongruencies and metaphors of your life so that they make more sense both in your waking and dream world.

In his book *10,000 Dreams Interpreted,* Gustavus Hindman Miller relates the case of a man who sometimes had dreams of walking through green fields of corn, grass, or wheat. When the man had one of these dreams, he discovered that for the next few days following the dream, he experienced prosperous opportunities. He found that if he encountered rocks or other adverse conditions in his dream, it usually meant that he would soon face some hardships. If he climbed a mountain and the top was barren in his dream, it meant that he would attain his goals, but the venture on the whole would be unprofitable. When he climbed the mountain and the top was green and springlike in his dream, it meant that the venture would yield excellent profits. In addition he found that muddy water in his dream signified sickness, business depression, or jealousy, and as such gave him a warning to be cautious.

Understanding what your dreams are trying to show you is what gives dream interpretation value. Often it's a matter of sitting down with your dreams and evaluating their effects on your life. You also need to evaluate what happens afterwards in your waking world when you have certain dreams, particularly ones that recur at regular intervals.

Keeping track of your dreams by recording and writing them down is essential for dream interpretation. That's why it's vital to keep a dream empowerment journal. By recording and writing down your dreams, you begin setting up a database with which you can observe comparisons, contrasts, and progressions within your dreams and your waking life. After all, the more complete the information you have, the better chance you have of interpreting your dreams accurately.

As a dreamer, you have many different types of dreams, from the significant to the nonsensical. Some dreams seem to act out the day's events, whereas other dreams portray information that is beyond your normal bounds of reality. Some short-sighted theorists have stated that dreams are something for the garbage disposal, whereas more open-minded theorists insist that dreams are valuable, often precognitive, and offer insights into your waking life. What this suggests is that there are many different types of dreams just like there many types of people.

As you write your dreams down in your dream empowerment journal, you will begin to see patterns in them, particularly with respect to dreams and themes that repeat themselves. If a dream is being continually repeated in one form or another, then chances are your dream self is trying to communicate something that it thinks is important to your waking self. Sometimes this information reflects your fears and anxieties, and other times it reflects problem-solving concepts, past life or future life memories, parallel lifetimes, precognition, impressions of the day, and creative ideas, to name a few. Sometimes as you are having a dream or writing one down, you might not see its relevance to your life, and only later, as you explore it further and begin interpreting what it's trying to tell you, do you see a dream's true meaning and importance.

Without a doubt, your dream empowerment journal is your most important tool when interpreting your dreams because it represents a basic communication link between your waking world and your dream world. The more you use your journal to record your impressions of your dream world, the more you open up the lines of communication, and the interpretation becomes easier and meanings of your dreams become clearer. This becomes even more true as you begin working on your empowerment goals, because they give more focus to both your dreams and waking life.

Approaches to Dream Interpretation

Along with the many varieties of dreams, there are also a multitude of approaches on how to interpret your dreams. These approaches represent the many psychological viewpoints of the roles dreams play in the context of your overall life.

In his book *The Interpretation of Dreams*, Sigmund Freud indicated that although dreams might be stimulated by external events, wish-fulfillment was the basis of most dreams. Because of this, he believed that dreams reflected a person's deepest desires, that they always had serious meaning, and that the roots were in a person's childhood. Freud saw dreams as windows into a world that was best kept at a distance. He felt the primary value of dreams were as psychological tools for dealing with and analyzing a patient's relationship with the "other self," which Freud termed the "unconscious" or "Id."

Originally a student of Freud, C. S. Jung agreed that dreams revealed people's deepest wishes and desires, but he also felt that dreams helped people realize and fulfill their unconscious ambitions. Jung saw dreams as meaningful messages that people send to themselves and, as such, were important to personal development. He would have warmed to the idea of dreaming as a tool for empowerment because he realized that the dream world represented something the dreamer wished to move toward.

Other innovative approaches to dreams include those of Frederic "Fritz" Perls, founder of the Gestalt therapy, who felt that every character and object in a dream represented some facet of the dreamer's life, and of Medard Boss, who saw the dream as a mirror or reflection, in a metaphorical sense, of what was happening in the dreamer's life.

Basically because there are so many different types of dreams, there are as many types of approaches to interpretation. The most valid as well as the most personally valuable is a personal approach, in which you interpret your dreams in terms of what is happening in your life—past, present, and future. You yourself know more about your life than anyone else, and this makes you the best one to interpret the meanings of your dreams.

Dreams are a reflection of the waking world, in all its many complexities. Like a computer, your mind is continually processing and responding to the multitude of stimuli that you experience every day. During the day, you experience your waking world, flying like a falcon over your perceived domain, and at night you are the dreamer, navigating like a bat through a world of fantasy. At a point the worlds of waking and dream come together, and as this happens, the communication link between the two becomes much more pronounced and magical and miraculous things begin to happen. You begin to realize that you can indeed attain your dreams on some level.

The main idea with dreams is to get them to help you make your waking world more enriching and enjoyable. This is the purpose of your dream empowerment goals and plans. In terms of goals and plans, start out simple and build from a basic foundation. No matter what you do, this seems to be the best way to begin manifesting your dreams.

Your dreams are a reflection of you and your relationship with the world, and also with the divine. This communication is oftentimes expressed in symbolic or metaphorical terms. Although symbols often have universal meanings, these only have depth within terms of who you are and what your goals are. This is again what gives focus to your life.

When looking at the dream empowerment symbols list in Appendix A and when referencing other books on dream symbols (many excellent ones are listed in Appendix B), remember that these meanings are provided by the authors and represent a collection of historical, cultural, and personal meanings. What is important is what things in your dreams mean to you.

For example, the image of an eagle to one person might mean danger while to you it might mean great power and insight.

By interpreting your own dreams in your own way, dream interpretation acts as a mode for personal transformation and empowerment. It also makes the process easier as dream symbol definitions can actually confuse your interpretation process, especially if the definition doesn't make any sense to you.

As a rule of thumb, the best way to make use of dream symbol books is as catalysts to activate your dream recall and help you brainstorm possible meanings of particular images in your dreams. Don't take any of the meanings verbatim. Instead use the meanings as a backboard for your thoughts. Also keep in mind that dream symbols constantly evolve and their meanings and significance change as you experience life.

Love

Within terms of love, it is often important to determine which amorous dreams are best left in the realm of fantasy and which ones you would like to honestly come true. Within your heart, you know the difference between the two. Just sit back quietly, take a few deep breaths, and check in with your inner self for clarity. There is an ancient wise light-filled part of you that knows exactly what you truly desire.

One of the best ways to better understand what you truly dream is to learn to move forward in your dreams, giving yourself a view of how things and relationships will look over time. This is called forward thinking and is what helps make successful people successful. By dreaming dreams, setting goals, making plans, and taking the steps to make those dreams come true, you give your life specific focus. By doing so, you tremendously elevate your chances for success both personally and professionally. You can help facilitate the flow of this dreams-to-reality process by creating and programming a dream crystal for love to help you remember and interpret your dreams regarding love and relationships.

Sacred Love Dream Space

Add a piece of rose quartz, a white taper candle, and rose-scented oil to your sacred love dream altar. Empower these ritual items by holding them in your hands, one at a time, and saying:

May this item be filled with divine and loving dream power.

Dream Ritual for Love

The purpose of this ritual is to empower a rose quartz crystal to help you better remember and more accurately interpret your dreams. You will need the rose quartz, white candle, and rose oil from your sacred love dream altar. You will also need matches and a ballpoint pen.

Imagine a bright sphere of white light completely encircling you and your sacred space. Invite the elements into your ritual space by saying:

May the elements of earth, air, fire, water, and spirit come into my sacred ritual space now.

Use the ballpoint pen to write the word "remember" on the candle three times. Then rub a thin film of rose oil on the candle body. Anoint yourself with the rose oil at the wrists and ankles and also put a drop of rose oil on the rose quartz. Wipe any remaining oil from your hands and light the candle. Dedicate it to your favorite divine energies.

Hold the piece of rose quartz in your power hand and imagine walking into the stone. Now say:

Dream stone of rose light
Guide my dreams tonight.
Help me to remember my dreams
And understand their meanings.
So be it!

Continue holding the stone and gaze into the candlelight for a few minutes. As you do this, imagine seeing images of your dream empowerment goals for love coming true in the candle flame. Take a few deep breaths to intensify your focus and the images of your love dreams.

When you are done, thank the divine and the elements by saying:

I thank the divine and the elements for their helpful presence and blessings.

Visualize stepping out of the sphere of white light and imagine the sphere diffusing into the air around you. Put the rose quartz on your dream altar for now. You will be using it for the love meditation, prayer, oracle, and affirmation that follow. Allow the candle to burn down safely. If you prefer, you can snuff it out and relight it the next day, allowing it to burn safely down at that time.

Dream Meditation for Love

Put a drop of rose oil on a cotton ball or handkerchief, and also anoint the piece of rose quartz from your dream altar with a drop of the rose oil. Then put the cotton ball or handkerchief close to your nose and breathe in the rose fragrance. Breathe in the essence of the rose and allow it to fill your senses completely. As you breathe out, release any anger, fear, and stress you may be feeling, neutralizing and balancing your overall energy field. As you continue breathing in and out, your breath becomes the connecting point between your body, mind, and spirit, between waking and dream.

Now, in your mind's eye imagine a beautiful, fragrant pink rose growing before you. Sense yourself moving into and through the soft, velvety pink petals toward the center of the rose. For an eternal moment, your essence becomes the rose and its essence becomes you.

From the essence of the rose, you follow a path of rose-colored light that leads you out beyond ordinary reality. In your journey you come across a river of darkness that separates your waking world from your dream world. From opposite shores, you can see your dream self and your dream self can see you, but from different sides of the river of darkness; your twin selves seem to never truly come together.

From out of the rose-colored light, you fashion a rainbow with which you build a bridge over the river of darkness that spans from your waking world to dream world. The colors of this world transcend into the colors of the other world until you finally perceive both worlds as one and the same. You notice that the rose rainbow bridge of remembering is complete.

Your waking self and dream self meet on the rainbow bridge, and as a result, you better remember and understand your dreams about love and life. The bridge allows you to move back and forth between your waking and dream worlds much like a shaman moves between worlds. To better remember and understand your love dreams, cross over your rose rainbow bridge and connect your dream and waking worlds into one.

Take a deep breath, and breathe in the knowing that you are the rose, you are the rainbow bridge, you are Oneness. As you breathe in again, you realize that love is always within your reach. Take another deep breath and slowly open your eyes, moving your fingers and toes and coming back to the present time and place. Stretch and shift your body, yet remain relaxed for the dreamtime prayer that follows.

Dream Prayer for Love

Hold the rose quartz in your receiving hand and say this prayer just before you go to bed:

Dear Goddess and God, I pray you
Help me to remember my dreams
When I wake from sleep
And guide me in interpreting
Their messages and meanings.
Thank you divine friends.
By the Lady and Lord, blessed be.

As you drift to sleep, keep the rose quartz in your receiving hand and repeat to yourself:

I clearly remember my dreams about love when I wake up and I easily interpret them.

When you wake up, hold the piece of rose quartz in your receiving hand as you write down everything you recall from your dreams in your dream empowerment journal. If you prefer, tape record your dreams and then transcribe them into your journal. Hold the stone in your receiving hand as you record them. Also, write down what the dream means to you.

Oracle of Dreams for Love

For Native Americans, stones are the oldest, wisest, and most enduring tribe. All stones are thought to be alive and have stone creatures inside them. In the Cherokee tradition, stones are used for divination.

In this oracle, you will be using the natural powers of rose quartz. Holding the piece of rose quartz between your hands, merge with the divine and say:

I empower this stone and the stone creature inside of it as a divine dream oracle to help me remember and interpret my dreams about love.

Take a few deep breaths to center yourself. Then turn your mind to a specific dream you had last night (or recently) about love. Think about the particulars of the dream, perhaps one or two elements that caught your attention. Now breathe in deeply, and as you breathe out, imagine sinking into the stone itself. Start with your toes and move up your body to your head. Imagine completely melding with the stone and becoming one with it. Once you are inside the stone, imagine a helpful stone creature inside the stone with you. Ask the stone creature inside the stone to help you understand your dream. Imagine the stone creature imparting a dream message to help you attain your dream empowerment goals for love.

When you are done, take a deep breath and imagine floating out of the stone. Now set the stone down and clap your hands once. Write down any messages you received from the stone creature about your dream in your dream empowerment journal.

Dream Affirmation for Love

Repeat this affirmation several times a day to enhance your dream recall and interpretation. Whenever possible, hold the piece of rose quartz in your power hand as you do so:

Each and every time I wake up, I clearly remember my dreams of love and I easily interpret them.

Health

In ancient times, dream messages often foretold a person's health. Hippocrates, the Greek father of modern medicine, believed that dreams reflected a person's medical condition. With this in mind, he could diagnose a person's ailments by means of that person's dreams.

Not all of us have Hippocrates's skill in dream interpretation, but at the same time, you can practically apply the messages you recall in your dreams to improve your health and attain your dream empowerment goals for well-being. For example, I have always dreamed of foods or vitamins that I need to eat or take for optimum health. Whenever I have a food or vitamin dream, I heed the message and immediately add the item to my diet for a few weeks. Each time I do this, I feel better.

In addition to personal healing, you can use your dreams to promote global healing. Many people throughout the world believe that we can dream together to create a healthy and joyful present and future for all of humankind. We are all human beings sharing a common experience of life on this planet Earth, and, in this sense, are living in one world.

Together, as one people living in one world, we can use our dreams to help heal ourselves, others, and the animals and plant life on our planet. By better remembering and understanding your dreams, you can actually use the dream messages you receive to heal yourself and the earth.

Sacred Healing Dream Space

Add a clear quartz crystal point to your sacred healing dream altar, or use the one you used in the dream empowerment techniques in the previous chapter. Also add a white tea candle and lavender essential oil. Hold the candle in your hands, merge with the divine, and say:

May the divine healing power of the universe fill this candle.

Next, roll the vial of essential oil in your hands for a few minutes until it gets warm, again merge with the divine, and say:

May the divine healing power of the universe fill this oil.

Dream Ritual for Health

The purpose of this ritual is to create a dream crystal to help you remember your dreams about healing and well-being as well as help you more accurately and easily interpret the message in your dreams. You will need the crystal, white tea candle, and lavender essential oil from your sacred healing dream altar. You will also need a tablespoon of sea salt, a bowl of water, and matches or a lighter.

First, cleanse your crystal by adding the salt to the bowl of water and soaking the crystal in the salt solution for about a minute. Then, rinse the stone for at least a minute in clear, cool water, with the point downward toward the drain. Dry the stone.

Next, create your sacred ritual space by imagining a luminous sphere of white light encircling you and your sacred space, above and below you as well. Then invite the elements into your ritual space by saying:

May the helpful elements of earth, air, fire, water, and spirit enter my sacred ritual space now.

Light the tea candle and invite any divine healing energies into your ritual by saying:

May the divine healing energies of the universe enter my ritual space now.

Anoint yourself and the clear quartz crystal with a few drops of the lavender essential oil. Then hold the clear quartz crystal between your hands and gently feel its contours and other details with your fingers.

Place the crystal in your left palm and cover it with your right palm. Now, in your mind's eye imagine one specific dream empowerment goal for health. Pulse that goal into the crystal by taking a deep breath and sharply pulsing your exhaled breath through your nose. Repeat this process three times. After programming the crystal, continue holding it in your hands, merge with the divine, and say:

Healing crystal of divine dreams,
Please help me remember my dreams of well-being.
Help me to understand their deeper meanings;
Empower me with healthy dreams. So be it!

Now hold the stone between your hands and imagine breathing your specific dream empowerment goal into it. Then put the crystal where it is illuminated in the candlelight. Gaze into the candle flame and visualize your dreams for good health coming true. Do this for a few minutes. If you like, put a mirror behind the candle to amplify its light. You can then gaze at the crystal, the flame, and their reflection. Moving your eyes between the reflection in the mirror and the flame eases eye discomfort. Keep your intention and expectation in mind as you gaze at the crystal and candle. Do this for a few minutes.

When you are done, thank the divine and the elements by saying:

I thank the divine and the elements for their helpful presence and blessings.

Imagine stepping out of the luminous sphere of white light you imagined at the beginning of the ritual, and visualize the sphere diffusing into the air around you. Put your healing crystal on your sacred healing altar for now. You will be using the crystal for the meditation, prayer, oracle, and affirmation that follow.

Dream Meditation for Health

Turn on some soft meditative music. Sit or recline comfortably with your healing dream crystal in your receiving hand. Begin breathing deeply and slowly. Breathe in boundless, unlimited life energy and breathe out any discomfort you may be feeling. Sense the muscles in your body letting go of any tension, releasing it out into the cosmos with your exhale. As you breathe in this way, you feel more relaxed and, at the same time, more aware. You realize that every breath you take is a sacred and divine one, and your mind is suddenly freed of the usual chatter. In its place is a beautiful, infinite clarity. Sense yourself flowing into that clarity. Set your spirit flying free, like a giant bird.

As you soar high up into the sky, things look much different than they do down on the ground. Stretching your wings, you soar above the rooftops and chimneys and realize you can move from place to place almost instantly. With one flap of your wings, you soar above majestic trees and high mountains. As you view the images below you, the smaller pieces fit seamlessly together into a larger whole. Flapping your wings faster, you soar into the clouds and toward the stars themselves. The higher you go, the more you perceive the whole of Oneness. It is at this point that you realize that you can go wherever you want to go and be whoever you want to be with a flap of your wings.

Now, in your mind's eye imagine a time in the near future when you are in optimum health. Imagine dreaming dreams of healing and well-being and becoming completely healthy. Sense what your body, mind, and spirit feel like in this healthy state of being. Check out some of the things the healthy you is doing, thinking, feeling, and saying. Take a deep breath to get a clearer image and sense of who you are when you are feeling healthy and in optimum health.

Once you have the image of your optimum health firmly in your mind's eye, spread your wings and begin winging your way toward the healthy you. Soar toward your dream empowerment goals for health, toward your vision of personal well-being. The harder you flap your wings, the faster you go.

As you soar higher and higher, you breathe in the divine healing breath of spirit and realize that as long as you practice forward movement, you will naturally flow toward a more healthy you. You choose how much effort you want to apply to attaining your dream empowerment goals for health. All you need to remember is to keep your flaps up as you soar higher and higher and achieve your dream vision. It's up to you to set the pace for yourself, to determine how quickly you want to attain your dream goals for health. So spread your wings and fly.

Now imagine you are dreaming a wonderful dream about flying toward an optimum state of health and well-being. In the dream, a divine light fills your entire being with healing energy as you soar through the skies. Imagine healing miracles happening with each flap of your wings, in every aspect of your life, and within every light-filled cell of your body. You realize that you have created your body and you have a deeper wisdom within, a wisdom that often speaks to you through dreams, that knows how to help heal you.

As you become one with yourself and the cosmos, you become one with Oneness, and upon doing so, you open up the door to an infinite cosmic library. Every particle of energy leaves an imprint upon the fabric of Oneness, and such is recorded in this energetic cosmic library that has records of the past, present, and future of all lifetimes, of everyone and everything.

Now imagine stepping into that cosmic library for a moment and viewing your own personal records in a video format so that you can better understand how to attain your optimum state of health. Imagine yourself as you are right now in present time, and know deep within that you can attain your dream empowerment goals for health. Believe with all your body, mind, and spirit that you are healthy and you will be healthy. Be your dream of well-being and good health and your dream will be you. You are one.

Take a deep breath, breathing in the knowledge that you can access the creative flow of the universe that shapes body, mind, and spirit whenever you need to. Take another deep breath, knowing that your breath is the breath of spirit. As you flow with your breathing, you welcome dreams for good health and well-being. You remember, understand, and heed those dream messages of importance. You also naturally glimpse things in your dreams that help you attain your dream empowerment goals for health. As you take another deep breath, begin moving your feet and hands and slowly open your eyes. Come back to the present time and place and stretch your body to get more comfortable.

Dream Prayer for Health

Anoint your pillowcase with a couple drops of lavender essential oil. Or if you prefer, put a few drops of lavender oil on a cotton ball or handkerchief and slip it inside your pillowcase. Then hold the clear quartz crystal in your receiving hand and say this prayer just before you go to sleep:

Dear Goddess and God, I pray you
Guide my dreams for healing and well-being.
Give me a message that I will attain
My dream empowerment goals for health.
Please help me to remember my dreams
When I awaken from my slumber,
And show me their deeper meanings.
I ask this in the Lady and Lord's name.
Divine ones dream with me, blessed be.

Continue to hold the crystal in your receiving hand, and if possible fall asleep on your right side to help assure a good night's sleep. As you drift to sleep, repeat over and over to yourself:

I clearly remember my dreams for healing and well-being when I wake up and I understand their messages.

When you wake up, anoint the crystal with a drop of the lavender oil and then hold it in your receiving hand as you write down everything you recall from your dreams in your dream empowerment journal. Also, write down what your dreams mean to you.

Oracle of Dreams for Health

Holding the clear crystal between your hands, merge with the divine and say:

I empower this stone and the stone creature inside of it as divine dream oracle to help me remember and interpret my dreams about health.

Take a few deep breaths to center yourself. Then turn your mind to a specific dream you had last night (or recently) about healing and well-being. Think about the particulars of the dream, perhaps one element that seemed most important in the dream. Now breathe in deeply, and as you breathe out, imagine sinking into the stone itself. Start with your toes and move up your body to your head. Imagine completely melding with the stone and becoming one with it. Once you are inside the stone, imagine a helpful stone creature inside the stone with you. Ask the stone creature inside the stone to help you understand your dream. Imagine the stone creature imparting a dream message to help you attain your dream empowerment goals for health.

When you are done, take a deep breath and imagine floating out of the stone. Now set the stone down and clap your hands once. Write the date and the message the stone creature imparted in your dream empowerment journal.

Dream Affirmation for Health

Anoint yourself with a drop or two of lavender essential oil, hold your dream stone for health and well-being in your receiving hand, and repeat the following affirmation several times a day for 28 days to enhance your dream recall and ease the interpretation process:

Each and every time I wake up, I clearly remember my dreams of healing and well-being and I easily interpret them.

Abundance

In dream interpretation, dream images of abundance and prosperity are good luck signs. Finding money in your dreams often indicates new opportunities and changes for the better, both personally and professionally. An inheritance in your dream may indicate that you will receive a legacy or boon. Gold, metals, coins, jewelry, and medals often symbolize financial gain.

Remember that abundance is not only things but can be found in love, enjoyable times, knowledge, good friends, pleasant dreams, a happy family, and fulfilling work. Use the following techniques to help you better remember and understand your dreams of abundance so you can attain your dream goals.

Sacred Abundance Dream Space

Add sandalwood incense and incense holder to your sacred abundance altar. Also add a stone that you have found in nature, one that you are particularly attracted to. You will be using this stone as your abundance stone for the dream techniques that follow.

Dream Ritual for Abundance

The purpose of this ritual is to create a dream stone to help you better remember your dreams regarding abundance and also to enhance dream message interpretation. You will need the stone, sandalwood incense, and incense holder from your sacred abundance dream altar and some matches or a lighter.

Imagine a bright sphere of white light encircling you and your sacred space, and invite the elements into your ritual space by saying:

I respectfully invite the elements of earth, air, fire, water, and spirit into my sacred ritual space.

Then carefully light the incense and invite the divine energies of abundance, prosperity, and wealth into your ritual sphere. Carefully bathe the stone in the incense smoke for a few minutes. This cleanses it of any unwanted energies. (If you are sensitive to incense smoke, you can use sandalwood scented oil instead. Simply rub the oil on the stone to cleanse it.)

Next, hold the stone to your forehead (third eye) for a minute. Then cup the stone between your palms and empower it by taking a few deep breaths, merging with the divine, and saying:

Stone of nature, stone of dreams,
Messages of abundance bring to me.
Help me remember my dreams of prosperity
And understand their deeper meanings.
So be it!

Continue to hold the stone cupped between your palms and imagine your dream empowerment goals for abundance filling the stone. Imagine the stone growing larger and larger as the abundance in your life also grows. Do this for at least five minutes.

When you are done with the ritual, thank the divine and the elements by saying:

I thank the divine and the elements for their helpful presence and blessings.

Visualize stepping out of the sphere of white light you imagined at the beginning of the ritual, and imagine the sphere diffusing into the air around you.

Use your dream stone by holding it in your receiving hand when you drift to sleep, or put it inside the pillowcase on your pillow. You will find that the stone has an immediate influence on your dreams. Continue doing this for 28 nights (a full moon cycle) to encourage helpful dream messages regarding your dream goals for abundance.

Dream Meditation for Abundance

In this meditation, once again you will be using the word "abundance" as a mantra. A mantra is a specific word or sound that has special meaning and is repeated over and over.

Begin by sitting or lying quietly and comfortably, holding your dream stone for abundance in your receiving hand. Begin to relax your mind by thinking of the word *abundance*. Think of only the one word as you breathe in and still your breath, and as you breathe out, say the word *abundance* aloud. Repeat this process several times and make an effort to focus your total awareness on the word *abundance* each time you repeat it. Empty your mind of everything but the word *abundance*. Don't force yourself to do this, just gently turn your mind back to the word *abundance* when it strays away from the word. As you continue doing this, you become more relaxed and calm, yet remain alert and aware.

Now, in your mind's eye imagine a single point of white light. As soon as you envision the white light, you sense it carrying you away on a bright beam that flows infinitely out into the cosmos. The luminous beam carries you through many layers of awareness until you finally come to a place where all beams of light come together into a brilliant, divine point of rainbow light composed of vivid colors.

Allow the rainbow light to flood your body. Now, in your mind's eye imagine flowing through a doorway where waves of multi-colored light envelop every part of your being. Moving deep within your essence, the light fills your body, mind, and spirit and whisks you gently further. Imagine flowing with the current of rainbow light as if it were a divine river. You flow with the rainbow spirit of abundance through the canyons of perception and move your awareness to a rainbow light-filled realm of joyful and prosperous possibilities.

As you enter this realm, a giant database opens up before you, a database that contains every bit of information that you ever wanted or will want to know. Every energetic impulse from everyone and everything is recorded, from thoughts and actions to dreams and realizations. You breathe in deeply and suddenly understand that all the information is there, waiting for you to access it in dreams and in waking consciousness. You suddenly realize that your breath acts as a natural carrier wave for the information as you breathe in and out. Breathe in and out, softly and completely for a few minutes, filling your being with information and energy as you do.

Now focus your awareness on your hands, fill them with rainbow light energy, and feel the energy as intensely as you can. Do this for a few seconds. Then focus your awareness on your feet, filling them with rainbow light energy, and feel the energy in them as intensely as you can for a few seconds. Next focus your awareness on the top of your head and flood that area with rainbow light energy. Do this for a few seconds. Then imagine the rainbow light energy in your body flowing like a wave from your feet to your hands to your head, back to your hands and feet, and back again.

Take another deep breath and begin gently moving your hands and feet. Slowly open your eyes and come back to the present time and place, yet remain in a peaceful state of mind.

Dream Prayer for Abundance

Hold your dream stone for abundance in your receiving hand as you say this prayer:

Dear Goddess and God, please hear my prayer.
Grace me with your divine presence
So that I may dream of joyful abundance,
And help me to remember my dreams
When I awaken once again.
Help me to interpret my dream messages
So that I may know their deeper meanings.
Thank you divine Lady and Lord, blessed be.

Slip the stone inside your pillowcase or put it next to your bedside with the point toward your head when you sleep. As you drift to sleep, repeat to yourself:

I clearly remember my dreams of abundance when I wake up and easily understand the dream messages.

When you wake up, hold the stone in your receiving hand as you write down everything you recall from your dreams in your dream empowerment journal. Also, write down what the dream means to you.

Oracle of Dreams for Abundance

Holding the dream stone for abundance between your hands, merge with the divine and say:

I empower this stone and the stone creature inside of it as divine dream oracle to help me remember and interpret my dreams about abundance.

Take a few deep breaths to center yourself. Then turn your mind to a specific dream you had last night (or recently) about abundance. Think about one element that seemed most important in the dream. Now breathe in deeply, and as you breathe out, imagine sinking into the stone itself. Start with your toes and move up your body to your head. Imagine completely melding with the stone.

Once you are inside the stone, imagine a helpful stone creature inside the stone with you. Ask the stone creature inside the stone to help you understand your dream. Imagine the stone creature imparting a dream message to help you attain your dream empowerment goals for abundance.

When you are done, take a deep breath and imagine floating out of the stone. Now set the stone down and clap your hands once. Write the date and the message the stone creature imparted in your dream empowerment journal.

Dream Affirmation for Abundance

Run your hands and your dream stone for abundance in cool water for at least a minute. Dry your hands and the stone. Then hold the stone in your power hand and repeat this affirmation several times a day for at least 28 days to increase your dream recall and help you better understand the dream messages you receive:

Each and every time I wake up, I clearly remember my dreams of abundance and understand the messages in them.

Chapter Five

Enacting Your Dream Plan

As you get better at remembering and interpreting your dreams, you start building your dream confidence. Rather than being afraid of your dreams, you come to terms with them and understand their value. Going to sleep and dreaming becomes an enjoyable experience that enriches many aspects of your life. This includes helping you to determine and achieve your dream empowerment goals, which moves you toward a life that is more harmonious with who you are as a whole.

Determining and achieving your dream empowerment goals builds your dream confidence. Every time you determine and achieve a goal, you gain dream confidence from the experience. When doing this, it's important to start with smaller goals and from there work toward larger goals. If your larger dream plan is to decorate or renovate your home, then a starting goal might be clearing out the clutter or painting the walls. Having achieved your smaller dream goals, you have the confidence to take on and achieve the larger ones.

Most of us have difficulty staying in the present moment because the natural inclination is to move back into the past or forward into the future. Within terms of dream empowerment, it is important to stay in the present. You must keep your awareness tuned in to what's currently happening around you and within you, otherwise you miss the cues and your timing suffers accordingly. You need to be aware of what's going on in your world right now if you expect to make any progress toward what you want in life.

It's important to flow with energy rather than struggle with it. You are like a sailboat on the waters of life. Depending on which way the wind blows, you set your sails accordingly so the wind works for you and not against you. There are times of contentment when the wind is at your back pushing you forward, and there are times that try your patience and initiative, when all you can do is finesse the energy in the hope of holding your own.

But remember, no matter what happens, don't give up hope because hope is the power that propels your dream boat when the wind isn't blowing. Without hope, life becomes pointless and meaningless. With hope, life is filled with meaning. It becomes a divine buffet of possibilities just waiting for you to sample its many delicious dishes.

Once you become more confident and comfortable with your dreams, it becomes easier to stay in the moment and flow with what is happening in a particular dream. At this point you begin to build upon your dreams and enact your dream plans. If your goal is to bake a cake and you have a recipe, then the next steps involve things like locating the ingredients you need; assembling the tools needed such as a bowl, spoon, and mixer; and doing any preliminary work such as preheating the oven and greasing the cake pan.

These steps represent the things you need to do to enact your plan for baking a cake. Obviously this formula is not limited to making cake. The process is universal in that once you have a goal and a plan, the next step is to enact that plan by taking the necessary actions.

Dream Incubation

Author Robert Louis Stevenson went through a period in his life when he experienced financial problems. Because Stevenson extensively used his dreams for inspiration in his writing, his use of dreams during this time of financial trouble was no exception. He decided to use dream incubation, a method where before going to sleep he gave himself the continual suggestion that he would dream about a story that would make him a good sum of money. As a result, the story "Dr. Jekyll and Mr. Hyde" came to him in a series of dreams. His incubatory suggestion and his ensuing dreams also had a precognitive component in that "Dr. Jekyll and Mr. Hyde" went on to become one of Stevenson's best-selling stories.

Easily one of the most powerful dream techniques you can practice, the essential concept of dream incubation compares to the idea of incubating an egg. You create an environment with the optimum conditions for hatching the embryo that is waiting to come to life within the shell of the egg.

In dream incubation you hatch a dream. You give yourself a suggestion and encase it within the shell of your mind, invite divine inspiration, and then dream on it. You set up the optimum conditions for this dream to arise within you and come to life. The resulting incubated dream then provides you with clarity as to your question or problem and how to achieve your dream goal.

Creating your personal sacred space, doing rituals, saying prayers, and meditating are all ways to optimize the conditions for dream incubation. Each process nudges you closer to positive results. Oracles and affirmation are ways to better understand and affirm the positive results of the dream incubation.

The ancient Egyptians, Celts, and Greeks all utilized dream incubation techniques and had special places for doing it. In particular, the Greeks were renowned for their dream temples, one of the most famous residing at the ancient seaport of Epidaurus, where people came to be healed through their dreams by the Greek god Asklepios. Son of Apollo, Asklepios was raised by the centaur Chiron, who taught him to be the most skilled of all physicians, to the point where he could restore the dead to life. His symbols were the staff and snake, which evolved into the caduceus, the symbol still used in medicine.

Asklepios's dream temples were like modern-day hospitals, where people would go to be cured of their ailments. The patient would go through a purification process and dream incubation rituals before being led into the sleeping chambers. One of the rituals used in the temples involved the patient writing his or her illness on a linen strip with myrrh ink. Afterward the patient wrapped the linen strip around an olive branch and placed it next to her or his pillow while sleeping.

Patients in Asklepios's dream temples most often dreamed of Asklepios healing them of illness or ailments. The God Asklepios would also come into a patient's dream to give a diagnosis and prescribe medical treatment. The temple attendants would then treat the patient as prescribed by the healing god.

This idea of being healed while in a dream is fascinating. Surprisingly, there are a great number of cases of this happening. Ancient Greek records describe a man who could barely see out of one eye going to the temple. In a dream Askepios came and made an ointment, which he applied in the dream. When the man awoke, he could see clearly out of the problem eye.

Modern cases of healing occurring in dreams include one described by Patricia Garfield in her book *Creative Dreaming*, in which a woman was afflicted by migraines for more than 40 years. One night in her dreams, a man came, put his hands on her head, and told her that her head wouldn't hurt any longer. When the woman awoke, she no longer was afflicted with migraines.

In a second case described by Robert Van de Castle in his book *Our Dreaming Mind,* a physician was afflicted with recurring acute bronchitis, until one night in a dream he was visited by his deceased sister, who told him she had come to heal him. As she vanished in the dream, the physician felt a burst of energy in his body. When he woke up, he found that he was healed from his ailment.

What these experiences point out is that there is an aspect to dreams that defies traditional, rational explanations. Dreams have a mystery that makes them all the more appealing, particularly when they have the power to heal and change the direction of your life. The idea of building on your dreams through incubation has enormous potential because it gives direction to that power so you can better utilize and benefit from it. After all, dream power is an untapped energy source with unlimited potential.

Incubation Techniques

In *The Lucid Dreaming Kit,* authors Paul and Charla Devereux cite the case of Nobel Prize–winning biochemist Otto Loewi, who noticed that when he stimulated a particular nerve to the heart, the result was that the heart slowed down. Loewi suspected that what happened was the nerve secreted something into the bloodstream that made the heart slow down, but he couldn't figure out how to prove it.

One night in a dream, he received an answer to the problem, but upon waking the next morning, he realized he had forgotten the dream. The next night he performed a simple incubation technique. He gave himself the suggestion to recreate and remember the previous night's dream. The incubation was successful and he had the dream again. This time he remembered it. Loewi went on to use the information he received from the dream to set up an experiment that proved that the nerve was indeed secreting a chemical that slowed down the heart. His dream discovery changed our understanding of biochemistry.

Dream incubation usually starts with your question or request seeking guidance or resolution of conflict within your life. Think of one of your dream empowerment goals and devise a statement or question that sums up the issue for incubation. Keep the question or statement clear and simple in no more than one or two sentences. Make it easy to remember and repeat to yourself.

Symbols are also excellent tools for dream incubation. They can be existing symbols or ones that you create yourself. These dream symbols are used to hatch a helpful dream by placing them next to your bedside where you can easily see them.

Scientists have shown that people are affected by symbols both on a conscious and subconscious level. That means that all information is being processed by your being on multiple levels of awareness, including the symbolic level. Knowing this, keep your symbols for dream incubation as simple and basic as you can. They will prove more effective when you do.

In the dream incubation process, rather than asking yes and no questions, it's better to make your questions open-ended. For example, you would ask, "What can I do to better communicate with my son (or daughter)?" rather than "Will my relationship get better with my son (or daughter)?" By asking open-ended questions, your dreams can then provide more expanded answers without the restrictions of the conditioned or ego-controlled mind.

When doing dream incubation, you are moving beyond the ordinary to an extraordinary place where you connect with all other forms of energy. In the dream incubation studies conducted by Dr. Henry Reed, dream incubation telepathy occurred when a group of people did dream incubation together. In one study, a group of people were asked to incubate a dream for a person who they were told had a problem, but they weren't told the nature of the problem. After their dreams, they met and discussed what the incubation was about. Amazingly, most of the group had dreams that pertained to the person's incubatory concern.

What this suggests is that people can come together as a group in dream. This, in turn, becomes the group or shared dream that continually moves humanity forward, even when some people try to fight it all the way. Like the oceans and the mountains, forward movement is something that comes naturally whether you like it or not. It's better to work and flow with it than to try to fight it. This is why people ask for divine help and inspiration when doing dream incubations, although the help can also come by way of a revered benefactor.

If you are a musician working on a piece of music, you might ask for the help of a musician whom you revere, such as Wolfgang Mozart, John Lennon, or Jimi Hendrix. Within the context of the dream, they become your dream helpers that you can call upon whenever you have a problem in your creative process. This is a dream incubation that you can use at any time, whatever your creative project may be.

When incubating a particular matter into your dreams, begin by perceiving that question or request in every imaginable way. Imprint it into your psyche so you know its essence from inside out. The idea in dream incubation is to know what you want to achieve through the incubation so when you incubate, you get it. This is why determining your dream empowerment goals and setting your plans are invaluable to the process, as it gives you a focus and direction.

Incubating Your Dream Plan

To incubate your dream plan, begin by selecting one of your goals and your plans for attaining it. Then write down a list of materials, tools, and preliminary work that you need to do to enact your plan. If you have any problems within this process, then use your dreams to incubate the problem and receive an answer.

Don't become discouraged if you don't receive the information right away. Keep dreaming; it will come to you. Sometimes it's a matter of persistence. Ask the question or request the information enough times, and eventually you are bound to get an answer. As with other dream techniques, the more you practice and do dream incubation, the better you will become at receiving the information from your dreams.

Depending on the problem you want to solve or conflict you want to resolve, select a one-sentence phrase or question that sums up what you want addressed and answered in your dreams. For example, if your health goal is to get more exercise and you don't know if you should join a health club, your incubation question might be, "What is likely to happen if I join a health club?" If your abundance goal is to build your dream house but you're stuck on what area or location you should build it in, your incubation question might be, "What is the best place for me to build my dream home?" Remember to keep the question as open-ended as possible, as this gives you the most possibilities and the most information.

Along with being open-ended, your dream incubation request or question needs to be simple so that it is easy to remember and repeat to yourself, as you will be using it as an incubation mantra throughout the dream incubation process. What this technique does is establish a communication link between the waking and dream minds and, in doing so, makes the incubation much more effective as a result of performing on multiple levels in multiple states of being. You bring the power of dream into what you are doing, giving you a higher chance for success.

Select a love, health, and abundance question or request, and decide on an incubation mantra for each. These mantras need to reflect where you are stuck with regard to your dream empowerment goals. After deciding on a mantra for each, write the mantras into your dream empowerment journal. This helps you remember and visualize it and takes it from being an abstract thought in your mind to something physically present, something written down on paper for you to see with your eyes. In this way, you empower the incubation even more by involving another of your senses in the process.

Love

Now is the time to begin incubating your goals and plans for love within your dreams. If you are not presently in a love relationship, ask yourself what kind of relationship you want. If you are in a relationship but don't have the kind of relationship you desire, ask yourself how you can change it into something that satiates your desires. By answering these questions, you can then begin enacting your love dream plan and transforming your relationships into more harmonious and loving ones.

Struggling with things takes too much effort. It's much easier to change the things you have the ability to change. With other things, sometimes you have to accept the way they are until you are finally able to make the necessary changes. Waiting for the right time and place is all part of the law of persistence. Apply persistence to dream incubation and you will find that your dreams often do indeed come true!

While persistence and drive are two of the primary elements that enable you to enact your plans and attain your goals, other important elements include having the skills needed and having a creative approach to your goals and the plans—for example, using dream incubation. Once you have a clear image of what you want and a basic idea as to how to attain it, you are ready to begin incubating your quest for love. As questions and requests arise on your quest, you can incubate them until you have an answer and the information you require. Then you can continue on your journey toward attaining your dream empowerment goals for love.

The following dream incubation techniques act essentially as transcendental psychological modalities. By going through the process and experience, you transcend ordinary reality and connect your many selves, including your waking self and dream self, together into one.

Before doing the following techniques, continually repeat your love incubation mantra aloud to yourself for several minutes. Like writing it down, when you say the mantra aloud it empowers it even more because you involve your sense of hearing and your power of speech. The more times you repeat the mantra, the stronger the bridge between your waking and dream selves, your conscious and unconscious. By doing so, you also greatly increase your dream incubation powers.

Sacred Love Dream Space

It's particularly helpful to add pictures, photographs, symbols, figurines, or other objects that represent some of the main elements of your dream incubation request or question to your dream space. First, add a symbol or picture of a divine benefactor or presence that you feel a strong kinship or rapport with. Second, add a symbol or picture of success in love. An example would be a photograph of you in your beloved's arms, a photograph of helping someone in need, or perhaps a photograph of your children. Third, add a symbol or picture of a well of dream knowledge for love to your sacred love dream space. Examples are photographs of a lake, the ocean, the universe, a small figurine of a wishing well, or even a glass or chalice filled with water.

Empower your three dream incubation symbols by holding them in your hands, one at a time, before placing them in your sacred space, merging with the divine, and saying:

I empower this dream incubation symbol with the divine power of love.

Dream Ritual for Love

The purpose of this ritual is to provide a successful dream incubation for love. You will need the three pictures or symbols that you added to your sacred love dream space. Select some special dream incubation sleepwear, for example a particularly sexy negligee or pajamas in silk, satin, cashmere, or soft cotton, in red or pink or white, that represents your dream intention. You will also need some fresh flowers in a vase of water, a red candle, a ballpoint pen, and a candleholder.

Begin by choosing a love question or request you want to incubate, and decide on an incubation mantra. Write the question or request and the mantra down in your dream empowerment journal and date your entry. Then throughout the day until you actually do this ritual, perform symbolic acts of purification and cleansing. For example, take a relaxing bath to purify your body, and give up sugar, caffeine, or cigarettes (if you smoke) for the day. As you do this, keep thinking about your question and request and frequently repeat your dream incubation mantra aloud and silently to yourself.

Just before you do this ritual, gather everything together that you will need and put on your special dream incubation sleepwear. Stand or sit before your dream altar. Imagine a bright luminous egg of white light completely encircling you and your sacred space. Then invite the elements into your ritual space by saying:

I respectfully invite the elements of earth, air, fire, water, and spirit into my sacred ritual space, right now.

Hold the vase of flowers in your hands and say three times:

It's a beautiful night, filled with dreams of love.

Use the ballpoint pen to inscribe your dream incubation mantra for love on the candle body. Then light the candle. As you do, say your mantra aloud three times.

Gaze into the candlelight and gaze at your three dream incubation symbols for love for at least five minutes. As you do this, repeat your dream incubation mantra for love aloud over and over.

Now focus your awareness on the picture or symbol of your divine helper. Merge with the divine presence and say:

Love, love, love, divine love, speak to me;
Love, love, love, divine love, fill my dreams.

Next, focus your complete attention on the picture or symbol of success in love, merge with Oneness, and say:

Love, love, love, successful love, come to me;
Love, love, love, joyful love, fill my dreams.

Then focus your awareness on the picture or symbol of the well of knowledge, merge with the elements, and say:

Love, love, love, divine knowledge flow into me;
Love, love, love, show me the well of dreams.
As I will, so shall I dream!

Continue gazing into the candlelight. As you do, imagine that you have had a successful dream incubation for love. Imagine all the necessary and pertinent information flowing to you from the well of knowledge in your dreams. Know that your dream incubation for love is a success. Step into the future for a few moments and imagine that you have already dreamed the helpful incubated dream, remembered it, and used the information to fulfill your request or answer your question regarding your dream empowerment goals for love.

When you are finished, remain within the luminous egg of light as you meditate, pray, and dream. Snuff out the candle or allow it to burn down safely. If you snuff it out, relight and burn it down all the way the next day. When the flowers fade and wilt, return them to the earth. As you do, repeat your dream incubation mantra for love aloud three times.

Dream Meditation for Love

You have done everything you can do to fulfill your request or answer your question in your dreams. You can now let go of it, giving it over to the universe. You are ready to completely relax.

Begin by taking a deep breath in and out. Raise your arms up slightly above the surface (any flat surface will do), and become aware of the heaviness that you feel trying to keep them elevated. Now drop them down, resting them on the surface. Feel the sensation of letting go of all your conditioned responses and, in the process, your points of stress and anxiety. Suddenly you realize the forces of gravity seem to be working for you.

Radiating out from your arms, sense all of the muscles in your body becoming more relaxed. Each time you take a deep, complete breath, release any tension that resides in your muscles with your exhale. Each breath helps you feel more and more relaxed. You sense all of your burdens being released, until you feel as light as air. You feel a sense of buoyancy that makes you feel lighter and lighter, flying free and easy.

Sense the particles of your being become less dense as you become the combination of earth, air, fire, and water. Imagine your eternal spirit becoming one with each of the elements, singing a harmonious tune that resonates through valleys and mountains from the deserts to the seashore.

When all are in harmony, your spirit sings within the breath of Oneness. You are all things, and all things are you. From this perspective you move from the now to the infinite now. Your perception moves from who you are in this lifetime, to a perception of who you have been in a multitude of lifetimes before and in the future. This momentary glimpse of eternity gives you a deep sense of relaxation that flows over you like the soft, gentle embrace of warm, radiant white light.

You have given your problem over to the inspiration of a higher power. In your mind's eye, imagine your picture or symbol of your divine helper for a few moments. You have done all you can do to establish the lines of communication between your waking and dream self, and now it's in the hands of a higher power. You no longer need to worry about it. The well of knowledge will provide the information you seek. In your mind's eye, imagine your picture or symbol of the well of knowledge for a few moments.

You are in contact with a higher power. All you have to do is dream. The well of knowledge becomes a tool that continually enables you to access information that can help you on your love quest.

As you breathe deeply, you feel relaxed and ready to sleep and dream. You begin moving your toes and fingers and come back to the present time and place, at the same time remaining relaxed for the following prayer.

Dream Prayer for Love

Put a glass filled with water next to your bed as you sleep. Hold the glass of water in your hands as you say this prayer just before you go to sleep:

Divine ones, please fill my loving cup
So that I may taste your divine wisdom.
Sacred spirits of the well of knowledge,
Please quench my thirst and guide me.
I pray you, open the dream door to love tonight
And give me the information that I request.
Blessed dreams. Amen.

Set the glass of water on your dream altar. As you drift to sleep, silently repeat your dream incubation mantra for love over and over to yourself. Ideally, the mantra is the last conscious thought you have before you drift to sleep.

Oracle of Dreams for Love

In this oracle you will be using an egg to interpret your incubated dreams. This ancient oracular form called "oomancy" was taught to humankind by the Greek god Orpheus and popularized in Europe in the 1600s.

Begin by filling a clear, eight-ounce glass with water. Set it aside for now. Then carefully hold the egg in your hand and say:

I empower this egg as a divine dream incubation oracle for love.

Now focus your mind on your incubated dream. Slowly and carefully hold the egg with your power hand and gently rub it against your body. After a few minutes of rubbing the egg over your body as you think about your dream, crack it open into the clear glass of water. Look into the glass of water with the egg and study the shapes and forms they create. Write these down in your dream empowerment journal. Also, make a note of any insights these shapes and forms represent to you. Take your time but don't think about it too much. Rather, feel the images and their messages and meanings.

After a few minutes, finish up by thanking the divine and the elements by saying:

I thank the divine and the elements for their helpful presence and blessings.

Visualize stepping out of the luminous egg of white light you imagined at the beginning of the ritual last evening, and imagine the luminous egg of light diffusing into the air. When you are done, return the water in the glass on your dream altar and the water and egg in the glass you used for the oracle to the earth.

Dream Affirmation for Love

To affirm your dream incubation for love, imagine your dream incubation picture or symbol for successful love, and then repeat the following affirmation several times a day for the next 28 days:

Today and every day, in waking and in dream, the well of knowledge provides me with the information and answers I request.

Health

Repeatedly recite your health incubation mantra to yourself throughout the time before you do the ritual. Become One with it, making it part of you. No matter what the health question or request may be, from "What would be the best means for treating my ailing back?" or "How should I change my diet?" to "What would be the best form of exercise for me?" and "In what ways can I attain optimum health?" the more you repeat the request aloud and to yourself, the more you move it into all aspects of your being, including your dreams.

Part of what you are incubating into your dreams and the other aspects of your being is your desire to be healthy. The expression of this desire is the first step to becoming healthy. You need to continually believe in yourself and your ability to be healthy with the help of your dreams. When you fulfill your dreams for healing and well-being, you complete a full circle and move to the next level.

Sacred Healing Dream Space

Add myrrh, lavender, and rosemary oils to your sacred healing dream altar. Roll the oil vials in your hands for a few minutes, one at a time, and empower them by saying:

I empower this dream incubation oil with divine healing energy.

Dream Ritual for Health

The purpose of this ritual is to provide a successful dream incubation for healing and well-being. You will need the three oils from your sacred healing dream altar, a strip of cotton or linen cloth, a ballpoint pen, a sprig of greenery, a makeshift tent (blanket and rope), and special sleepwear that symbolizes good health to you.

Begin by selecting one health question or request and decide on an incubation mantra. Write the question or request and the mantra down in your dream empowerment journal. Then date your entry. For the entire day and night of the ritual, eat healthy foods such as fresh, organic fruits and vegetables.

About an hour before you go to sleep, draw a warm bath and add a few drops of the lavender and rosemary oils to the bathwater. As you add the oils, chant aloud:

Blessed ones of divine healing light,
Please share your sacred knowledge with me tonight.

Relax in the fragrant waters for several minutes. As you soak, think about your dream incubation request or question. Also, state your dream incubation mantra over and over as you bathe.

When you are done with your bath, dry off with a soft towel and anoint yourself with the myrrh-scented oil at the ankles and wrists. As you do, repeat the chant:

Blessed ones of divine healing light,
Please share your sacred knowledge with me tonight.

Next, put on your special dream incubation sleepwear that represents good health to you. Now erect your incubation healing tent temple by stringing the rope across the room, about four to five feet above your bed, from head to toe. Anchor the rope ends, and then drape the blanket over the rope. You should be able to lie in bed and be covered with the makeshift tent.

Sit in your newly constructed dream incubation tent temple. Now imagine a bright luminous egg of white light completely encircling you, the tent, and your sacred space. Invite the elements in by saying:

I respectfully invite the elements of earth, air, fire, water, and spirit into my sacred ritual space, right now.

Write your dream incubation mantra for healing and well-being on the strip of cloth with the ballpoint pen. Then wrap the strip of cloth around the sprig of greenery. Anoint the wrapped cloth with several drops of myrrh oil. Hold the bundle in your hands, merge with the divine, and say:

Divine dream helpers from north, east, south, and west,
Generous and wise dream spirits of the inner quest,
Please assist me now, this is my request
[State your dream incubation request or question for health]
Blessed ones of divine, healing light,
Please share your sacred knowledge with me tonight.

When you are done, put the wrapped sprig with your dream incubation mantra for health next to your pillow. Remain in the luminous egg of white light as you meditate, pray, and dream.

Dream Meditation for Health

Sit or recline comfortably inside your dream incubation tent. Your dream incubation preparation is complete, and now it's time to relax and get ready for dreamtime. Sense yourself giving control of your incubation over to divine inspiration, and with this you feel a relief, like a weight being lifted off your being. You have faith in the divine inspiration that is akin to the faith you have that each breath you take provides oxygen to your body.

Take a deep breath and hold it in your lungs for a count of three, and then exhale completely, releasing any tension that has built up in the muscles and tissue of your body. As you breathe in, arch your shoulders upward and hold them there until you exhale, and then drop them down, feeling like someone has just taken a great weight off of them. Do this exercise with your arms and legs, by raising them up while you inhale and hold your breath, and then when you exhale, drop them down, feeling all of the muscles and tissue releasing any energy that has been collected in them. Breathe in, hold it, then breathe out, until your body starts to feel relaxed and at ease.

Now close your eyes if they aren't already closed, and in your mind's eye imagine being in a divine temple of healing. The attendants lead you to an alcove where they anoint you with sacred herbs and oils, readying you for the dream incubation chambers. Now imagine taking the piece of cloth that you inscribed with your incubation mantra in the ritual into the dream incubation chamber and placing it next to your pillow.

Imagine your divine benefactor visiting you, telling you she or he has been thinking about your incubation question or request and will be giving you an answer soon, either in dream or waking. The divine presence tells you to be aware of the signs around you at all times. These are oftentimes communicated on a subtle level. Your divine benefactor is constantly trying to communicate with you, both in waking and in dreams. As you become more aware of the signs, you can better understand the messages being given. It is at this point that you become in sync with your divine benefactor. You know that you will be given the necessary help in your dreams and know you will clearly remember the messages.

Sense the healing energies of the divine presence envelop your being, and for a moment feel yourself in an embryonic state. Like an egg, your inner being is waiting to hatch and emerge from its shell in order to realize your divine potential.

You are an aspect of the divine, and the divine is an aspect of you. Together you are One. When you are at One with yourself, you are healthy. Your divine nature is your true nature. When you become One with your divine nature, you realize you truly are free from all the exterior trappings.

Everyone has a divine beauty within that needs to be expressed in order to give fulfillment to the spirit. Know that your questions and requests will be answered and that your dreams will help breathe energy into your dream goals for healing and wellness. Sense your energy coalescing into a singe point of light, and then into a single pulse, as the light spreads out into every corner of the universe, becoming all there is, was, and will be.

As you take another deep breath, begin moving your toes and fingers. Shift your body slightly, and open your eyes. Stretch and come back to the present time and place.

Dream Prayer for Health

Say this prayer while in your dream incubation tent:

Divine and sacred ones, please guide me to the healing temple in my dreams. I pray you, grant me messages of healing. May your divine wisdom empower my mind. May your healing energy empower my body, and may your breath inspire my spirit. Thank you, divine ones. Blessed dreams.

As you drift to sleep, repeat your dream incubation mantra for health silently to yourself.

Oracle of Dreams for Health

Fill the clear, eight-ounce glass with water. Set it aside. Then carefully hold the egg in your hand and say:

I empower this egg as a divine dream incubation oracle of health.

Now focus your mind on your incubated dream for health. Slowly and carefully hold the egg with your power hand and gently rub it against your body. After a few minutes of rubbing the egg over your body as you think about your dream for health, crack it open into the clear glass of water. Look into the glass of water with the egg and study the shapes and forms. Write these down in your dream empowerment journal and make a note of any insights they symbolize to you. Get a feel for images and their messages and meanings.

After a few minutes, finish up by thanking the divine and the elements by saying:

I thank the divine and the elements for their helpful presence and blessings.

Visualize stepping out of the luminous egg of white light you imagined at the beginning of the ritual last evening, and imagine the luminous egg of light diffusing into the air. When you are done, return the water and egg to the earth.

Dream Affirmation for Health

Say this affirmation for health aloud several times a day and night for at least 28 days for best results:

Today and every day, my body is a temple of divine healing light and wisdom. In waking and in dream, I am healthy and full of life.

Abundance

During your day, repeat your dream mantra for abundance to yourself every hour on the hour. It is an expression of your expectations, the beginning of any energetic pattern or plan. The idea is to answer one question or request at a time as they arise within the context of enacting your dream plan.

Problem-solving and answering requests and questions are some of the things dreams are good for. When you incubate the question or request within your dreams, you give your dreams the opportunity to help you with your empowerment. Within this framework, dreams may be one of the greatest tools you have at your disposal both for personal development and professional development.

Dreams access the database of Oneness that includes all things for all times. It's just a matter of knowing how to dip into the well and access the information. With a little practice, incubating dreams becomes something you do without consciously thinking about it, like breathing.

Sacred Abundance Dream Space

Add a soft fleece blanket, rose-scented oil, and a picture of a garden to your sacred abundance dream space. Roll the vial of oil between your palms for several minutes until it is warm. As you do this, chant:

I empower this dream incubation oil with divine abundance.

Dream Ritual for Abundance

The purpose of this ritual is to provide a successful dream incubation for abundance. You will need the fleece blanket, rose-scented oil, and picture of a garden from your sacred abundance dream space. And you will also need your picture or symbol of a divine benefactor.

Begin by choosing a question or request regarding your dream goals for abundance. Create a simple incubation mantra. Write your question or request, your dream incubation mantra, and the date in your dream empowerment journal.

Put the picture of the garden where you can easily see it from your bed. Then anoint the four corners of your blanket with a few drops of the rose-scented oil. Anoint yourself at the ankles and wrists. Now imagine a bright luminous egg of white light completely encircling you and your sacred space. Invite the elements in by saying:

I respectfully invite the elements of earth, air, fire, water, and spirit into my sacred ritual space, right now.

Gaze at the picture of the garden for a few minutes. Breathe in the beauty of the picture, and say three times:

Divine abundance flows and grows
As I sleep, I dream it so.

Next, focus your awareness on the picture or symbol of your divine benefactor or presence, and say three times:

Divine one, show me what I need to know
As I sleep, I dream it so.

Now close your eyes and imagine being in the garden. Imagine your divine benefactor or helpful presence in the garden with you answering your dream incubation request or question. Know that you are divinely inspired as you sleep and incubate your dream for abundance.

Remain in the luminous egg of white light, wrapped in the soft blanket, as you meditate, pray, sleep, and dream.

Dream Meditation for Abundance

You have done all the preparation for your dream incubation for abundance, and now it's time to give it over to divine inspiration. Like a garden in which you plant your seeds, now it's time to wait to see what sprouts and grows. You sense complete faith and trust in the divine inspiration. You know your question or request will be answered in your dreams and you will remember when you wake up.

A wave of great relief spreads across your being as if a heavy weight has been lifted, leaving you feeling lighter. Starting down in your toes, feel the wave of relief and relaxation move up your body into your feet, ankles, and then into your legs, bringing a soothing, calming sensation of energy with it. The wave continues upward into your thighs, stomach, and up into your chest, and out through your arms and fingers, spreading its relaxing energy wherever it goes. The wave of relaxation moves up your neck, chin, to the top of your head, where it sends tingling sensations dancing in slow, soothing motions throughout the crown of your head. At this point you feel completely relaxed and at peace with yourself.

You visit your magical garden of dream incubation, where your question or request is incubating in a fragrant and lovely white rosebud. When the rose opens, it will have the information you seek to help move your dream plan forward. Until then, you relax in the garden, enjoying the abundant beauty of nature.

While in the garden, you call on your dream helpers, who help you access the divine inspiration of dreams. When the time is right as with the rose, they will give you helpful messages that will answer your question or provide insights that will fulfill your request. You will receive the information you need to move the pattern of your life forward.

Sense yourself letting go of all control in terms of your dream incubation for abundance. It is now part of a higher power, whose access to information is unlimited. This higher power will communicate the information to you through both through your waking and dream worlds.

Take a deep breath and feel yourself moving into a peaceful, calm state of being. You feel confident that your dream incubation for abundance is successful. Now take another deep breath and begin moving your toes and fingers. Shift your body slightly, slowly open your eyes, and return your awareness to the present time and place, remaining relaxed as you say the following prayer for abundance.

Dream Prayer for Abundance

While wrapped in the blanket, say this prayer just before you go to sleep:

Divine and blessed ones,
Tonight I pray that I may find
Helpful messages in my dreams.
Please grant me this request.
May my dreams be blessed.
Thank you, divine ones. Amen.

Remain wrapped in your dream incubation blanket. As you drift to sleep, repeat your dream incubation mantra for abundance silently to yourself, again and again.

Oracle of Dreams for Abundance

Traditionally, dreaming of eggs signifies abundant wealth, and an egg with a double yolk is a powerful sign of good fortune. Begin this oracle by filling a clear, eight-ounce glass with water. Set it aside. Then carefully hold an egg in your power hand and say:

I empower this egg as a divine dream incubation oracle of abundance.

Now focus your mind on your incubated dream for abundance. Gently rub the egg against your body. After a few minutes of rubbing the egg over your body as you think about your dream for abundance, crack it open into the glass of water. Look into the water with the egg and study the shapes and forms. Write these down in your dream empowerment journal, making a note of any insights they bring to mind. Get a feel for images and their messages and meanings.

After a few minutes, finish by thanking the divine and the elements by saying:

I thank the divine and the elements for their helpful presence and blessings.

Visualize stepping out of the luminous egg of white light you imagined at the beginning of the ritual last evening, and imagine the luminous egg of light diffusing into the air. When you are done, return the water and egg to the earth.

Dream Affirmation for Abundance

Repeat this abundance affirmation several times a day for at least 28 days for optimum results:

Today and every day, I am divinely inspired. In waking and in dream, my life is a garden of abundance, beauty, and harmony.

Chapter Six

Dream Empowerment Steps

Every time you go to sleep and dream, you are like the shaman, crossing over into that "other world." Your dream self is essentially an energetic double that you create so that you can travel beyond the confines of this particular reality into the great beyond. Like the shaman, you travel to this "other world" in order to gain information that can help you empower your dream goals for love, health, and abundance.

Your dream self or energetic double is an entity that you come to know intimately as it is a reflection of you. A product of both your conscious and unconscious mind, your dream self is not only your communication link with the "other world," but it is also a way of reaching into the inner regions of your being and exploring the many aspects that combine to make you who you are. This is an integral part of body, mind, and spirit development.

Now that you have determined your dream empowerment goals, drawn up your plans, and begun implementation, it's important that you continue with your dream empowerment steps. As you follow through by making the necessary effort and taking the appropriate steps, you continue to move forward with your plans.

It's essential not to be waylaid by things that come up in the interim, but rather that you deal with problems as they arise. Avoid letting problems and pitfalls take away from your dreams, which are often the desires that drive you forward in your quest for something you really want to experience in life. In this sense, dreams are an essential element in evolution. Without them, we would still be in the Stone Age, accepting everything the way it is without question. Our dreams are the force that nudges us, caresses us, and moves us forward.

You need to continually update your perceptions and database with regard to the changing world. The technological age has made this issue even more paramount in that the tools and methods you use for dream empowerment are changing at a faster and faster rate. What this means is that you have to adapt to the events around you at a faster pace than you are normally used to. As the world around you changes, you most likely will need to adapt your dream goals and plans accordingly.

As things change and you change, it's important to maintain your focus in order to be successful and empowered. This means applying the steps of your dream plan so that you are continually moving toward your dream empowerment goal. Once you achieve one goal, move to the next. Oftentimes one goal sets up the next, building up to your ultimate goals for love, health, and abundance.

If one of your ultimate dream goals is to find your dream career, your first step might be researching the jobs available that you find interesting. The next step might be designing your own entrepreneurial dream job. Further steps might be networking with helpful people, creating a terrific resumé, or selecting or purchasing an outfit or suit that is perfect for the job. In other words, there is a sequence of steps and goals that move toward your ultimate dream empowerment goals.

By dividing your ultimate dream goals down into their smaller sequential parts, they become more within your immediate reach. Suddenly you don't feel quite so overwhelmed by the task at hand. Again, there is an overall movement from the small to the large in terms of dream empowerment goals. No matter how large the goal, as long as you continue to take positive steps toward it, chances are you will eventually reach it.

Dream Guides and Helpers

Beads of sweat drip from the shaman's face as he dances along the lines of light that form the sacred circle. He beats his drum with a sustained and frenzied passion that sends him and the other tribal dancers into an altered state of being. As the shaman tilts his head, he hears the voice that speaks quietly to his spirit. The beat on the drum becomes more pronounced as he tunes himself in harmony with a voice that vibrates through every part of his body, mind, and spirit.

For thousands of years, tribal shamans bridged the gap between this world and the dream or spirit world. Whether it had to do with an individual's health or the survival of the tribe, shamans used traditional techniques and skills to successfully access information from the other world. They did this by keeping an ongoing relationship with the spirits of nature, the elements, ancestral spirits, and divine beings. Power and knowledge derived from the shaman's interaction with these helping spirits in whatever form they took.

Shamans realized the inherent connection of all things. They knew that humankind, the creatures and plants of Earth, as well as the stones and soil, the water and the wind, the sun, moon, planets, and stars are all a collective whole.

In the shaman's perception, the spirit world and waking world were mirrored images of one another. Modern research has given credence to this perception. In his book *River's Way*, Arnold Mindell writes that "One of the most exciting discoveries of process science is that the evolution which results from amplifying primary and secondary processes is always mirrored in dreams." This confirms the concept that your dream self is your mirrored double.

Dream guides and helpers can come in many forms, including Goddesses, Gods, devas, guardian angels, animal helpers, and alien beings, to name a few. In particular there seems to be a connection between humans and animals that extends beyond this reality into the dream world.

Many ancient folktales tell of a time when animals and humans were on basically the same level and spoke the same language. In some cultures this connection is upheld, such as in Chinese folklore, which maintains that people have two souls: the animal soul called the "po" and the spirit soul called the "hun." The souls join together to create the whole of who you are. One without the other is half of what it could be. This is why your dream guides and animal helpers are important to your dream empowerment process. They can help you gain answers and insights about both your immediate plans and future goals.

In essence, animals represent your primordial self and, as such, represent aspects of your self that often remain hidden, but nevertheless need to be expressed. When you seek out your animal helpers, for example in ritual and guided meditation, a door opens to them, and they will enter into a relationship with you, often guiding and protecting you both in dream and waking.

Through this relationship with your animal helpers, you absorb their knowledge and abilities. You come to know about "tiger-ness" or "hummingbird-ness". You commune with the totality or spirit essence of the animal. You feel as they feel, hear as they hear, taste as they taste, smell as they smell, see as they see, intuit your world as they do, and dream as they do.

When you dream with your animal helpers, remember that they won't necessarily appear as they do in ordinary reality. Often their shape, size, coloring, and movements change in dream. In his book *Medicinemaker,* shaman Hank Wesselman says that his animal helper called "leopard man" represents the group soul of all leopards, which he entered into a relationship with. Wesselman writes that "He ('leopard man') usually appeared first as a feline, looking much like a real leopard. But as the connection between my conscious awareness and his became active, he almost always shape shifted to become bipedal, a stance that mimics the way humans habitually stand and walk."

Love

Even though people in modern times have strayed from their wild nature and shamanic roots, we still have intricate relationships with animals. As children, we are surrounded by animals—from our early pets and the stuffed ones that adorn our living spaces to the animate characters that occupy our bedtime stories and cartoons.

Early on in our development we learn that animals symbolize humans because of the underlying theme that animals act like humans. The *Winnie the Pooh* stories by A. A. Milne are an excellent example. All the main characters except for Christopher Robin are animated stuffed animals who display human characteristics. From Tigger's boundless energy and Rabbit's need to stay on schedule, to Piglet's helpful ways and Pooh's unending love of honey, each character represents human aspects. Their adventures in the Hundred Acre Wood tell stories of sharing, caring, and friendship while imparting precious bits of information that begin our learning and socialization process.

Because of our early relationships with animals, we come to perceive them as our friends and allies in life. This perception and close relationship with animals carries over into our dreams. In terms of symbolism, certain animals in our dreams can be interpreted to mean certain things in terms of our lives, and with respect to allies, certain animals can come into our dreams and help us achieve our goals. As in our early associations with animals, they continue to impart information and knowledge in our lives in many ways, including dreams.

Sacred Love Dream Space

Add images of animals that you are attracted to in picture form, figurines, or even toy animals to your sacred love dream altar. These images are symbolic of the living creature and its power. Also add jasmine-scented oil, a white candle, and sandalwood incense and censer.

Empower these items by holding your hands over them, palms down, taking a deep breath, and running divine loving energy into them by saying:

May the divine loving dream power of the Great Spirit fill this ... [Say the name of the item, for example, animal figurine, jasmine oil, white candle, and so forth.]

Dream Ritual for Love

The purpose of this ritual is to dream with your divine animal friends and obtain protection and helpful messages regarding your dream empowerment goals for love. You will need the images of the animals, jasmine oil, white candle, sandalwood incense from your sacred love dream altar, and a lighter or matches.

This ritual is best done during a waxing or full moon on a Friday night. Just before doing the ritual, take a few minutes to study the images of the animals on your altar. In your dream empowerment journal, make a note of any animals you recall dreaming about recently, your favorite childhood animal, and any pets, either ones you have now or in the past that you dream about. Date your entry.

Begin by imagining a bright sphere of white light completely encircling you and your sacred space. Invite the elements into your ritual space by saying:

May the elements of earth, air, fire, water, and spirit come into my sacred ritual space now.

Next, rub a thin film of jasmine oil on the candle body. Anoint yourself with the oil, and then wipe any remaining oil from your hands. Light the candle, dedicating it to your animal friends. Then say:

Candlelight, candle so bright,
Light the way so that I may
Dream with my animal friends tonight.

Light the incense from the candle flame, once again dedicating it to your animal friends. Then say:

Divine animal friends of mine
Familiar spirits through lifetimes
Ancient helpful friends hear my call
Come dream with me, one and all.

Now close your eyes and imagine dreaming with your divine animal friends. Imagine the candlelight as a beacon that reaches out into the night sky, into the dream world. In this light you clearly see your animal friends and feel the joy and wonder of your divine friendship. Imagine your animal friends magically floating down the beacon of light, closer and closer. As they come closer to you, communicate with these divine animal friends and ask them to dream with you tonight, to protect you while you are dreaming, and to bring helpful dream messages regarding your dream empowerment goals for love. Continue doing this for a few minutes.

When you are done, imagine stepping out of the sphere of white light, and visualize the sphere diffusing into the air around you. Allow the candle to burn down safely, or if you prefer snuff it out and burn it down the next day. Anoint your pillowcase with a couple of drops of jasmine oil to enhance your dreams with your divine animal dream friend.

Dream Meditation for Love

For this meditation you will need an animal friend to help you. If you do not have a pet companion, envision an imaginary pet for the meditation. Begin by softly stroking the animal, feeling the fur beneath your fingertips. You sense a warmth of energy as you continue to stroke your pet, scratching its chin and rubbing behind its ears. Tuned in, the animal responds happily to your attention, and you sense a strong rapport of friendship and love.

Begin matching your breathing to the strokes you are giving your pet. Breathe in as you stroke down along the fur, feathers, or skin, still your breath, and then exhale as you move your hand back up, and once again stroke your pet. Cats begin to purr, dogs act like they're in heaven, and most other animals love the attention.

In nature, animals are constantly grooming one another as both a practicality and show of affection. When you stroke your pet, you are showing the animal that you love it just like a mother cat or dog shows her love and care for her young by licking them. In the mind of your pet, the gesture is basically the same. Just as you respond to your conditioning and upbringing, animals do, too.

Now rest your hand gently on the animal, and begin to sense a Oneness between your two spirits. In a mutual exchange, you give your pet your energy, and it in return gives you its energy. Within the animal, you feel a sense of loyalty and devotion. No matter what realm of being you exist in, your pet is always your helper, there to defend and help you not only in this world but also in the dream world. Your energies continue to forge a strong lasting bond with one another.

Just like your relationships with animals can help you in your waking world, they also can help you in your dream world. They can help discover the answers to your dream incubations and problems in your empowerment plan. Again, dreams often speak in terms of metaphor, and your dream animals are often part of the symbolism.

Your animal friends can help you on your quest for empowerment. It is important to ask for the help of your animal friends and allies. Ask them to come into your dreams and help you on your quest. Tell your animal friends what it is you are searching for in your dreams and how they can help you.

When you are done meditating, take a deep breath, move your toes and fingers, and return your awareness to the present time and place.

Dream Prayer for Love

Place your hands over your heart chakra as you say the following prayer just before you go to sleep:

Great Spirit, Divine One,
Please listen to my prayer
And help me live my dream for love.
May I care for my animal friends
And feed them and keep them from harm.
May I dream with my animal friends
And remember their helpful messages.
Happily, may I dream loving dreams
And remember them well when I awaken.
By the Great Spirit, in love it is done.

As you drift to sleep, repeat the following over and over:

Divine animal friend, dream with me, and I remember my dream when I wake up.

When you wake up, write down everything you recall from your dream in your dream empowerment journal and date your entry.

Oracle of Dreams for Love

What is the last animal you dreamed about? In your dream empowerment journal, write a description of it as if you were a child who has never seen the animal before and examine it for oracular messages. Now place your hands over your heart chakra and focus your awareness on that animal. What do you associate with the animal?

Now place your hands over your throat chakra and continue to focus your awareness on the animal. Does the animal have any special message to communicate to you concerning your dream goals for love? Sometimes the animal message is conveyed in words, and sometimes it is more mind talk without actual spoken words. Sometimes the message is conveyed in actions, moods, or events within the dream itself. At other times, the message is imparted in the waking world: in your surroundings, in nature, on your drive to work, on billboards, signs, buildings, on television, the radio or the computer, or in books and magazines. Today, for the rest of the day, write down in your dream empowerment journal all the animal signs, messages, and images you notice that may be relevant to your dream empowerment goals for love.

Dream Affirmation for Love

Place your hands over your heart chakra as you repeat this love affirmation several times a day, both aloud and silently to yourself. Continue doing so for at least 28 days for the most powerful dream results:

Today and tonight, in waking and in dream, my divine animal friends protect me and give me messages that help me attain my dream empowerment goals for love.

Health

In healing, visualization, guided imagery, meditation, prayer, and affirmation, in conjunction with dreaming, are especially powerful. One of the reasons for this is that as a human being you are teleological, which means your awareness moves toward what you imagine in your mind. This also holds true for healing and wellness. When you imagine yourself as healthy and vibrant, for example in meditation or dreaming, you open the door to a much healthier and more vital you.

To be healthy, it's necessary to have both the intention and expectation to be healthy. Otherwise you will undermine the healing process. You also need to make a mental note of your thoughts, feelings, actions, dreams, and other behaviors during the day, so that you can see how you are empowering or disempowering your health.

Becoming healthy is a matter of transforming into a healthy person. Animal helpers can help you make that transformation or shape shift happen. They provide important messages both in dream and in waking that help you attain your dream goals for health and well-being. To receive these messages, it's important to keep an open mind and a kind heart.

The animals you most resonate with often make the best animal helpers. They can bring balance and connectedness to your life. As time goes on, you will likely be drawn to different animals, depending upon the kinds of healing energy you need.

You need to determine which animals you resonate with. Look through a book with pictures of animals or surf the Internet and look at animal images. Then write down the answers to these seven questions in your dream empowerment journal.

1. What kind of animals repetitively come into your environment?
2. What animal do you or your movements most resemble?
3. What kind of animals are you drawn to?
4. What kind of animals are drawn to you and come up to you?
5. When visiting a zoo, aquarium, animal preserve, farm, ranch, or the country, what animals do you pay the most attention to?
6. Do you find yourself thinking about one animal more than others?
7. What kind of animals do you dream or daydream about?

When you are finished answering the questions, look over your answers and check for any recurring animals or types of animals. These animals are likely your most powerful dream helpers.

Sacred Healing Dream Space

Select an animal helper from the ones you have listed in the previous section. Do so by asking yourself which animal you are most interested in right now as you read this sentence. Go with your gut feeling and write down your first response.

Next, add a picture or other item that symbolizes the specific animal you have selected. For example, if you selected a tiger, use a picture of a tiger or a figurine of a tiger. Also, add a drum (or an item that will act as a drum if you tap against it) and a white candle to your sacred healing altar.

Empower these items by holding them in your hands, one at a time, and merging with the divine animal spirits of Mother Earth. Then say:

May the divine healing and dreaming energies of Mother Earth and Father Sky empower this ritual item.

Dream Ritual for Health

The purpose of this ritual is to connect with your animal helper and obtain messages of healing and well-being in your dreams. You will need the image of your animal helper, the drum and white candle from your sacred healing dream altar, and a lighter or matches.

This ritual is best done during a waxing moon on a Sunday night. Begin by gathering everything together. Then imagine a bright sphere of white light completely encircling you and your sacred space. Invite the elements into your ritual space by saying:

May the elements of earth, air, fire, water, and spirit come into my sacred ritual space now.

Light the candle, dedicating it to your animal helpers. Hold the drum and play it rhythmically for a few minutes. Then pause and face the altar and say three times:

Hello to my animal helpers of land, air, and sea;
I bid you welcome, and ask you to dream with me.

Play the drum for a few minutes and merge with its tone and rhythm. Then set the drum down. Gaze into the candlelight and imagine your animal helper before you in the light. Keep breathing deeply. Ask the animal its name, and give yourself the suggestion to clearly remember its name. Repeat your animal helper's name over and over again to yourself.

As you continue to merge with your animal helper in the candlelight, imagine its strength and energy merging with you, increasing your overall health and well-being. Do this for a few minutes.

Now face the altar once again and say three times:

Animal helpers of land, air, and sea,
Tonight, please come dream with me.

When you are done, thank the divine and the elements by saying:

I thank the divine and the elements for their helpful presence and blessings.

Visualize stepping out of the sphere of white light, and imagine the sphere diffusing into the air around you. Allow the candle to burn down safely. If you prefer, you can snuff it out and relight it the next day, allowing it to burn safely down then. Write down your animal helper's name in your dream empowerment journal and date your entry. Whenever you want to communicate with your animal helper, you need only call its name.

Dream Meditation for Health

Turn on some soft meditative music, and then sit or recline comfortably. In your mind's eye, visualize an immense tree that stretches from the ground up to what looks like infinity. Its branches are like steps on a stairway to the sky. Taking a deep breath, step onto the first branch, and then slowly exhale. Taking another deep breath, step onto the second branch, and again slowly exhale. Continue to take deep breaths and climb the branches of the tree.

Once you have climbed partway up the tree, you encounter a great white crane who communicates with you mentally. The crane invites you to climb onto its back; and as you do so, the crane spreads its wings, and begins soaring higher and higher into the sky. The branches of the immense tree move by faster and faster until you sense yourself moving up through the clouds. You fly through the clouds into the blue sky and see the top of the tree which extends into what looks to be another world. The great white crane sets you down in this other world and then bids you good-bye before spreading its wings, flying away, and disappearing into the distance.

In your travels around this other world, you find a garden unlike any other you have ever encountered. You feel peacefully calm and safe in this special garden filled with its flowering plants, many colored stones, and mysteriously shaped trees. In the center of the garden is a small pool with beautiful blooming flowers in it. You can smell the scent of the water and the flowers that float on its surface. You breathe in deeply several times, drinking in the heady healing scent of the flowers, and feel yourself relaxing even more.

You suddenly sense a friendly presence nearby, and from the corner of your eye you see a flash and then a strange shimmering that flows over you and vibrates throughout your being. On the other side of the pool, your animal helper emerges from the center of this shimmering light. You sense its power and wisdom, and without fear you move over next to it and touch it. You sense a union that extends from this world to the other world, and within this union your power and the power of the animal come together as One. It is at this point that the helpful knowledge from this magnificent animal passes into you as healing energy. Bathe in this healing energy for a few minutes.

Now communicate with your animal helper. Ask your animal helper a specific health question. Ask your animal helper to come into your dreams and help you find the answer or information you need to move forward. Also, ask your animal helper its name so you can call upon her or him when you desire.

Now take another deep breath, move your toes and fingers, and slowly open your eyes, coming back to the present time and place. Remain relaxed and allow a calm peacefulness to cover your body like a warm blanket. You are now ready for your prayer and dreamtime.

Dream Prayer for Health

Say this prayer just before you go to sleep:

Father Sky, please hear me and make me strong.
Mother Earth, please hear and sustain me.
Divine Ones, source of life and health,
I pray you, please guide me on a path of healing and wellness.
In dreams and in waking, may I understand
The natural wisdom of my animal helpers.
In dreams and in waking, may I be touched
By the healing grace of the animal spirits.
In dreams and in waking, may every creature of nature
Abound in well-being and health.
I ask this in the names of Father Sky and Mother Earth.
Blessed be my animal helpers. Blessed be my dreams.

As you drift to sleep, repeat silently to yourself, over and over:

Tonight, I welcome healing dreams with my animal helpers, and I remember my dreams when I wake up.

When you wake up, write down everything you recall from your dream in your dream empowerment journal and date your entry.

Oracle of Dreams for Health

Think about the last animal you dreamed about. Describe it as if you were a child. Write this in your dream empowerment journal and examine it for oracular messages. Now place your hands over your heart chakra and focus your awareness on that animal. What do you associate with the animal?

Now place your hands over your throat chakra and continue to focus your awareness on the animal. Does the animal have any special message with regard to your dream goals for healing and well-being to communicate to you? The message might be conveyed in words, thoughts, or images. The message may come to you in the waking world, in your surroundings, on television or the computer, or in magazines. During the day, make a note of all the animal signs, messages, and images you notice that are relevant to your dream empowerment goals for health in your dream empowerment journal.

Dream Affirmation for Health

Sound your drum a few times before repeating this affirmation aloud several times a day for 28 days. The tone of the drum reinforces the power of the affirming statement:

Today and tonight, in waking and in dream, my animal helpers protect me and give me useful dream messages for health. I know that the natural healing energy of nature is empowering me.

(If you can't use your drum at work, use the drumming of your fingers on your file cabinet or tap your pencil or pen to mimic the sound of the drum.)

Abundance

All of nature is divine. It is naturally abundant in beauty, harmony, creativity, delight, growth, and hope. You, too, can enrich your life with natural, divine abundance by communing with nature and dreaming with your animal helpers. Your animal helpers can provide messages and information you need to transform and enrich your life.

One way to access the knowledge and powers of your animal helpers to help you with your dream goals for abundance is to make an animal fetish out of stone. American Indians, especially those of the Southwest, have employed the extraordinary powers of fetishes in waking and dream for thousands of years.

Traditionally, fetishes relate to animals of prey, those admired for their power and strong hearts. They are used to energetically guide, help, and protect you and can be made from just about anything into any form. Most often fetishes are made from semi-precious stones, coral, or shells, and fashioned into jewelry or small animal figurines.

Once you have made or procured a fetish, it is your responsibility to feed and care for it. You need to keep it in its special pouch, take it out to admire it once in a while, and then feed it a pinch of cornmeal when you put it back in the pouch. The better you take care of your fetish, the more powerful it becomes.

Sacred Abundance Dream Space

Add a brown candle and a woodsy incense such as cedarwood or pine to your sacred abundance dream altar. Also, add a piece of turquoise or malachite (if you prefer, you can use a carved stone fetish that you purchase or make), a small green or gold pouch, and a pinch of cornmeal.

To empower these items, hold them in your hands one at a time, and merge with the animal spirits of Mother Earth. Then say:

May divine and abundant dream power fill this item.

Dream Ritual for Abundance

The purpose of this ritual is to make an animal fetish to help access the knowledge of your animal helper in waking and in dream. You will need the brown candle, incense, piece of turquoise or malachite, pouch, and cornmeal from your sacred abundance dream altar. You will also need some matches or a lighter.

This ritual is best done during a waxing or full moon on a Thursday. During the day, pay attention to animals you see and hear. These animals may be in your surroundings, on television, on the Internet, or on billboards, in magazines, cars, jewelry, and so forth. Write down a list of the ones you encounter in your dream empowerment journal and date your entry. Select one of the animals you have written down in your journal for this ritual, ideally the most powerful of those listed. Write down the animal you have selected in your journal.

Now imagine a bright sphere of white light encircling you and your sacred space, and invite the elements into your ritual space by saying:

I respectfully invite the elements of earth, air, fire, water, and spirit into my sacred ritual space.

Then carefully light the candle, dedicating it to your animal helper by saying:

I dedicate this candle to my animal helper [name animal].

Then light the incense from the candle flame, once again dedicating it to your animal helper.

Bathe the piece of turquoise or malachite in the incense smoke for a few minutes, and then hold the stone in your power hand. Face north, imagine breathing in the color yellow for a minute or so. Then empower your fetish with the natural energies of the north by saying:

Dream animal helpers of the north,
Share your knowledge and wisdom with me tonight.

In your mind's eye, imagine a helpful tawny-colored mountain lion.

Now face east and imagine breathing in the color white for a minute or so. Then empower your fetish with the natural energies of the east by saying:

Dream animal helpers of the east,
Share your knowledge and wisdom with me tonight.

In your mind's eye, imagine a helpful white wolf.

Next face south and imagine breathing in the color red for a minute or so. Then say:

Dream animal helpers of the south,
Share your knowledge and wisdom with me tonight.

In your mind's eye, imagine a helpful badger.

Then face west and imagine breathing in the color blue for a minute or so. Then say:

Dream animal helpers of the west,
Share your knowledge and wisdom with me tonight.

In your mind's eye, imagine a helpful and protective bear.

Spread your arms toward the earth below you. With your stone still in your power hand, imagine breathing in the color brown for a minute or so, and then say:

Dream animal helpers of the inner Earth below me,
Share your knowledge and wisdom with me as I dream.

In your mind's eye, imagine a helpful groundhog.

Spread your arms toward the sky and imagine breathing in all the colors of the rainbow for a few minutes. Then say:

Dream animal helpers of the air above me,
Share your knowledge and wisdom with me as I dream.

In your mind's eye, imagine a magnificent bald eagle.

Now focus your attention on the candle flame. If you prefer, you can use a mirror behind the flame and gaze at its reflection. As you gaze at the light, imagine being in a peaceful place in nature. Focus your awareness on this peaceful place. Imagine the animal helper you have selected and written down in your journal being there with you in this peaceful place in nature.

Next, put the stone fetish up to your mouth and take deep breaths in and out for a minute or so. By doing this, you fill yourself with the power of the animal helper and are able to communicate with your helper. As you and your animal helper commune, there is no fear, just a calm rapport between the two of you.

Ask your animal helper if she or he has a message for you. If you have a specific question, ask it and listen for a response. Write down messages or other information you receive from your animal helper in your dream empowerment journal and date your entry. Your animal helper may speak softly like a morning breeze or loudly like thunder, or the message may be thought to you mentally without words. You will know when the communication is complete because the energy recognizably shifts. You will feel a coolness or the image of your animal helper will fade or move away from you.

When you are done, put your stone fetish into the pouch. Feed it the pinch of cornmeal by putting the cornmeal in the pouch with the stone. Place the pouch with your animal helper fetish next to your bed as you sleep. Now and again, feed it cornmeal and take it out and breathe with it as you did in the ritual.

Then thank the divine and the elements by saying:

I thank the divine and the elements for their helpful presence and blessings.

Also thank your animal helper and ask her or him to dream with you tonight. Imagine stepping out of the sphere of white light you imagined at the beginning of the ritual, and imagine the sphere diffusing into the air around you. Allow the candle to safely burn down.

Dream Meditation for Abundance

Before beginning the meditation, stand before your sacred abundance dream space and study the area and the objects in it. Now sit or recline comfortably for the meditation, and begin breathing slowly and deeply. Look at your sacred abundance dream space, and beginning on one side of the space, allow your awareness to drift from one item to the next. What are your thoughts about each item? What emotions and feelings does each thing evoke? How do these items relate to your life?

Now step clear of your rational mind for a moment. Ways of doing this are:

- Chanting either aloud or silently to yourself for a few minutes. The chant can be one word such as "abundance" or a sentence such as "My life is fruitful and abundant."
- Closing your eyes and imagining being immersed in a warm, clear pool of water that cleanses your body, mind, and spirit. Take a deep breath and pulse your breath out your nose instead of your mouth, pulsing out the energy stored in your being.
- Merging with Oneness through swaying, dancing, singing, drumming, praying, and so forth for a few minutes. Feel yourself and your awareness become fluid, pure energy.

Look at your sacred abundance dream space again, but this time become aware of the spiritual essence of each item. Use your senses, including your intuition and psychic ability, to experience both the individual item and how it relates to the whole of your sacred space, dream empowerment plans, and life itself.

Now focus on your animal fetish. Imagine merging with that one specific animal helper. As you transform into your animal helper, you become one with the spirit animal. You see, hear, smell, taste, and feel from the animal's perspective. While this transformation happens, you become your animal helper and your animal helper becomes you for a few moments.

You are like a shaman who moves into another world in order to gather information. With practice, you become the shape shifter, who can become all things. At this point, you realize you can transform your life and attain your dream goals just as you can transform into your spirit animal helper.

As you experience the essence of your spirit animal helper, practice staying in the moment. Whenever your focus strays from your animal helper, take a deep breath and turn your awareness back to the spirit animal. Do this for at least 10 minutes.

Now take a deep breath in and move your hands and feet slightly, wiggling your toes. Stretch your body and bring your awareness to the present time and place.

Dream Prayer for Abundance

Hold your animal helper fetish in your receiving hand and say this prayer just before you go to sleep:

I pray to the helpful animal spirits of nature,
To the divine creatures of Mother Earth.
Please fill me with your grace and wisdom,
And share your knowledge with me in waking and dream.
Please guide and protect me
By north, east, south, and west,
By firmament, land, air, and sea,
Above and below, before and behind.
Thank you cherished ones. Blessed be!

As you drift to sleep, repeat over and over:

Animal helper, share your wisdom, and I remember my dreams when I wake up.

When you wake up, write down everything you recall from your dream in your dream empowerment journal and date your entry.

Oracle of Dreams for Abundance

Focus your awareness on the animal you recently dreamed about. Describe the animal as if you were a child. Write your description down in your dream empowerment journal and examine it for oracular messages. Now place your hands over your heart chakra and focus your awareness on that animal. What do you associate with the animal?

Next, put your hands over your throat chakra and continue to focus your awareness on the animal. Does the animal have any special message with regard to your dream goals for abundance?

The message can be conveyed in words, thoughts, images, and so forth. The message may come to you in the waking world. During the day, make a note in your dream empowerment journal of the relevant animal signs, messages, and images you notice.

Dream Affirmation for Abundance

Hold your animal helper fetish in your power hand and repeat aloud this affirmation for abundance several times a day for at least 28 days:

Today and tonight, in waking and in dream, my animal helpers give me useful messages to help me attain my dream empowerment goals for abundance.

Chapter Seven

Expanding Your Dream Awareness

In his book *Recollections of Abraham Lincoln,* Ward Hill Lamon relates a story about a dream that President Lincoln had shortly before he was assassinated at the end of the Civil War. Lincoln had been up late waiting for news from the front. When he finally went to sleep, he had a dream in which he described a "death-like stillness" that hovered around him. Then there came subdued sobs, as if a number of people were weeping. Lincoln's dream body got up out of bed and wandered downstairs, where he went from room to room, but there was nobody in the rooms. As Lincoln reported, "It was light in all the rooms and every object was familiar to me, but where were all the people who were grieving as if their hearts would break? I was puzzled and alarmed. What could be the meaning of all this?"

Not one to shy away from a challenge even while dreaming, Lincoln was determined to find the source of this sorrow. Arriving at the East Room of the White House, he saw a casket with a body whose face was hidden. The casket was guarded by soldiers, and there was a throng of people around it weeping. In the dream, President Lincoln questioned one of the soldiers.

"Who is dead in the White House?" he demanded.

"The President," came the soldier's response. "He was killed by an assassin!" The words brought a loud burst of grief from the crowd, awaking Abraham Lincoln from the dream.

President Lincoln had been handed a glimpse of the future. Unfortunately, he didn't act quickly enough upon the information given to him in his extraordinary dream.

Precognitive dreams occur regularly and, as such, are one of the key reasons you should never ignore and always respond to what your dreams are attempting to tell you. Even if you think your dreams are nonsense, it's important to allow for the possibility that there is an aspect of your dreams that may be helpful to you in your future.

The concept of "déjà vu," which is an experience that seems like it has already happened, relates to the precognitive aspect of dreams. It's quite feasible that many déjà vu experiences arise not because the person has experienced the same experience in ordinary waking reality but because the person has experienced the situation in dream and is replaying it in "real life."

Like a tape recording that is out of sync or time with itself, the waking and dream worlds work differently with respect to time and space. This is why dreams can sometimes seem to echo reality in both the past sense and the future sense, which are always working together to compose the present moment. As expressed by the philosopher Kahlil Gibran, "Trust in dreams, for in them is the hidden gate of eternity."

Eternity is an interesting precept because metaphysically it exists beyond linear time. Like a serpent swallowing its tail, time is a concept that can be accessed at many points of view. In some ways, waking reality is more like a cassette tape where you have to move the tape forward and backward, depending on the place in the tape you want to be. When dreaming, time on the other hand is more like using a CD's Random Access Memory. By pushing a button, you instantly arrive at your destination, without moving either forward or backward. You are simply there.

Past and Future Lives

In his book *The Cathars and Reincarnation,* Dr. Arthur Guirdham describes a patient who came to him because she was being plagued by nightmares of murder and massacre. As he began to treat her, she started describing some of her other dreams that involved being another person in another lifetime. She showed him some of the things she had written down, including songs where the verse was written in Medieval French, a language his patient did not know. In researching some of the facts with regard to the things his patient had written down, he found that they related to the Cathars, a religious group brutally persecuted in the Middle Ages. He found in particular that four of the songs she had written down were in the historical archives.

From the evidence at hand, it appeared that the patient's dreams and subsequent nightmares related to a past life. What makes the case even more interesting is that once his patient realized it was a past life she was living out in her dreams, she quit having the nightmares which had been recurring since she was 12 years old. There was a definite healing aspect to her understanding of the deeper meanings of her dreams. This suggests that precognitive dreams move into some future lifetime or event, whereas past life dreams move back in time to a prior lifetime or event. It's amazing that dreams do such things, but what's even more surprising is that dreams do it with a seamless ease.

Because dreams move through time so easily, they lay beyond the physical boundaries of the time/space continuum. During dreams, we move into a world akin to the world of the shamans, visionaries, and prophets, a world of imagination and possibilities that exists outside the normal constraints of time and space. In the dream world, time stands still, moves forward thousands of years, folds into nothingness, or changes completely into something else, depending on the dreamscape we experience.

When you dream, you are able to access the great circle unbounded by time and space. That great circle is Oneness, a wholeness that contains virtually everything that has happened, is happening right now, and will happen. It is through directed dreaming as well as spontaneous dreaming that you can tap into this universal energy and truly begin living your dreams for love, health, and abundance.

Dreamtime

In the cosmology of the Australian Aborigines, "dreamtime" is the epoch that existed before time and form came into being. It is symbolic of a time when the world was in a state of dream. Then the world awoke and was born into its natural state of being.

When the world was born, it forgot the dreams of dreamtime; and since that time the people in the world have been constantly trying to remember and connect back to the larger cosmic dream. In this respect, we are constantly dreaming ourselves and our world into being.

Mythological stories are enacted, chanted, painted, costumed, danced, sung, and imagined in ways that create a bridge from the dreamtime through to the world of natural creation. This is done by contacting and listening to the voices of the ancestors echoing from the great dreamtime. The result of this is to bring into the conscious realm the subtle creative energies and relationships that are normally hidden, establishing a link between the spirit existence and the bodily existence.

As with many ancient spiritual traditions, the tradition of the Aborigines being the oldest known, there is a connection between ancestral energy and the land or natural environment. Oftentimes this ancestral energy resides within the natural environment, waiting to be released from its slumber—for example, the sleeping kings and queens in Celtic spirituality. This ancestral energy, when awakened, shapes a bridge between the waking world and the dream world.

The metaphysical beings of the dreamtime give definition and order to the natural world. When people experience the dreamtime, they bring back the flowing order which is inherent in everything. In this way, dreams give definition to life, and life gives definition to dreams. The relationship is often divine. To the Aborigines, a person's experiences within the dreamtime gives direction to that person's life. This idea is succinctly expressed in the Aboriginal saying, "Those who lose dreaming are lost."

By keeping one eye on ordinary reality and one eye on your deepest dreams, you continue to move toward your dream empowerment goals for love, health, and abundance. Mirroring the dreamtime concept, your dreams give focus to your empowerment goals, and your empowerment goals, in the form of your needs and desires, give focus to your dreams. When fully integrated, they are a sublime example of a mutually beneficial and empowering relationship.

Overall, the dreamtime expresses the idea that the dream world exists outside the realm and confines of linear time. Let's add the concept that it also exists outside the boundaries of manifested form. This means that given the "right" dream, anything is possible, which explains some of the influences behind magic and miracles.

Many of the physical boundaries you experience in your daily life are more matters of perception rather than actual matters of physical space. You set your own limitations, just as you set your own dream empowerment goals. It's essential to focus on how high you can soar rather than how low you can sink.

Be prepared to dream your life into being and live your dreams. The choice is yours to make. Take your time, use some common sense, and pay close attention to your dreams. Follow your heart, head, and spirit, and make the best choices possible. Remember, it's primarily your choices that determine who you are and the life you live.

Love

In a flight-or-fight world, it can be an arduous task to move toward love. Just as there is a certain amount of trust in relationships, there is a certain amount of distrust. The problem that inevitably arises is that in the twenty-first-century world, it's difficult to truly trust anyone. Trying to create relationships that move beyond this axiom can be a tremendous challenge, but the positive results are worth the effort.

It's important to first find people you can connect with, but make sure that connection is true. Make sure that there is a mutual exchange of energy and effort. Otherwise the relationship is one-sided and creates resentment. If there is a mutual exchange of goodwill and genuine effort and affection between you and another person, then the relationship will be empowering for both of you.

Relationships are built upon mutual trust and agreement. In order to move beyond superficial relationships, you need to be willing to trust the person you want to have a relationship with. If you don't feel this trust, maybe that's something you should look at before attempting a relationship with that person.

Dreamtime is the time when you look at your relationships for what they are, without all of the trappings normally associated with them. In dreamtime, the dream windows and doors open, and your conditioned mind steps aside for a while. Because of this, dreams often provide you with dream messages with regard to love.

Love is a wonderful thing, but it needs to be tempered with what works in your dreams and life. Oftentimes your dreams tell you what you need to know as long as you tune in to what they are trying to tell you.

Because dreams move through time so easily, they can tell you things that are important to your relationship right now, something the buddhists call the "eternal now." This is a point in metaphysical time when the present moment is continually happening, unimpaired by any other moment in time. When you reach this point in your awareness, then you will begin seeing dreams and experiences in terms of their whole, rather than individual, meanings.

Sacred Love Dream Space

To your sacred love dream altar, add a vial of lavender essential oil and a ring that symbolizes eternal love to you. The circular shape of the ring also symbolizes the "eternal now" of dreamtime. Empower the ring by holding it in your hands. Merge with the divine and say three times:

May the divine love of dreamtime fill this ring.

Empower the lavender oil by rolling the vial between your palms until it is warm. As you do this, chant several times:

Lavender oil bring loving dreamtime dreams.

Dream Ritual for Love

The purpose of this ritual is to create a dreamtime love ring and dream song to encourage dreams of love in the eternal now of dreamtime. You will need 2 tablespoons honey, linden-flower, or chamomile tea, and the ring and lavender essential oil from your sacred love dream altar.

For best results, do this ritual on or just before a full moon on a Friday night. Make a cup of tea, sweeten it with a bit of honey to taste, and then sip the tea slowly. Set the ring aside on your altar. Next draw a warm bath. Imagine a bright sphere of white light completely encircling you, the bath, and your sacred space. Invite the elements into your ritual space by saying:

May the elements of earth, air, fire, water, and spirit come into my sacred ritual space now.

Then invite the divine energies of your preference into your ritual space.

Next, pour the honey and six drops of the lavender essential oil into the warm bath water. As you do, say three times:

Sweet powers of lavender and honey,
Bring loving dreamtime dreams to me.

Step into the water and immerse yourself. Relax in the warm, fragrant bath, and as you bathe, either make up a dream song or sing a song you especially like that you think represents your dream goal for love. If you make up your own dream song, remember that it can be as simple or complex as you desire. When you finish singing, say three times:

Everything I dream is an eternal part of me.
My song gives wings to dreamtime love dreams.

Step out of the tub when you are done soaking. As you towel off, once again hum, sing, or play your dream song. Anoint your wrists and ankles with a drop or two of the lavender essential oil, and anoint the ring on your altar with a drop of the essential oil. Then put the dreamtime love ring on a finger of your receiving hand and say three times:

With this ring I do dream
Loving dreamtime dreams.
Eternal wisdom come to me.
As I ask, so it shall be.

Thank the divine and the elements by saying:

I thank the divine and the elements for their helpful presence and blessings.

Visualize stepping out of the sphere of white light, and imagine the sphere diffusing into the air around you. Leave the ring on as you sleep and dream to encourage meaningful dreams of love in the eternal now of dreamtime. Put the ring on your dream altar for love during the day, and slip it on before you go to sleep every night. After you slip it on, reaffirm it's dream power by repeating:

With this ring I do dream
Loving dreamtime dreams.

Dream Meditation for Love

Sit or recline comfortably next to a clock with an audible tick as you do this meditation. Close your eyes and breathe in deeply and for a moment hold your breath, and then pulse it out as if you are freeing yourself from anything that may be burdening you. While again breathing in, focus on a single point of white light, and as you exhale, sense this point spreading throughout your body, into your environment, and into the universe. Within an instant, your breath acts as a carrier wave from the human to the divine and back again. Take several more deep and complete breaths.

In your mind's eye, imagine you are the seconds of a clock, ticking away. Each second gives way to the next in an endless procession that gives the perception of linear time moving forward. From seconds, you become minutes, and you suddenly feel your awareness has expanded sixty-fold. Next you become days, then years, decades, centuries, and millenniums. With each step, your awareness expands to new levels—both in the waking world and the dream world. Eventually you become eternity, which is the state of being when all time comes together as One.

Breathe in deeply and for a moment hold your breath, and then pulse it out as if you are freeing yourself from everything that burdens you. When you become One with the eternalness of time, then you move to the level where you can access any period of time—whether in the past, present, or future—just by focusing on it with your mind. With your expectations, you can go wherever you want to go.

Time and space cease to be limitations but instead are gateways to dream empowerment. Perceive your world in terms of positive opportunities that are there to help you move forward in your quest for fulfillment in terms of relationships and love. Believe that you can have the relationships that you wish for in your soul.

Now take a deep breath, and breathe in the knowing that you are worthy and deserving of the love that you so desire. As you breathe in again, you realize that love is always within your reach. You are a loving person who deserves to live a loving life. Take another deep breath, and slowly open your eyes, moving your fingers and toes and coming back to the present time and place. Stretch and shift your body, yet remain relaxed.

Dream Prayer for Love

Say this prayer just before you go to bed:

Great Spirit, please pray with me.
May I start my day with love
And end my day with love,
In this world in this time
In the dream world in dreamtime.
By the Great Spirit,
May my dreams be filled with love.
Thank you for sharing my prayers.

As you drift to sleep, sing or hum your dream song to yourself or play it on a CD. When you wake up, write down or record all the details you remember from your dreams plus your insight in your dream empowerment journal and date your entry.

Oracle of Dreams for Love

In this oracle you will be using the power of time to divine your answers. Time is related to motion, like the dawning of the sun and the rising of the moon as day flows into night. The wheels of time roll on. You can use the motion of the wheels of time, in the form of a clock or watch with a second hand sweep, as a simple, yet effective divination technique. Temporally speaking, it allows you to peek around the divine corner into the future.

You will need a clock or watch with a second hand sweep and your dream empowerment journal. Write down one specific question about your dream empowerment goal for love in your journal. Read the question aloud three times. Hold the timepiece in your hands, take a deep breath, merge with the divine, and say:

I empower this timepiece as a divine dream oracle for love right now.

Continue to hold the timepiece in your hands, and think about your dream empowerment question regarding love. Take your time and spin the question around in your mind a while. Take a few deep breaths to focus your awareness even more. If your mind wanders, just gently return your attention to the question. Open your eyes when you feel you are ready—usually a few minutes—and make a note of the exact time in your dream empowerment journal: the hour, minute, and second on the timepiece.

Add the total numbers of the exact time. For example, 3:45 and 15 seconds would be 3 + 4 + 5 = 12, then 1 + 2 = 3. 15 seconds is 1 + 5 = 6. 3 + 6 = 9. The oracle number is 9. Exceptions are 11 and 22, which are master numbers and often remain as they are and are not added together. Refer to the following Dream Number Chart for the meanings of the numbers you receive in the oracle.

For best results, ask a maximum of three questions at a time. Make a note of the date, your questions, and the oracular responses in your dream empowerment journal.

Dream Number Chart

1—Personal dream empowerment, Oneness, attaining your goals, action, new beginnings.

2—Helpful partners, the union of the waking and dream worlds, shared dreaming, shape-shifting dreams, dream inspiration, creativity in dream.

3—Divine dreams, ancestral dreams, moving beyond time/space, sacred unity, harmony.

4—Lucid dreaming, elemental dreaming, attaining dream goals, dream creativity, organizing your dream empowerment goals for the better.

5—Dream adventures, lucid dreaming, transformation, changeable dreams and goals.

6—Dreams of children, love, beauty, home, family traditions, muses, and ancestors; dream messages for creative artists.

7—Spiritual dream messages, time-travel dreams, dream cycles, lucid dreaming, masterful and transformational dreams.

8—Dreams of the eternal now, dream gifts and rewards, dreams of abundance, business, and career path.

9—Dream goal completion and transformation, knowledge, wisdom, and creativity through dreaming, humanitarian dreams, global dreaming, shamanic dreaming.

11—Dream insights and inspiration, telepathic and precognitive dreaming, lucid, healing, shared, and intuitive dreams.

22—Dream visions, lucid dreaming, mastering and attaining your dream empowerment goals for love, health, and abundance.

Dream Affirmation for Love

Tap the middle of your breastbone with your fingers for a minute or so to stimulate your thymus gland and boost your energy, and then repeat this love affirmation. Repeat this process several times a day for at least 28 days for optimum results:

In this time and in all times, I follow my plan for attaining my dream empowerment goals for love and receive and remember helpful dream-time signs and messages.

Health

One of the areas you access when you enter dreamtime is that of perfect health. Rather than a physical state of being, dreamtime deals with your spiritual health. Perfect health is, in this sense, an aspect of the divine, which then serves as a template for what you strive to achieve in terms of health.

When you access these divine aspects of perfect health, you are reminded of your own divine qualities and how these qualities make you healthy in a spiritual sense, then, as a result, improve both your physical and mental health as well. When all three are working together, you move into an optimum state of health.

Dreams are an excellent method for tapping into this divine aspect of perfect health. By giving yourself the suggestion, in your dreams you can go to this epoch of perfect health and bring its health benefits back into your waking life. Just as the Aborigines travel into dreamtime in order to maintain the natural order of the universe, you travel into dreamtime in order to maintain the natural order of your health. By accessing the divine aspects of perfect health, you realize an innate healing wisdom and potential within your body, mind, and spirit.

Sacred Healing Dream Space

Add a calendar and a cedar and sage smudge stick to your sacred healing dream space. Empower the smudge by holding it in your hands, merging with the sacred powers of dreamtime, and saying:

May the sacred and eternal healing powers of dreamtime empower this smudge stick.

Hold the calendar in your hands, merge a little deeper with the sacred powers of dreamtime, and say:

May the sacred and eternal healing powers of dreamtime empower this calendar.

Dream Ritual for Health

The purpose of this ritual is to establish a time frame and six specific steps to take toward your dream empowerment goal for health and well-being. You will need the calendar and smudge stick from your sacred healing dream altar and a pen.

Do this ritual on or just before a full moon. First, smudge your sacred space with the cedar and sage smudge stick. Smudge smoke purifies your sacred space. Use a bowl, dish, or pan to catch any burning ash from the stick. When you are done smudging, carefully extinguish the stick by dipping the burning smudge in water.

Next, imagine a bright sphere of white light completely encircling you and your sacred healing space. Invite the elements into your ritual space by saying:

May the elements of earth, air, fire, water, and spirit come into my sacred ritual space now.

Then, invite any helpful divine energies or presences into your ritual space by asking them to now be present.

Use the pen to write one specific dream goal for health in your dream empowerment journal, and then under the goal list six steps you can take toward attaining that dream goal in the next year. These steps can be ones that you can take both in your waking and dream worlds. Date your entry.

Next, copy your dream goal for health onto the front of the calendar, and write down on the calendar in temporal order the steps of your plan to attain your goal. Write down the first step on the first week, the second step on the second month, the third step on the third month, the fourth step on the sixth month, the fifth step on the ninth month, and the sixth step on month twelve.

These time divisions make time seem more absolute and give you a time frame to work with. By assigning a time frame to a specific dream goal for health, you breathe temporal power into your dreams, which helps you manifest your goal. (You may need to use two calendars—this year and next year—depending upon when you do the ritual. Or you can simply add a few months needed to your calendar so that they total 12 by attaching blank pages and labeling them with the appropriate month and year.)

Read over what you have written down on your calendar and tweak your entries in any way you feel necessary. Feel free to slot in any dream requests, questions, incubations, shape-shifting dreams, and lucid dreaming adventures to make your calendar for attaining your dream goal for health even more exciting and powerful!

After you have filled in your calendar, sit back for a few minutes and imagine moving toward your dream goal for health one step at a time just as you have written down on the steps your calendar. Begin imagining by moving a week forward in time toward your dream empowerment goal for health. Then imagine moving ahead in time a month, three months, six months, nine months, and a year. Imagine a healthier and happier you as you progress in time. Then go even farther by imagining yourself three years in the future, five years in the future, and ten years in the future. Use your imagination to color your future with beauty and harmony. Picture the future as bright and clear, filled with joy, happy adventures, and good health. Continue doing this for at least five minutes.

When you are done, thank the divine and the elements by saying:

I thank the divine and the elements for their helpful presence and blessings.

Visualize stepping out of the sphere of white light, and imagine the bright sphere diffusing into the air into a million points of lights drifting out in all directions around you.

Put the calendar in your sacred healing space and refer to it every morning and every night just before you go to sleep for the next year to help you stay on track to a healthier and happier you.

Dream Meditation for Health

Sit or recline comfortably. Uncross your hands and legs and shift your body slightly to get even more comfortable. If you like, you can turn on some soft, meditative, New Age or instrumental music during the meditation and prayer.

Begin by breathing in deeply and slowly for three heartbeats, stilling your breath for three heartbeats, and then exhaling for three heartbeats. Count to three before again repeating the breathing exercise of breathing in for three heartbeats, holding your breath for three heartbeats, and breathing out for three heartbeats. Do this several times until you begin to sense the rhythm in your breathing and it starts to become a natural part of your breathing pattern.

Now imagine that every time you breathe in, you breathe in bright white light. Imagine that each time you breathe out, you release any negative, unwanted, or unhealthy energy in your body out through your breath to be recycled by the universe. In the time you still your breath for three heartbeats, imagine neutralizing the energy in your body. As you continue breathing rhythmically in this way, you feel free of any unwanted energies and ready for dreamtime.

Now, in your mind's eye imagine standing in front of a magnificent, stately oak tree. Also, imagine that the oak tree has a knot in its trunk at eye level that looks just like a doorknob. Grabbing hold of it, you turn this natural knob, and as it turns, a portal to other worlds and other times opens before you. The portal opens to whatever time you want to go to and to wherever you want to go.

You notice that when you move the natural wooden knob counterclockwise, you move backward in time, and if you move it clockwise, you go forward in time. When you merely touch it without turning it, you remain in the present moment.

As you turn the knob forward and backward, you realize that the oak tree is a powerful portal into dreamtime. Any time you desire, you can imagine the oak tree in your mind's eye, and then depending on whether you want to go forward or backward in time, imagine yourself turning the knob accordingly. Imagine it as your very own time machine that can transport you into eternal and complete health and well-being. Turn the knob left and right for a few minutes, and use your imagination to explore the different times and realms.

As you turn the knob to several different times and realms, you understand that to be truly healthy, it is necessary to integrate your past and future into what is happening to you in the present. All times influence all other times. It's all one. Each thing and every time is connected. You suddenly realize that it's time to integrate your waking and dream worlds into one where they complement and empower one another.

Now take a deep breath in and out, welcoming dreams for good health and well-being, in waking and in dreamtime. Take another deep breath, feeling healing energy flow through you. As you take another deep breath, move your feet and hands, and slowly open your eyes. Come back to the present time and stretch your body, yet remain relaxed for prayer.

Dream Prayer for Health

Just before you go to sleep, say this dream prayer for health and well-being:

Divine and sacred ones, I pray you,
Cosmic Mother and Cosmic Father,
Please hear my prayer
In this time and in all times.
In the eternal now of dreamtime
Please grace me with healing dreams
Of wellness and well-being.
Bless you eternally.

When you wake up, write down or record all the details you remember from your dreams in your dream empowerment journal and date your entry.

Oracle of Dreams for Health

Use a clock or watch with a second hand. Write down one specific question about your dream empowerment goal for health in your dream empowerment journal. Read the question aloud three times. Hold the timepiece in your hands, take a deep breath, merge with the divine, and say:

I empower this timepiece as a divine dream oracle for health right now.

Continue to hold the timepiece in your hands and think about your question. Take your time and spin the question around in your mind. Take a few deep breaths to focus your awareness. If your mind wanders, gently return your attention to the question regarding health. Now open your eyes when you feel you are ready—usually a few minutes—and make a note of the exact time in your dream empowerment journal: the hour, minute, and second on the timepiece.

Add the total numbers of the exact time. Refer to the Dream Number Chart for the number meanings. For best results, ask a maximum of three questions at a time. Make a note in your dream empowerment journal of the date, your questions, and exact times, as well as the oracular responses and any personal insights you may have.

Dream Affirmation for Health

Tap the middle of your breastbone with your fingers for a minute to stimulate your thymus gland and boost your energy, and then repeat this healing affirmation. Repeat this process several times a day for at least 28 days for the most powerful results.

Today and every day, I am filled with the sacred healing energies of Oneness. My waking and dream worlds connect into one and complement and empower each other in the best possible ways.

Abundance

Within dreamtime, abundance can be all things to all people, depending on their perceptions. There is a *Twilight Zone* episode where a man gives the leading character a pair of scissors, telling him that it's very important to his livelihood. Reluctantly the man takes the scissors. Moments later his tie gets caught in an elevator door, and suddenly those scissors become the crucial element in his survival as he cuts the tie just before he's about to choke.

Dreams are much the same way in that sometimes you don't always realize what they are giving you, but as your life progresses, you begin to understand why certain things and certain dreams come into your life at different times.

Overall, the perception of abundance is subjective within terms of the self and who you are as a person. To some people, composing a hit song is abundance, to others making a million dollars is abundance, and to still others it's reaching a Oneness with the spiritual Tao. Although the goals may be different, the sensation you feel when you attain them is very much the same. This is essentially what empowerment is all about. It is a feeling that defies the boundaries of time and space and, as such, it propels you forward within your overall quest for abundance.

Expanded, the perception of abundance is objective within terms of the overall perspective of time. Individual actions come into terms of their holistic intent. Holistically, each action brings about a larger series of events that spread out from the original event.

Perceiving how past and present events affect future events is the key to precognition. People who exhibit this quality have been known to become wealthy. When you pay attention to your dreams, you can come to know unlimited wealth. By asking the right questions, your dreams can give the answers to help you attain your dream goals for abundance.

Sacred Abundance Dream Space

Add four white tea candles and holders and cedarwood-scented oil to your sacred abundance dream altar. Roll the capped vial of oil between your palms until it is warm. Merge with the divine and say three times:

May this oil be filled with abundant dream power.

Hold the candles and their holders in your hands, one at a time, and empower them for dreaming. Merge with the divine and repeat three times:

May this candle be filled with abundant dream power.

Dream Ritual for Abundance

The purpose of this ritual is to ask for and receive a dream gift of abundance from the eternal well of dreamtime. You will need a clear glass filled with water, the tea candles with holders, and cedarwood oil from your sacred abundance dream altar.

On or just before a full moon, gather together everything you need for the ritual and place it on your bedside altar. Next, write down in your dream empowerment journal a specific dream gift you would like from the eternal well of dreamtime which embodies all knowledge to help you attain your dream goals for abundance. Use as few words as possible, be exact, and keep it simple and to the point. Date your entry.

Now imagine a bright sphere of white light completely encircling you and your sacred space. Invite the elements into your ritual space by saying:

May the elements of earth, air, fire, water, and spirit come into my sacred ritual space now.

Put the glass of water in the center of the altar (this water is not for drinking). It represents the eternal well of dreamtime and the wisdom within. Put a drop of cedarwood oil on each of the candles. Then anoint your wrists with the oil. Wipe the oil from your hands. Place the candles at the four directions of north, east, south, and west (in that order) around the glass of water on the altar. Light the candles, one at a time, in the same order as you placed them around the glass of water, and each time you do, dedicate the candle to the divine by saying:

I dedicate this candle to the divine ones and ask them to join me in this ritual now.

Once you have lit the candles, carefully spin each of the candleholders clockwise three times. As you do, chant:

From the eternal well of dreamtime
May abundant dream wisdom be mine.

Gaze at the candle flames and the illuminated well of water in their center (the glass filled with water). Merge with the divine energy of your preference and say:

Divine Ones, blessed Ones, please hear my request.
I [state your full name] ask for a dream gift from the eternal well of dreamtime.
[Read what you wrote down in your journal three times aloud with feeling.]

Now think about the good things you have done in your life—for example, times you have unselfishly shown love to others, when you have truly helped someone else, shared food and your good fortune, helped heal Mother Earth, done good deeds, or helped make the world a little brighter. Gaze at the candles and the symbolic well in the center of them again and say:

I have done these good things in my life.
[State aloud some of the good things you have done.]
You know of my sincere actions and efforts.
Please, Divine Ones, grant me this dream gift
From the eternal well of dreamtime
To help me attain my dream goal for abundance.
Many thanks to you, divine and generous Ones,
Blessed be the eternal well of dreamtime.

Close your eyes and imagine the eternal well of dreamtime before you. Shape it in any way you like in your imagination. Visualize reaching into the well and pulling up your dream gift. Imagine receiving the exact information, creative idea, insight, inspiration, or answer you need to attain your dream goal for abundance. Continue doing this for a few minutes.

When you are done with the ritual, thank the divine and the elements by saying:

I thank the divine ones and the elements for their helpful presence and blessings.

Visualize stepping out of the sphere of white light, and imagine the sphere diffusing into the air around you. Allow the candles to burn safely down as you meditate and pray. As a safety precaution, be sure to snuff out any candles before you go to sleep. If needed, you can always relight them the next day and burn them down completely. Keep the glass of water on your bedside altar as you sleep and dream. The next morning, pour the water outside on a plant or down the drain. Do not drink it.

Dream Meditation for Abundance

Get as comfortable as possible and uncross your hands and legs. Begin to breathe in and out, and imagine that your breath turns a giant wheel. As you breathe inward, you tighten the springs of the wheel, and as you still your breath, you stay within the moment and think about what you want. When you exhale, you release your mind energy toward your goals and the wheel spins forward.

Breathing in, you bring into focus one specific dream empowerment goal for abundance, and stilling your breath for a few seconds, you focus your energies and set your plan in place to make it happen. When you exhale, you invoke the natural power within you as well as the timeless and eternal divine energy of the universe to help you attain your genuine, heartfelt goal for abundance.

As you continue to breathe in and out, spinning the wheel forward in your imagination, you realize that dreams can help you begin to understand the holistic and timeless quality of your life. Rather than seeing your life in terms of specific moments of time, you begin to view things in terms of the grander picture of time. You begin to comprehend the timeless quality of your spirit.

Spinning the wheel with your breathing, you start to understand how your present choices, thoughts, and actions affect your life, now and in the future, just as they have in the past. Everything is connected. Taking a deep breath and spinning the wheel forward, imagine stepping through a door into the future, into a positive, joyful, and abundant world that you are very much a part of.

Allow yourself to become one with that positive world in the future for a few minutes. Shape and fashion it with your imagination. See, feel, hear, taste, and smell your positive future. Turn your attention completely to this future world for a few minutes and enjoy attaining your dream goals. Enjoy your success and empowerment. Look at how your life has changed for the better. Imagine how it would feel to be in this abundant and joyful future. Know in your body, mind, and spirit that you can and will experience this abundance, this joyful and successful future. Know that with the help of your dreams and the messages and information you are provided in them, your powers of imagination and your active efforts of taking the steps toward your empowerment goals combine to carry you into this image of the future, an image that becomes your waking reality.

Take a deep breath and spin the wheel to the present time and place. Take another breath, knowing that the image and energetic patter of your joyful and abundant future is set in place and the wheel is now in spin. Breathe in deeply once again, exhale completely, and begin gently moving your hands and feet. Slowly open your eyes and stretch your body, yet remain in a peaceful state of mind for prayer, sleep, and dreaming.

Dream Prayer for Abundance

Say this prayer as you go to bed:

Tonight may I dream of a joyful and abundant world, filled with beautiful green valleys. May I dream of attaining my deepest dreams of abundance.

May my dreams of abundance flow like Mother Earth's clear, rushing rivers and streams, and may I remember their helpful dream messages when I awaken. Thank you, Dear Mother, for your kind blessings and for empowering my dreams.

When drifting to sleep, give yourself the suggestion that your dreams will provide you with the information you need and desire to attain your dream goals for abundance. This works best when you focus on one goal at a time for a period of 28 nights.

By giving yourself this positive suggestion just before you go to sleep, you are, in a sense, programming your mind to provide you with dreams that become your connection point with the eternal database that exists both in the waking and dream world. It is at this point when all things become One, and you connect with your higher self. This is the point in dream when everything is possible, when complete personal transformation becomes possible.

When you wake up, be sure to write down or record all the details you remember from your dreams in your dream empowerment journal and date your entry. Keep in mind, you may be doing this several times a night.

As a rule of thumb, make an effort to write down or record at least one dream each night. As you continue in the process, you will find that you write down and record multiple dreams throughout the night. One way to do this is by just jotting down a few words of association or strong images in the dream in your journal, or you might record what you remember into a handheld tape recorder. In the morning, go over what you have written, drawn, or recorded, and write a more complete description of the dream and your dream insights in your dream empowerment journal.

Oracle of Dreams for Abundance

Write down one specific question regarding your dream empowerment goal for abundance in your journal. Read the question aloud three times. Hold your timepiece in your hands, take a deep breath, merge with the divine, and say:

I empower this timepiece as a divine dream oracle for abundance right now.

Continue to hold the timepiece in your hands and think about your dream empowerment question regarding abundance. Focus on your question for a while. Take a few deep breaths to focus even more. If your mind wanders, gently return your awareness to the question. Open your eyes when you feel you are ready, and make a note of the exact time in your dream empowerment journal: the hour, minute, and second on the timepiece.

After you add the total numbers of the exact time together, check the Dream Number Chart for the meanings of these numbers. Ask a maximum of three questions at a time. Make a note of the date, your questions, and exact times, as well as the oracular responses, in your dream empowerment journal.

Dream Affirmation for Abundance

For the most powerful results, write this affirmation in your dream empowerment journal:

Today and every day, my vision of a joyful and abundant world moves from my imagination into my waking world. My true nature is eternal and boundless, and each moment is filled with divine abundance as I attain my heartfelt goals for an empowering, enriching, and joyful life.

Also write the affirmation on 10 or more notes and put them around your home—for example, taping them to the refrigerator, mirrors, and doors—so you will see and read the affirming message often. In addition, write the affirmation on a small card or cards you can put in your pocket, wallet, purse, and top drawer.

When you repeat the affirmation, either aloud or silently to yourself, tap the middle of your breastbone with your fingers for a minute or so to stimulate your thymus gland and boost your energy. Read the notes around your home when you see them, and also take the card out and read it several times a day. You can do this aloud or silently to yourself. Continue repeating this affirmative process several times a day for 28 days or more.

Chapter Eight

Transformation Through Dreaming

The transformation aspect has always been one of the essential qualities in mythology and fairy tales. In "The Ugly Duckling," the duckling becomes a beautiful swan, and in "Cinderella," the poor servant sister becomes the princess. The transformation is what makes mythological tales more interesting because each of us can identify with these sets of circumstances. When you get stuck in a rut, through a dream, you are able to move out of this rut and get back on track. This is the essential element of transformation, whether in a waking or dream state of being.

A story that has come to take up mythological proportions, particularly within terms of transformation through dreaming, is Charles Dickens's *A Christmas Carol*. The main character, Scrooge, is confronted in his dreams by three ghosts who represent his past, present, and future. The three ghosts show Scrooge events from all three time periods that then alter his awareness and perception of life. The experiences he has in the dreams transform Scrooge's relationships with the people around him by letting the light of love and sharing into his life. Thus he learns the value of giving as well as receiving.

Scrooge doesn't have to die in order to be aware of what life would be like without him, but, instead, he senses and experiences it within terms of the dream. The experience is essentially only real in his dream, but that doesn't matter because the effects carry over from the dream to the waking world, making transformation through dreams very real. This means you can experience certain transformative events in dreams rather than having to face them in waking reality. This is one of the key reasons dreams are invaluable for transformation and empowerment.

Moving Forward Through Your Dreams

This is the point in the process when you begin to become more aware of the connection of the dream and waking worlds and how this connection could be invaluable in transforming your life into more of what you want and often need. By transforming who your dream self is, you in turn change your waking self-image. This gives you more confidence and helps attain your dream empowerment goals and live your dreams.

The idea that you have past and future lives gives rise to the idea that you are indeed working out energetic issues often over lifetimes. These issues can and do affect your love, health, and abundance in the context of this lifetime. When the idea of multiple lifetimes added to this formula, it suggests that as a human being, you are definitely dynamic, and as such, you are continually moving and changing, hopefully in a positive direction.

These changes and forward movement are driven by your experiences both on the dream and waking level. Evolution is all about learning from experience, otherwise you continually repeat your mistakes. The key is to hone your skills for observation and then to transfer this into techniques that work to move you forward in life.

This becomes the essence of empowerment—at each point you reach a plateau of forward movement, and you form an energetic base camp. Much like a mountain climber, you then move methodically up the mountain from this point, so that the whole expedition is completed in segments that when fitted together work as a seamless whole.

No matter how high the goal you set, if you utilize your dreams and helpful dream techniques to move toward your empowerment goals step by step, you can attain amazing heights. Dreams are an important tool for transformation for two reasons:

- There is a close energetic connection between your waking self and dream self.
- Dreams happen every time you go to sleep, which generally happens at least once in every 24-hour period of time. You have the potential for transformation every time you sleep.

This means that every day of the week, you can move toward where you want to be in life. If your dream empowerment goal is to be more prosperous and financially stable and you determine that at the rate you are going it will take you perhaps a hundred dreams and dream steps to get there, then it becomes possible to reach your goal in less than a year. For what you get out of it, the amount of time is insignificant because, after all, empowerment is an eternal process that is continually unfolding and opening up new opportunities and awareness in this lifetime and in all lifetimes.

Changing Your Life, One Dream at a Time

Avid dreamer and poet Ralph Waldo Emerson felt that each person has to dare to live the life she or he has dreamed of. To do so, you have to go forward and make your dreams come true. This is what transformation through dreams is all about—becoming the person you want to be. That way you can be at ease with who you are at all times, and when this happens, you complete an essential energetic cycle that progresses you to another level in your personal empowerment.

This transformation aspect of dreams is in ways more observable and, as such, more practical than the theoretical or metaphysical aspects of dreams. As Carl Jung so appropriately summed it up, "I have no theory about dreams. I do not know how dreams arise. On the other hand, I know that if we meditate on a dream sufficiently long and thoroughly—if we take it about with us and turn it over and over—something almost always comes out of it."

Because dreams tap into a divine collective database, they give you answers that aren't always available to your waking state. To fully access this collective database, you need to move beyond your familiar maps into new, uncharted territory. Termed the "reflective consciousness," it deals with the highest levels of cognition that tune in to an environment in more subliminal ways than determined by your instinctual, reflexive, and conditioned reactions.

The wonderful thing about dreams is that you move through them reflectively instead of acting out conditioned responses. This moves you, the dreamer, beyond your compulsion for habit, into a world that is both reflective and creative, depending on your needs.

Obviously, when you open yourself up to your dreams, you in turn open yourself up to anything that is a problem in your life. Sometimes these problems escalate and present themselves as nightmares that sometimes can disrupt your sleep and activities in your waking world. This is all right because it's part of your process of dealing with the problems that arise out of life, particularly as you begin to make forward movement in your endeavors. One of the biggest parts of success is being able to deal with problems as they arise, rather than waiting for them to avalanche on you.

Positive transformation happens one dream at a time and one step at a time. If you want to become a stronger person who deals with problems better, then start envisioning yourself that way just before you go to sleep and also in your dreams. Dream that you are in a successful, loving relationship, and you are at least half the way to attaining that goal. In this way, dreams are important to your overall self-image, both internal and external. If you can dream it, you can experience it in the waking world.

Love

Your dreams can help you solve the problems of your present relationships and at the same time help you see the direction in which you want to move your future relationships. Start perceiving your dream self as who you want your waking self to be. If you want to be smarter, stronger, more sensuous, or more intuitive, then become more that way in your dreams.

If you can't particularly deal with certain emotions and feelings within the waking world, then try dealing with these emotions in your dreams. The loss of a loved one or feelings of love toward someone who doesn't yet know you're alive are two examples. Every time you deal with an issue of this nature, you move a little bit forward, like a play piece on a board game. You move to the next level, but at the same time, the wheel's still in spin and the game is still in play.

Sacred Love Dream Space

Add a sea shell, a white candle, and sandalwood-scented oil to your sacred love dream altar.

Empower these items for your dream ritual by holding your palms over them, merging with Oneness, and saying:

May the transformative power of love fill this sea shell, white candle, and sandalwood oil.

Dream Ritual for Love

The purpose of this ritual is to identify one specific aspect of your present or prospective love relationship that you want to transform and then make that transformation. You will need a sheet of paper, a pen, 1 tablespoon sea salt in a glass of water, and the white candle, sandalwood-scented oil, and sea shell from your sacred love dream altar.

Do this ritual on or just before a full moon on a Friday night. Imagine a bright sphere of white light completely encircling you and your sacred space. Then invite the elements into your ritual space by saying:

I respectfully invite the elements of earth, air, fire, water, and spirit into my sacred ritual space.

Invite any helpful Goddesses and Gods or other divine powers of your choice into your ritual space now. This imbues your ritual with sacred power.

Bathe the sea shell in the salt water for a minute or two, and then take it out of the water. Pour the water down the drain. Rub a drop of the oil on the sea shell, a drop on the tea candle, and a drop or two on your ankles and wrists. Wipe any remaining oil off your hands, and light the candle, dedicating it to your beloved or prospective beloved.

Next, write down one specific aspect in your love relationship that you want to transform into your dream empowerment journal and date your entry. If you don't have a mate, then write down the most important aspect you want to transform within yourself with regard to a prospective love relationship.

Copy this onto the sheet of paper in large, legible letters. Put the paper on your altar where you can easily read it. Pick up the sea shell, hold it in your hands, and say:

Bring transformative dream messages to me tonight.

Hold the sea shell over your ear and listen to the ocean waves for a minute. Then whisper what you have written down on the paper into the shell three times.

Softly gaze into the candlelight for a few minutes, holding the shell in your power hand and imagining the details of your transformation coming to life in the flame. As you do this, review your dream empowerment goals, and ask that you will be given the plan for transforming your love life in your dreams, tonight, tomorrow night, and so forth until you receive a clear message.

Anoint the four corners of the paper with a few drops of the oil, put it on your dream altar, and read it often until the transformation is complete. Also, anoint the sea shell with another drop of oil and place it on your bedside altar. It is a symbol of your positive transformation.

When you are done, thank the divine and the elements by saying:

I thank the divine and the elements for their helpful presence and blessings.

Imagine stepping out of the sphere of white light you imagined at the beginning of the ritual, and visualize the sphere diffusing into the air around you.

Dream Meditation for Love

Recline comfortably where you won't be disturbed. Uncross your hands and feet and close your eyes. In your mind's eye, imagine being on an ocean beach with the waves before you moving inward and outward. Taking a deep breath, imagine the wave being drawn into the ocean; then exhale while imagining the wave being released onto the shore.

The scent of the salt air fills your nostrils as the water from the wave touches your skin. The bubbles that form on top of the water tingle as the wave again moves back into the ocean and you again inhale deeply. Hold your breath for a moment before exhaling and sending the wave crashing into the sandy shore. Do this several more times, feeling yourself becoming more and more in syncopation with the rhythm and essence of the ocean with each breath you take.

Sense the tide moving in and carrying you away on a throne made from the whitecaps of the waves. You sail across the sea of dreams to an island of your own imaginative design. The island represents that special place you have created for yourself where you can go to actualize your love empowerment dreams.

Stepping out onto the island, your feet sink into the sand, and the cool breeze blows gently in your face. Still in syncopation with the ocean, you sense the rhythm of the waves moving through your being. Each wave is like a veil being lifted from your perception so that you can continually see things clearer, creating a transformation within the dynamics of who you are. Following your dream empowerment plans for love, you set the path for more positive transformations to follow. As you do so, you give yourself the following suggestion:

Each time I dream it's like a wave transforming me into a more loving person. Step by step I gradually change my life for the better, giving way to relationships that are more fulfilling and joyful.

Remember to visit your island of dream transformation for love often in your quest for empowerment. Rather than try to transform your world overnight, transform it aspect by aspect. Each dream brings with it more helpful messages and images, moving you forward and carrying you along the path toward attaining your dream empowerment goals for love.

Take a deep breath now, feeling peacefully relaxed, knowing you are worthy and deserving of love. As you take another deep breath, you know that a more loving life is within your reach. As you breathe in again, slowly open your eyes, move your fingers and toes, and come back to the present time and place. Stretch and shift your body, yet remain relaxed.

Dream Prayer for Love

Say this prayer just before you go to bed:

God and Goddess, I pray you
Please share with me the meaning of love
So that each time I dream

I transform into who I want to be.
Guide and protect me as I make these positive changes
With divine blessings, now and eternally.
Thank you, God and Goddess.

As you drift to sleep, repeat softly to yourself:

My dreams transform me, and I clearly remember my dreams of transformation when I wake up.

When you wake up, record or write down everything you remember from your dreams, as well as any personal insights about your dream in your dream empowerment journal.

Oracle of Dreams for Love

Go outside on a starry night and gaze at the stars for a few minutes. Take a deep breath and say:

The stars provide me with a divine oracle tonight.

Then think of one question regarding your dream goals for love and transforming your life into a more loving one. Focus your awareness completely on your question as you look closely at the stars and notice any patterns or symbols in their formations. Also make a note of any stars or constellations present that you are familiar with. Write these down in your dream empowerment journal along with any insights you may have regarding the patterns and constellations. If you see a shooting star within 30 minutes after asking your question, it confirms your positive transformation.

Dream Affirmation for Love

Write the following dream affirmation for love in your dream empowerment journal:

Today and each day, I transform my life, in waking and in dream, into a more loving one in every way.

Then write the affirmation on several notes and post them around your home, so you will see and read the affirming message often. Also write the affirmation on a small card or cards you can put in your pocket, wallet, or purse. Take the card out and read it several times a day. Continue repeating the affirmation several times a day for 28 days or more.

Health

Dreams can reveal the mental and spiritual causes of disease before the actual physical symptoms develop. Once dreams reveal these causes, you can then deal with them on the spiritual and mental level, preventing the disease from ever reaching your physical body. In this way, your dream self can be a powerful protector from disease. If you find your dream self and use it appropriately, it can offer you another means for getting healthy and staying healthy.

Physical reality is a result of your choices. This is why it is important to choose wisely. Dreams can often help you in this process because they open up doors and windows to other choices that you might not normally perceive.

Dreams open up the doors and windows of your perception in ways that at times seem as nonsensical as Lewis Carroll's *Through the Looking Glass*. This world is one of polarities, from good and bad and hot and cold to hard and soft and male and female. You are continually trying to create a balance between these polarities in life. When you obtain this balance, you move much closer to transforming into a healthier you.

Sacred Healing Dream Space

Add a picture or pictures of some of your favorite butterflies to your sacred healing dream space. Butterflies are a universal symbol of transformation and change. Empower these images for transformational dreaming by placing your palms down over the picture(s), merging with Oneness, and saying:

May the healing dream power of Oneness fill this transformational image.

Dream Ritual for Health

The purpose of this ritual is to access the natural transformative powers of the butterfly spirits to help you attain your dream goals for good health. You will need a compass and the picture of the butterflies in your sacred healing space.

Imagine a bright sphere of white light completely encircling you and your sacred healing space. Invite the elements into your ritual space by saying:

May the elements of earth, air, fire, water, and spirit come into my sacred ritual space now.

Then, invite the helpful butterfly spirits into your ritual space by saying:

I invite the helpful butterfly spirits into my ritual space.

Face north. Use the compass to get your bearings. Now raise your arms upward. Merge with Oneness, and say:

I welcome the helpful and transformative butterfly spirits of the north into my dreams tonight.

Next, face east, raise both arms upward, merge with Oneness, and say:

I welcome the helpful and transformative butterfly spirits of the east into my dreams tonight.

Then face south, raise both arms upward, merge with Oneness, and say:

I welcome the helpful and transformative butterfly spirits of the south into my dreams tonight.

Now face west, raise your arms upward, merge with Oneness, and say:

I welcome the helpful and transformative butterfly spirits of the west into my dreams tonight.

Face center, raise your arms upward, and say:

Helpful butterfly spirits of the four directions,
I ask that you grant me your transformative powers and wisdom
On the wings of healing and well-being.
Please dream with me tonight.

Remain within the sphere of white light as you meditate, pray, and sleep. When you wake up, after you write down or record your dream details, thank the helpful butterfly spirits and elements by saying:

I thank the butterfly spirits and the elements for their helpful presence and blessings.

Visualize stepping out of the sphere of white light, and imagine the sphere diffusing into the air in all directions around you.

Dream Meditation for Health

Turn on some soft meditative music to facilitate deeper relaxation and encourage your powers of imagination. Then recline comfortably and close your eyes. Begin by breathing deeply and completely. Imagine breathing in warm, white, healing light and exhaling any tension or stress you may be feeling.

As you take another breath, imagine a strand of warm, white, healing light moving across and around your being. In that moment you envision your empowerment dream of health. Exhaling, you sense yourself moving a step closer toward that dream.

Breathing in again, another strand of white, healing light wraps itself softly and warmly around you as you solidify your positive image of good health. Taking several more deep breaths, the white light continues weaving soft, white, healing strands around you until you are completely encircled in a marvelous cocoon of warm, white light.

Imagine merging with the infinite and eternal energies of Oneness, with all things, animate and inanimate, as you dwell in the cocoon of healing light. In an instant you become a part of everything. You are filled with a healing power that makes every part of your being sing with bliss and joy. You are filled with the everlasting light that connects you to all levels of your health, physical, mental, and spiritual. For an eternal moment, your connection to Oneness transforms your entire being, bringing your body, mind, and spirit into balance as you breathe in and feel the natural healing energy move through you.

In your mind's eye, imagine that your arms have become giant wings, and as you spread them and they split the cocoon of white light in half, you sense yourself emerging with all your beautiful splendor into the world. Emerging from your cocoon, you flap your magnificently colored wings and take flight on the breeze. You fly higher and higher, until from way up above, you see the larger picture and realize that your problems seem less significant and easier to resolve than they did before. Your dream goals for good health and well-being also seem within your reach now.

As you fly, you feel like a different person. You feel healthier and more positive about yourself. You realize you are positively transforming, both in dream and in waking. As you transform, you emerge a healthier and happier person, more vibrant and filled with light and life. Continue flying and transforming in your imagination for a few minutes.

Take another deep breath, once again breathing in white light, feeling peacefully relaxed. Breathing in again, move your hands and feet, slowly opening your eyes and coming back to the present time and place.

Dream Prayer for Health

Say this prayer just before going to sleep:

Divine Mother and Father,
Please help me to transform in waking and in dream.
Guide me on the path to good health and well-being
And share your healing light with me tonight.
Thank you, divine Mother and Father.

As you drift to sleep, repeat softly to yourself:

My dreams transform me, and I clearly remember my dreams of transformation when I wake up.

When you wake up, record or write down everything you remember from your dreams as well as any personal insights about your dream in your dream empowerment journal.

Oracle of Dreams for Health

Go outside on a starry night and gaze at the stars for a few minutes. Take a deep breath and say:

The stars provide me with a divine oracle tonight.

Then think of one question regarding your dream goals for good health and well-being and transforming into a healthier you. Focus completely on your question and look closely at the stars, noticing any patterns or symbols in their formations. Note any constellations and stars you are familiar with. Write these down in your dream empowerment journal and include any insights you may have regarding the patterns and constellations. If you see a shooting star within 30 minutes after asking your question, it confirms your positive transformation.

Dream Affirmation for Health

Write down the following affirmation and then repeat it aloud and silently to yourself several times a day for 28 days or more. When you do, actually imagine yourself dreaming the dreams and taking the steps you have marked on your calendar:

Today and every day, I take one more step, both in waking and in dreaming, toward positive personal transformation and good health.

Also write the affirmation on notes and put them around your home and workplace. Write it on a small card and carry it with you, pulling it out now and again during the day and reading it over.

Abundance

Oftentimes you will find yourself struggling with the things around you. Whether something intrusive or different, you need to learn to deal with the things around you rather than react to them. Like a shadow dancer, you respond to and mirror the images that transform around you. Like a shape shifter, you transform yourself into anyone you want to be. You are pliant, especially in your dreams, and, as such, you can transform into the person you truly want to be.

Your dreams are one of the things that make your life pliant and give it suppleness in that they represent your hopes and visions for the future. They become that vision or focal point that you are working toward as a way to make yourself happy and satisfied in terms of your personal experience.

Once you dream about something you genuinely want to transform in your life, you then move your mind toward experiencing your dream in waking reality. Dreaming it first actually makes this process much easier. Your thoughts, both in dreaming and waking, produce a certain amount of energy. When you direct sufficient thought energy toward attaining your goals, in your dream and waking worlds, you have a much better chance at success.

Sacred Abundance Dream Space

Add a small figurine of a frog, preferably made of metal, stone, or clay, to your sacred abundance dream altar. Frogs embody the qualities of stillness and complete focus. They traditionally represent the qualities of abundance, flexibility, and transformation.

Empower the frog figurine for your dream ritual by holding it between your hands, merging with Oneness, and saying three times:

May the transforming energy of Oneness fill this object.

Dream Ritual for Abundance

The purpose of this ritual is to make a talisman to encourage positive transformation in dreaming. You will need a cedar and sage smudge stick and the frog figurine from your sacred abundance dream altar.

Imagine a bright sphere of white light completely encircling you and your sacred space. Invite the elements into your ritual space by saying:

May the elements of earth, air, fire, water, and spirit come into my sacred ritual space now.

Light the sage and cedar smudge, dedicating it to the Great Spirit (or the divine energies of your preference). Catch any falling ash in a fireproof bowl or plate. Pass the frog figurine through the smudge smoke several times to cleanse it of any unwanted energies.

Now hold the frog in your hands, merge with Oneness, and say three times:

Talisman of dreams transform me.

Then put the frog in your left hand, covering it with your right and pulse the power of transformation into the figurine by taking a deep breath in, holding your breath for a few seconds while imagining your dreams transforming you in the best possible ways. Then pulse that image into the frog by exhaling sharply through your nose. Repeat this process a total of three times.

Hold the frog talisman in your hands for a few minutes as you close your eyes and imagine being transformed through your dreams and attaining your dreams for abundance, personally, locally, and globally.

When you are done with the ritual, thank the Great Spirit and the elements by saying:

I thank the Great Spirit and the elements for their helpful presence and blessings.

Visualize stepping out of the sphere of white light, and imagine the sphere diffusing into the air around you.

Place your dream talisman next to your bedside while you dream, or better yet, hold it in your receiving hand while you sleep. Each time you dream, turn your awareness toward that positively transformed image of yourself that you imagined, the one where you have attained your dreams of abundance and prosperity, and then repeat the words:

Talisman of dreams transform me.

Dream Meditation for Abundance

Sit or recline comfortably, and close your eyes. Slowly breathe in to a count of 1-2-3, then hold your breath for three counts, and then exhale while counting to three. Pause for three counts, and then do the whole process again. By counting slower, you slow down your breathing process and become more relaxed. Sense yourself becoming one with the cadence of your breathing; inhale 1-2-3, hold it 1-2-3, exhale 1-2-3, pause 1-2-3. Continue breathing in this way until you begin to sense your awareness subtly shifting.

Now, in your mind's eye imagine that you are swimming through a thick cosmic soup. At your sides, you have smooth, flipperlike fins that you use to steer yourself, and at the end opposite your head, you have a giant and powerful tail fin that you use to move yourself around in the watery womb of the Great Mother.

As you breathe in the cosmic soup, your gills naturally and easily take the oxygen out of the liquid and you exhale what's left. As before, inhale 1-2-3, hold it 1-2-3, exhale 1-2-3, pause 1-2-3. After doing this several times, you again sense your awareness shifting to a familiar place. You are filled with the joyful feeling that you have returned to your spiritual home. You feel the gentle and affirming embrace of the Cosmic Mother and Father as they encircle you with their ever-present love, healing light, and abundant gifts. Allow yourself to experience the divine energy of the universe for a few minutes. Breathe it into your being, 1-2-3. Each time you breathe in and out, you feel more and more empowered.

Imagine yourself emerging from the cosmic soup; your side-fins becoming your arms and your tail-fin your legs, you walk about. Your gills become lungs that take the oxygen in directly from the air, an element that you gradually become more in tune with. Your emergence from the cosmic soup transforms you, and you become the person you truly want to be, living an abundant, caring, and joyful life. Breathe in this knowledge, 1-2-3.

As you continue to breathe in 1-2-3, hold it 1-2-3, exhale 1-2-3, and pause 1-2-3, imagine that your arms transform into giant wings and transport you on the wind to a marvelous dream world. Allow yourself to fly freely in this world for a few minutes.

Now take another breath in 1-2-3, and begin moving your fingers and toes. Open your eyes slowly and come back to the present time and place, feeling peacefully aware.

Dream Prayer for Abundance

Say this prayer just before you go to sleep:

Cosmic Mother and Father,
Movers and shakers of evolution,
I've come down out of the trees.
Now help me with the next step, please.
I pray you, share your wisdom with me
And help me transform my life as I dream.
In the name of the Great Mother and Father
May I enjoy peace, harmony, and abundance
Now and forevermore.

As you drift to sleep, repeat softly to yourself:

My dreams transform me, and I clearly remember my dreams of transformation when I wake up.

When you wake up, record or write down your dream details, as well as any insights in your dream empowerment journal.

Oracle of Dreams for Abundance

Go outside on a starry night and gaze at the stars for a few minutes. Take a deep breath and say:

The stars provide me with a divine oracle tonight.

Then think of one question regarding your dream goals for abundance and transforming your life into an abundant one. Turn your mind completely to your question. Focus all of your awareness on it. Now look closely at the stars and notice any patterns or symbols you see in them. Write these down in your dream empowerment journal along with any insights you have regarding the patterns. If you see a shooting star within 30 minutes after asking your question, it confirms your positive transformation.

Dream Affirmation for Abundance

Write the following affirmation in your dream empowerment journal, and then repeat it several times a day for at least 28 days to encourage your personal transformation through dreaming:

Today and every day, my dreams transform me in very beneficial ways, and my life is filled with abundant joy, creativity, and prosperity.

For best results, also write the affirmation on several notes and put them here and there where you will see them around your home and workplace. In addition, write the affirmation on a small card and carry it with you, pulling it out and reading it during the day.

Chapter Nine

Lucid and Conscious Dreaming

Piercing through the darkness, the dark shadow moves closer and closer. I move away, but from over my shoulder I see the shadowy figure mirrors my every action. It seems as though death itself is stalking me. I call out but my voice is muffled. I look down and notice that my ring is on the wrong hand and know I am dreaming. Immediately, I yell "STOP," and stop the dream much like a film director switching cameras. I turn my dreaming mind to a dream world I am familiar with and find myself lying under a shady palm tree on a quiet, secluded beach. The shadow of the palm tree is cooling and welcome, and I feel completely relaxed and at peace.

In a dream experience, I can use several lucid dreaming indicators such as my hands, pet companions, and people I know who have passed over. For example, when I look down at my hands in the dream, if my ring is on the wrong hand or a different ring altogether, I know I am dreaming and can go lucid. If I see one of my dogs or cats, either living or deceased, in my dream, I know I'm dreaming and immediately go lucid. Once I go lucid, I alter the dreaming scene before me and direct my dreaming awareness to a more pleasant dreaming world or image I am familiar with, or I simply wake myself up.

In an interview with Brandon Boyd, who is the composer and lead singer for the popular rock 'n' roll band Incubus, he mentioned that his mother always encouraged him to enjoy dreaming. At an early age, she taught him to look at his hands and snap his fingers three times whenever he was having a bad dream. The third time he snapped his fingers in his dream, he would wake up. The action of seeing his hands in the dream and snapping his fingers made him aware of the fact that he was dreaming. From there Brandon went on to further develop his lucid dreaming skills, and now uses his dreams to fuel his creativity.

Once you realize you are dreaming, your dreams cease to be threatening as you literally and figuratively have the controlling influence. You can direct your own dreams much as you direct your waking day. From this point of realization, your dreams can then become especially beneficial and empowering.

Facing Your Fears in Lucid Dreaming

Troubled dreams and nightmares are often your fears manifesting themselves in dreams. These fears can take many forms, usually physical and mystical creatures that you fear on some level, whether it be snakes, spiders, death, or your in-laws. Dreams, by their nature, help you cope with your fears and anxieties. Troubled dreams and nightmares, rather than being bad things, can help you pinpoint your fears and in the process help you move beyond them and move forward in positive and empowering ways.

We are all born in this world essentially strangers to ourselves and the world around us. As such, we immediately fear both. We are afraid to become who we truly are because it might not work out the way we planned. And additionally, we have become disconnected from Mother Nature and many of her misunderstood aspects, for example, snakes, spiders, and mountain lions, as well as bees, cockroaches, and ticks.

If you have a bad experience with one of these animals or insects, you have a tendency to remember the pain and develop a fear of the entity. That fear is like a shadow that follows you around wherever you go.

The good news is that you can easily alleviate your fear by facing and confronting it, and dreams are one of the best ways of doing this.

Through dreaming, especially lucid dreaming, you can move through your fears in the form of nightmares or troubling dreams by directly influencing them.

Once you become aware of the concept that you are dreaming when you are dreaming, you suddenly realize that your fears can't hurt you because they are merely another aspect of the dream. It's actually a simple process that everyone can learn and implement for personal empowerment and enrichment.

Lucid dreaming is a state of mental clarity that brings with it the concept of dreaming while being conscious that you are dreaming. Leading dream researcher and author Stephen LeBerge has shown that lucid and conscious dreaming has the potential of being a most effective therapy for nightmares. Once you become aware that you are dreaming, the next step is to realize that nothing, no matter how unpleasant, can cause you physical harm in your dreams. You need not struggle or run from the monsters in your dreams because, after all, they are manifestations of your mind and will continue to haunt you until you deal with the source of the problem and overcome it. The best way to permanently get rid of your nightmares is to rid yourself of the fear and anxiety that drives them.

The fear you sense in your dreams is in some ways real, but the immediate physical danger encountered within the dream is not real. When you become conscious of this, you realize you can direct the flow of your dreams and the monsters cease to be threatening, and as such transform into things such as shady palm trees on warm sandy beaches. This seemingly magical transformation is another clear indication that you are dreaming.

Lucid Dreaming Focals

If you suddenly find yourself in a troubling dream or nightmare that you want to end, the first thing you need to do is to go lucid and become conscious that you are dreaming. One of the most effective means of achieving this is by using a lucid dream focal.

A lucid dream focal is something that you are especially familiar with in your waking world. It can be a part of your body that is usually visible, such as your hands or feet, or it can be a personal object, such as a ring, wristwatch, bracelet, or your keys. You can also use a personal symbol, special photograph, painting, or even your teddy bear.

Because you are very familiar with your lucid dream focal while in your waking state, you are more apt to notice any irregularities, thus clueing yourself in to the fact that you are dreaming. For example, if your wristwatch has words on it that you have ingrained into waking awareness, in a dream these words often appear altered and look different. At that point, you know that you are dreaming.

Once you know that you are dreaming, you can either wake yourself up or continue dreaming, but when you continue, it's in a state of lucidity. At this point you direct your dreams and influence their images, making them less threatening and more enjoyable. Essentially, when you notice your lucid dreaming focal in your dream, it's like turning on a light switch. It instantly makes you aware that you are dreaming, and once you are aware, you are lucid dreaming and are free to change the action or immediately stop the dream.

If you choose to remain in a state of lucid dreaming, you have several options. You can move on to another, more enjoyable dream, or you can stay in the bad dream but play it out in your mind so that you overcome the obstacle or fear within the dream. For example, if you encounter a threatening rattlesnake in your dream, deliberately find your hands in your dream. Then go lucid, become Steve Irwin of the popular television show *The Crocodile Hunter,* and become one with the snake. Or you can bring the incredible powers of Steve Irwin into your dream and have him deal with the snake—for example, relocate it out of your dream. In these lucid ways, instead of being harmed by the snake or fearing it in your dream, you learn to respect its natural power. This transfers over into your waking world as well.

Other ways to get rid of nasty things and creatures in your dreams are limited only by your imagination. For example, you can zap them with your magic dream laser wand, banish them to the outer reaches of the universe by dream shouting "GO" at them, or laugh so hard in your dream that the fear or obstacle just vanishes into thin air. In these lucid ways, you can alleviate and overcome your fears, but under more "controlled" circumstances within your dream that are more to your liking as well as less physically harmful.

Love

Lucid and conscious dreaming opens the door to a different way of dreaming. Besides using it as therapy for nightmares, lucid dreaming has also been used for fulfilling the need for adventure and fantasy, rehearsals and play acting for success, creativity and problem solving, healing, out-of-body travel, shape shifting, and spiritual evolvement.

As with any skill you have learned in the past, the more you practice something, the better you become at it. This applies to walking, talking, reading, driving, and lucid dreaming. The more often you practice lucid dreaming, the better your skills become and the easier it is to go lucid. After a time, lucid dreaming becomes a natural and automatic part of your sleeping cycle.

When you combine lucid dreaming with the intention of attaining your dream empowerment goals for love, you discover an infinite potential for enriching your life. Once again, the choice is yours to make and the dreams are yours to dream. First imagine and dream it, and then go lucid. As you do, you step through the dream door into an amazing and intriguing new avenue of empowerment.

Always remember to trust your innermost feelings in waking and in dream. They act as your compass, giving you direction in your life. Learn to hone and listen to your inner sensations so they can help you become a better person. To ignore them is to live a life of nightmares, whereas to heed them is to live a life where your dreams come true.

The following dream techniques show you how to use your hands as a lucid dream focal, thus triggering your dream awareness and inducing lucid dreaming.

Sacred Love Dream Space

Add a red candle and a vial of rose-scented oil to your sacred love dream altar. Empower the candle by holding it in your hands and saying three times:

Divine energies of love, empower this candle with lucid dream power.

Then gently roll the vial of oil between your hands until it warms up. As you do, chant several times:

Divine energies of love, empower this oil with lucid dream power.

Dream Ritual for Love

The purpose of this ritual is to focus on your hands in your waking world so you can use them as a lucid dream focal for love when dreaming. You will need natural skin moisturizer and the red candle and scented oil from your sacred love dream space.

Imagine a bright sphere of white light completely encircling you and your sacred love space. Invite the elements into your ritual space by saying:

May the elements of earth, air, fire, water, and spirit come into my sacred ritual space now.

Light the red candle, dedicating it to the divine powers of your preference. Place the candle in its holder on a flat surface large enough for both of your hands to fit spread out in front of the candle. Begin by applying the moisturizer on your hands and rubbing it in. Then spread your hands out with the palms down in front of you. Look at their general characteristics, such as size, shape, coloration, tone, fingernails, wrinkles, lines, freckles, any scars, and other markings. As you do this, chant:

I see my hands in my dreams and go lucid.

Now stare intently at your left hand, starting at your fingertips and moving toward your wrist. Focus your complete attention on your left hand. Notice and become aware of every aspect of your left hand, from your fingernails and the lines where your fingers bend to the look of your knuckles. Then turn your hand over and examine the back of your hand as well. Continue doing this for at least 15 minutes to become more familiar with your left hand.

Next, shift your awareness to your right hand. Do the same thing as before, starting at your fingertips and moving toward your right wrist. Focus your complete attention on your right hand. Slowly make a mental note of every aspect of your right hand, front and back. Continue doing this for at least 15 minutes.

Once you have finished with the right hand, then take time to notice ways in which both hands are the same and ways they are different. First notice any general characteristics; then focus on your left hand and then your right, becoming aware of every aspect of your hands. As you do this, chant:

I see my hands in my dreams and go lucid.

Next, rub a few drops of the rose oil over the fronts and backs of both hands. Use your right hand to begin massaging the oil into your left hand, starting with your little finger and moving across finger by finger to your thumb. As you massage the oil into your hands, continue chanting:

I see my hands in my dreams and go lucid.

After massaging each of your fingers, move on to the back of your hand, palm, and wrist. In addition to observing how the hand looks, also check out how it feels to the touch.

Once you are finished massaging your left hand, reverse the process and massage your right hand with your left, again paying special attention to how your hand looks and feels, while you chant:

I see my hands in my dreams.

Put the fingers of both your hands together, and sense the energy that runs between them for a few minutes, completely focusing your attention on your hands as you do.

When you are finished, thank the divine and the elements by saying:

I thank the divine and the elements for their helpful presence and blessings.

Imagine stepping out of the sphere of white light you imagined at the beginning of the ritual, and visualize the sphere diffusing into the air around you. Allow the candle to safely burn down, or if you prefer, snuff it out and relight it the next day and let it burn completely down.

Repeat this ritual just before you go to sleep every night for at least 15 minutes until you see your hands in your dreams. When you do see your hands in your dreams, check out to see if you are wearing a ring, wristwatch, or bracelet. You can use these details to also go lucid. Most everyone has success with this easy-to-do lucid technique within a week or two.

Dream Meditation for Love

Sit or recline comfortably as you uncross your arms and legs. Close your eyes, breathe in deeply, and hold the breath for a moment before exhaling. Now, in your mind's eye imagine your physical world in terms of love coming together as One with your dream world. Breathe in love, breathe out fear until your being is filled with love, a sensation that is like a fountain within your inner being. You feel refreshed and revitalized with every breath you take.

Now imagine your hands as they are in your waking world. In the "Dream Ritual for Love," you observed your hands so that your eyes perceived every aspect. Now transfer this observation to your imagination, where you see your hands in your mind in the same way as you perceived them with your eyes. Visualize the length, shape, wrinkles, and color of your hands. The more details you remember, the better the lucid dream focal they become. Start with your fingers and envision every characteristic. Move on to the base of your hand, backs and fronts, and onward to your wrists.

Continue to picture your hands in your mind's eye. Take a deep breath, and as you do, imagine the details of your hands even more clearly. By memorizing all the details of your hands, they become a lucid template for whether you are dreaming or not. You know that when looking at your hands in your dream, you are dreaming.

As you take another deep breath, you realize that whenever you observe your hands in waking and in dream, you will pay attention to how they appear. When they appear, you realize you are lucid dreaming. If the appearance of your hands starts to deviate from normal in unusual or surreal ways, you know you are lucid dreaming.

Take another deep and complete breath in and out, and as you exhale, slowly open your eyes. Stretch your body and come back to the present time and place, remaining peacefully alert.

Dream Prayer for Love

Say this prayer just before you go to sleep:

Divine energy of Oneness,
I ask for your help tonight as I dream.
Help me to see my hands when I am dreaming;
Help me to experience lucid dreaming.
Show me how to direct my dreams in positive ways.
Please share your wisdom with me tonight

And help me to attain my dream empowerment goals for love.
Thank you, divine energy of Oneness.

While drifting away into sleep, repeat to yourself:

As I dream I see my hands, and I know I am lucid dreaming. When I awaken, I recall my dreams.

When you wake up, write down or record everything you remember about your dreams in your dream empowerment journal. Add any impressions you have with regard to what went on in your dreams and why. Do you remember how you felt when you became lucid in your dreams?

Oracle of Dreams for Love

Go outside on a cloudy day, and take some time to look up at the clouds. My young nephew, who loves to do this, is always quick to point out all the things that the clouds remind him of, from elephants to snow castles. As you are looking up at the clouds, say:

I recognize the clouds in the sky as a divine oracle.

Remember a recent dream that has been on your mind, and begin seeing the deeper meanings of the dream. Or if you prefer, think of one question regarding your dream goals for love.

Now take a deep breath, look upward into the clouds, and let their shapes suggest things to you that may be pertinent to the dream. If you run into problems or if things just don't make sense, then take another deep breath and look deeper into the clouds, in the different sectors of the sky for the meaning behind the meaning. Everything is connected together, but sometimes you have to dig around to find the connecting points. Sometimes the answers are right before your eyes, subtly blended in with everything so that at first it's hard to see, but if you keep looking, you'll find it.

After you are done gazing at the clouds, write down in your dream empowerment journal the date, your dream or question, any shapes that the clouds suggested to you, and other insights you have.

Dream Affirmation for Love

Write down the following affirmation in your dream empowerment journal, and then say it aloud to yourself several times each day:

Today and every day, I know I am overcoming my fears and anxieties. As I see my hands in my dreams and go lucid, I direct my dreams into loving and empowering ones.

Write this affirmation down on notes and put them around where you sleep as reminders of your newfound awareness. For at least 28 days, repeat this affirmation several times a day until the affirming message becomes firmly planted in your waking and dream consciousness.

Health

Health can be divided into two basic areas—the prevention of disease and healing once disease has happened. The most emphasis should be placed on the first because if you are successful at preventing disease, you need never bother with the second, healing part. If you do become sick, then the greater emphasis is placed on healing the illness itself.

Oftentimes good health is simply a matter of changing a few of the patterns in your life so they work better for you. Other times, it is just a matter of changing *how* you do things, for example, eating, exercising, using positive thinking, and so forth.

Many health problems start in the spiritual and mental before manifesting in the physical. Positive visualization is a key element in both the prevention and healing aspects of health, in waking and in dreaming.

Through research, dream imagery has been proven to be beneficial in terms of health. Lucid dreaming, in particular, can help you determine the underlying causes of your physical illness and help you heal yourself and strengthen your immune system so you are less likely to become ill again.

Sacred Healing Dream Space

Place three pinches each of dried thyme and rosemary in a bowl on your sacred healing dream space. Empower the herbs in the bowl by rubbing your hands briskly together for a few minutes, and then placing your hands, palms down, over the bowl, merging with Oneness, and saying three times:

Divine energies of health, imbue these herbs with lucid dreaming and healing powers.

Dream Ritual for Health

The purpose of this ritual is to focus on and learn to use your feet as a lucid dream focal for health. You will need a flashlight, a pan of warm water big enough for both your feet, a mesh bag or knee-high nylon, and the dried thyme and rosemary from your sacred healing dream space.

Imagine a bright sphere of white light completely encircling you and your sacred space. Welcome the elements into your ritual space by saying:

I respectively request that the elements of earth, wind, fire, water, and spirit come into and empower my sacred ritual space now.

Take the bowl of dried thyme and rosemary, pour it into the mesh bag or nylon, and close the bag or tie the nylon off. Then place the mesh bag or nylon in the pan of warm water. Next, place your feet into the water and allow them to soak.

Feel the warm water as it caresses and soothes the skin on your feet, from the tips of your toes and balls of your feet to your arches and ankles. Sense the healing effects of the thyme and rosemary encircling every part of your feet. Rub your toes together and rub your feet together, becoming aware of how they feel when touched and soaked.

Continue bathing your feet as long as you want before taking them out of the water and drying them with a soft towel. This and the bath is your way of telling your feet how much you like and appreciate them. After all, the only reason they're tired and sore is because they've been hauling around the rest of you all day.

After you have dried your feet, then get the flashlight and sit down in a comfortable spot where you can easily view your feet. Place both your feet together and click on the flashlight and begin using it to spotlight your feet. Say three times:

I see my feet in my dreams and go lucid.

Shine the light on both feet first and notice their general characteristics, such as shape, size, and coloration. What features do you notice about them immediately?

Now, shine the spotlight on your left foot only, and beginning with your toes, scan your foot. Become aware of every detail as you move your focus to the various parts of your left foot. After you feel you know all the details of your left foot, close your eyes and see your left foot in your mind's eye just as if you were viewing it with your open eyes. As you do, chant three times:

I see my feet in my dreams and go lucid.

Repeat this process with your right foot. Again start at the toes and move across the foot until you are familiar with every feature and detail. When you know it well, then close your eyes and see your right foot in your mind's eye as clearly as you saw it before with your open eyes. Then chant three times:

I see my feet in my dreams and go lucid.

When you are done, place both your feet together, sole-to-sole. Sense the energy that runs between them for a few minutes. As you do, chant:

I see my feet in my dreams and go lucid.

When you are done, thank the divine and the elements by saying:

I give my thanks to the divine and the elements for their help in this ritual and their continued assistance in my empowerment process.

Imagine stepping out of the sphere of white light you imagined at the beginning of the ritual, and visualize the sphere diffusing into the air around you. Return the water and herbs to the earth.

Dream Meditation for Health

Relax by taking several slow, deep breaths and sense yourself resting on a cloud. Your lungs are like balloons. When you fill them up with air, you begin to rise up off the cloud, and when you exhale, you float like a feather back down to the cloud. After doing this several times, fill your lungs with air and hold your breath as long as you comfortably can. As you do this, you float higher and higher and feel brighter and brighter. When you finally let your breath out, sense that your surroundings have shifted. You feel joyful, at ease, and filled with light.

Imagine being in a temple of lucid dreams, preparing for sleep and lucid dreaming. You look down at your feet and begin focusing on every detail from the tips of your toes to your ankles. You become One with your feet, and they become One with you. Give your fullest attention to your feet and whatever the moment presents.

As you breathe in deeply, close your eyes and visualize your feet in your mind. From this perspective, you see them on many levels and in ways that move beyond the physical realm of waking reality.

In your mind's eye, you give yourself the suggestion that your feet are your lucid dream focal for health, and when you see them in your dream, you will know you are dreaming. You also give yourself the suggestion that if you are ever having an unpleasant dream, you will see your feet, know you are dreaming, and thus know nothing can hurt you. Every time you witness your feet in your dream, you go lucid and either wake up or continue to dream. If you continue to dream, you direct the dreamscape in the direction you want it to play out, moving your dreams toward your dream empowerment goals for good health and well-being.

Still in the temple of lucid dreams, take another deep, relaxing breath and imagine lying down and getting ready to go to sleep and dream. You look down at your feet for a few minutes and become more and more lucid. As you lie there, you feel empowered in knowing that you now are the director of your own dreams and can select what and how to dream. Any time you don't like your dream, you see your feet in your dream and go lucid as a means of shape shifting the dream. Or when you like, you see your feet in your dream and halt the dream completely.

Now breathe in deeply with joy and ease, and exhale, knowing you are becoming more conscious and bringing more consciousness into your life, both in waking and dreaming. As you breathe in again, feel a sense of quality, well-being, and good health within yourself. And as you exhale, become more aware of your present surroundings. Slowly opening your eyes, look down at your feet and become more conscious of the present time and place. Stretch your body, yet remain relaxed for prayer and sleep.

Dream Prayer for Health

Just before you go to sleep, say this prayer:

Sacred energies of good health,
Let me dream of perfect health.
Where I am One with your healing light,
Help me to be conscious of this insight
By making me aware that I am dreaming,
And go lucid as a way to good health.
Thank you, sacred energies of health.

As you drift to sleep, repeat to yourself:

As I dream I see my feet in my dreams and know I am lucid dreaming.
When I awaken I remember my dreams.

Upon awakening, write down or record everything you remember of your dreams in your dream empowerment journal. Include any impressions you have regarding the dreams and what they mean. Also write down or record any sensations or conscious dreaming selections you made when you went lucid.

Oracle of Dreams for Health

Tribal shamans were some of the earliest lucid dreamers. The information they brought back from their lucid dreams often dealt with issues of health. By being aware and asking questions in your dreams, like a shaman, you bring back information that can be used to heal yourself and others. Again, the hard part is determining what information your lucid dreams are trying to convey to you. Start by choosing a dream from your dream empowerment journal regarding your health that has been on your mind lately.

Go outside on a cloudy day and find a quiet spot where you can lie back and comfortably view the clouds. Look upward at the clouds and say:

I recognize the clouds in the sky as a divine oracle.

Now, formulate a question expressing what has been troubling you about the dream. Repeat the question several times to yourself with your eyes closed, sensing any impressions that you get. Next, open your eyes and begin observing what images and impressions you receive from the shapes of the clouds. If you don't sense anything at first, then take another deep breath to center your awareness and look deeper into the cloud shapes until you begin getting impressions. What do these impressions tell you about your question? Look for and be aware of the larger message and greater images in the cloud formations.

After you are done with the oracle of dreams for health, write down the date, your question, the shapes you saw in the clouds, your impressions, and how the oracle relates to your dream question.

Dream Affirmation for Health

Copy the following affirmation into your dream empowerment journal. Read it aloud or repeat it silently to yourself several times each day:

Today and every day, I am more conscious of my health in waking and in lucid dreams. Through my lucid dreams and my active efforts, I move one step closer toward attaining my dream empowerment goals for good health.

Write the affirmation on notes and tack them in places such as the door of your refrigerator and on your computer. Also write the affirmation on a note card that you can carry with you. Take the card out from time to time and read it to yourself. Do this for 28 days or more until you are lucid dreaming on a nightly basis.

Abundance

Lucid dreaming is the ideal way to rehearse and play-act your plans for success. You can play them out like movies, seeing how different circumstances and actions produce a variety of results, focusing on the ones that connect more closely with your dream empowerment goals and plans. This is the point when you can start developing the ability to make anything you dream happen in the waking "real" world. After all, if you can find your hands and your feet in your dreams, you can pretty much find anything you can focus your dream awareness on.

The more lucid you become, the thinner the division between waking and dream. When this division ceases to exist, except on a practical level, your ability to attain your goals becomes stronger, and you become that much closer to empowering your dreams and, in the process, enriching your life.

Sacred Abundance Dream Space

Add a wristwatch, a sage and cedar smudge stick, and three pieces of clover to your sacred abundance dream altar. Empower these items by rubbing your hands briskly together for a minute or two and then placing your hands, palms down, over the items while you say three times:

Let divine abundance flow through these items and fill them with lucid dreaming power.

Dream Ritual for Abundance

The purpose of this ritual is to create a lucid dream focal for abundance out of your wristwatch to help you lucid dream. You will need the wristwatch, smudge stick, and three pieces of clover from your sacred abundance dream altar.

Begin by imagining a bright sphere of white light totally encircling you and your complete sacred space. Invite the elements into your ritual space by saying:

I welcome the elemental powers of earth, air, fire, water, and spirit. I respectfully call upon you and ask for your help in giving this ritual as much power as possible so that it will be successful in its purpose.

Light your smudge stick and softly blow at the embers to get it to smoke. Catch any hot ashes in a fireproof place or bowl. Next, pass the wristwatch carefully through the smoke for a minute or two to cleanse it of all unwanted energy.

Set the wristwatch on a flat surface so that you can comfortably sit before it, easily seeing all the details of the watch face. Next, place the three pieces of clover around the watch in a triangle—one piece at the top and the other two on either side of the base.

Begin by concentrating on the watch as a whole, noticing the general characteristics that it displays. Look at the numbers, the hands, the writing on it, and the watch band. As you do this, softly chant over and over:

I see my watch in my dreams and go lucid.

Next, moving from left to right, begin focusing on the watch face, becoming aware of every aspect of it. Notice any details that make the watch similar or different from other watches. Continue chanting:

I see my watch in my dreams and go lucid.

Once you feel that you are aware of all the details on the watch, close your eyes and in your mind's eye, view the watch. How much detail is there in your visualized image? Open your eyes and check your visualization with how you perceive the watch with your eyes. Close your eyes again, and see if you can add more detail to the image in your mind's eye. Do this until you feel comfortable that you know the watch both with your physical eyes and the image that you see when you close your eyes.

When you are done with the ritual, thank the divine and the elements by saying:

I thank the divine and the elements for their help in making this ritual successful.

Conclude by imagining that you are moving out of the sphere of bright white light that you imagined when you began the ritual. Visualize the sphere diffusing into the air around you. Put your wristwatch on your bedside altar or wear it to bed. Return the clover pieces to the earth.

Dream Meditation for Abundance

Sit or recline comfortably and uncross your hands and feet. Close your eyes, and take a deep breath in and out to center yourself. In your mind's eye, imagine little droplets of white light streaming across your consciousness. One of the drops lands on your lips, and as you breathe in, you move the white light into your lungs and then throughout your body. Breathing out, you create a giant bubble of white light that you send out into the universe with your wishes for abundance. Another drop of white light lands on your lip and again you breathe in deeply, holding for a moment, and then out, creating another bubble of white light, this time carrying your wishes for peace on Earth.

Now imagine your wristwatch in your mind's eye. Fine-tune the image, bringing into focus all the details of your lucid dream focal for abundance. If you have any problems getting all the details of the wristwatch into focus, then take yourself back to the ritual, where you scanned every detail of the watch with your eyes. Put yourself back in the moment and see all the details come to life in your mind's eye.

Looking at the watch, you study its every facet until it is a part of you. There are those that count the hours of your life, and there are those that count the minutes, but the most interesting to watch are the ones that count out the seconds. Tick, tock, tick, tock, the seconds seem to go on forever, one after another. You count as the seconds move from 55, 56, 57, 58, 59 ...

You breathe in again and realize that your wristwatch is a key to your dream empowerment. It allows you to slow your dreams down, stop them, or change them altogether. With your watch, you can enter the eternal now of dreamtime and navigate throughout the universe, gaining knowledge and personal power at every stop along the way.

Take another deep, empowering breath and imagine that you are protected by a giant golden white halo that surrounds you at all times, in waking and in dream. Take another breath, knowing that when you dream, your magic watch is there to help you go lucid and move to whatever time and place you desire. As you breathe in again, begin moving your hands and feet, slowly opening your eyes, and coming back to the present time and place.

Dream Prayer for Abundance

Before drifting off to sleep, say this prayer:

Dear God and Goddess, I pray you
Please help me to know when I am dreaming,
So that I can realize the full potential of my dreams.
Empower my dreams with your divine powers of abundance,
So that when I look at my watch, I know I am lucid
In both my waking and dream worlds.
Dear God and Goddess, thank you for your help.
In the name of the Lord and Lady, blessed be.

As you go to sleep, give yourself this suggestion:

I see my watch in my dreams and know I am lucid dreaming, and I remember my dreams when I wake up.

When you awaken, record or write down in your journal everything you remember about your dreams. Include the date, any impressions you have, and any dream messages you received. Did you become lucid or conscious in your dreams? If yes, record or write down any sensations and dream directing you did while lucid dreaming.

Oracle of Dreams for Abundance

Go outside on a cloudy day and find a quiet, comfortable place for gazing at the clouds. Take a deep breath and say:

Divine clouds, show me your deeper meanings and become my oracle of dreams for abundance today.

Now think of a question regarding your dream empowerment goals for abundance that has been on your mind lately. Repeat the question several times to yourself. Focus all your awareness on it, becoming one with your question.

As you gaze at the clouds, sense yourself diffusing and becoming One with them. Within their infinite shapes and contours are the answers to all questions; you just have to know where to look. Ask your question aloud while still gazing intently into the layers of clouds that blanket the sky. Sense yourself moving closer and closer toward the answer until it is within your perception.

When you are done gazing at the clouds, write down the date, your question, the shapes of the clouds, and any insights.

Dream Affirmation for Abundance

Write the following affirmation in your dream empowerment journal, and read it aloud to yourself several times a day:

Today and every day, I am abundantly lucid in waking and in dreams, and I am moving one step closer to my dream goals for abundance.

Write the affirmation on notes and stick them where you will see and read them often. Also, put a note card in your purse or wallet in such a way so that you see it first when you open your purse or wallet. Continue repeating this affirmation for 28 days or more until it becomes a part of you and you are ready to move farther on your path to abundance and personal enrichment.

Chapter Ten

Manifesting Your Dreams

Visionary poet and artist William Blake felt that the source for his creative efforts was in his head, dreams, and divine visions. "God put his head to the window," William Blake told his parents at the age of four. Later on in childhood, he told of a waking vision where he saw a tree filled with angels. Blake's extraordinary visions nourished his creative process, both in waking and dream.

William Blake trained his younger brother Robert in the crafts of drawing, painting, and engraving, but in the winter of 1787, Robert became sick. At the time of Robert's death, William saw his brother's spirit rise up through the ceiling while clapping its hands for joy.

Blake's brother Robert continued to visit him in spirit. At a time when he was trying to sell his work *Songs of Innocence* but had been unsuccessful in getting it published, Robert came to Blake in a dream with a plan for publication of the work, complete with a new way of engraving. Blake invested all his money in the process and was successful in publishing this work of art and others, such as *Songs of Experience,* using the techniques his deceased brother Robert had taught him in the dream. After 200 years, these engravings are still held in high regard because of their craftsmanship.

William Blake's dream experience has, on one side, the traditional concept of using dreams to solve problems, but, on the other side, it has the elements of deceased people coming into dreams, visions, or waking dreams and helping someone out in life. Interestingly, deceased people or pets with whom you had a strong connection when they were alive is an excellent way to become lucid in a dream. The reason for this is because when you see the deceased person or pet, you immediately know you're dreaming.

Visions and waking dreams are moments when your waking and dream world overlap as One, and in these moments you essentially become lucid while awake. This brings on a dreamlike image or vision that you experience in your waking state. This is a technique used by both shamans and masters of Eastern spiritual traditions such as Hinduism and Sufism. In this sense, lucid dreaming becomes part of the larger theme of lucid living, where you are in a higher state of awareness both when awake and dreaming.

Manifesting Your Dream Empowerment

The information and techniques in this chapter and those that follow are intended to help you get at the deeper meanings of your dreams and what they are trying to tell you about your waking life with regard to your relationships, your health, and your lifestyle and level of abundance.

In terms of both dreams and waking events, there is a great deal of natural overlapping between these three areas. A dream where a dream messenger comes and takes you to another place, such as a garden, can have meanings and significance with regard to love, health, and abundance, depending on your perceptions about what the dream is trying to tell you. Often on multiple levels all aspects connect together into one complete picture.

Because of the multilayered quality, you often have to look into the deeper meanings of dreams. The oracles given in each section are a way of helping you see and become aware of the larger picture and how things connect together in this picture.

Carl Jung called this connectedness "synchronicity," a term that stems from the idea of "collective unconscious," meaning we all create these connections with our unconscious minds. It's just a matter of getting your conscious mind in on the process.

Jung believed that "big" or "meaningful" dreams were the ones that came from the deeper level of the "collective unconscious" and thus impacted our lives on a grander scale. A dream calling you to follow a particular spiritual or occupational path for the good of yourself and others would be an example of a "meaningful" dream.

As Robert Moss states in his fascinating book *Conscious Dreaming*, "Dreams provide a context of meaning. They demonstrate how our ailments are related to our whole psycho-spiritual condition." In other words, health is not a separate part of your life; it's part of your whole being. Separation is an illusion. When you become conscious of this concept both in waking and dream, you begin to be aware of the synchronicity that continually happens all around you. You take that giant step, and your empowerment process begins to quickly accelerate.

This is the intention behind learning to become a lucid dreamer—accelerating your empowerment process and manifesting your dreams. Rather than being a method of control, lucid dreaming instead gives your dreams focus so that you can more easily work with them. Once you learn to become lucid, you can use other methods for becoming lucid, such as seeing a deceased relative or pet or seeing something surreal and out of the ordinary such as a yellow canary driving a taxi.

When you become lucid in your dreams, you begin rapidly increasing your awareness of the connections and synchronicity occurring in your dreams and waking life. You begin to notice how the two connect together as a whole. Suddenly you delve into another layer of your dreams that you only caught momentary glimpses of before .

The techniques in this chapter are intended to help you become more lucid in your dreams and more aware of the synchronicity in your life. As you do this, use your energy and dream skills to focus on attaining your dream goals for love, health, and abundance in your waking world.

Love

You have dreamed the dream, made the dream a goal by putting a deadline on it, and then constructed plans for making these dream goals a reality. This is the part of the empowerment process where you bring your plans to fruition, thus attaining your dream.

The techniques in the love section are for helping you become more aware of your natural energy field and become lucid in your dreams. The oracles are "everyday oracles." The concept is to become aware of the everyday events around you and what they are telling you about your dreams in particular and about life in general.

Sacred Love Dream Space

Add a clear quartz crystal and white candle to your sacred space.

First, cleanse the crystal by rinsing it in cool water. While you do, say three times:

Elemental power of water, cleanse this stone.

Cup the clean stone in your hands and take a deep breath in, and then pulse your breath out through your nose while in your mind's eye imagining an image of a pure mountain stream flowing into the crystal.

Second, empower the candle by saying:

May the divine and lucid dream power of love fill this candle.

Dream Ritual for Love

The purpose of this ritual is to focus and expand your energy field. You will need the clear quartz crystal and white candle from your sacred space.

Take the quartz crystal in your dominant hand, and draw an imaginary line of white light all around the parameter of your sacred space. Next, imagine a sphere of white light completely encircling you and your sacred space, and then invite the elements into your ritual space by saying:

Elements of earth, air, fire, water, and spirit, I respectfully request your presence in this ritual.

Light the white candle and dedicate it to your divine ancestors and dream helpers by saying:

I dedicate this candle and its light to my divine ancestors and dream helpers, who eternally protect and guide me on my path to empowerment.

Set the candle and its holder on your altar. On the floor in front of your altar, use your crystal in your power hand to draw a circle of white light that is about six feet around. Go over the circle several times, reinforcing the energy field with your intention and imagination.

Stand in the middle of the circle of white light, and take the palms of both your hands and begin rubbing the top of your head. After you sense a flow of energy moving from your hands to your crown chakra at the top of your head, begin moving your hands down both sides of your body, rubbing all the parts on the way down. When you reach the lower half of your body, sit down in the middle of the circle and rub your feet.

Take a few minutes to get in tune with the energy field that continually moves around your body. Once that happens, sense your energy field expanding out around your body for one foot. Keep it there for a few moments before bringing it in against your skin.

Now, expand your energy field out three feet and then six feet so that it fills the entire circle of white that you drew with your crystal. Each time you expand your energy field, remember to bring it back in against your skin.

Next, take a deep breath in, and as you exhale, imagine expanding your energy field outward until it first encompasses the candle on your dream altar and then includes everything within the room.

From this energy, imagine crafting a ball of luminous white light that you spin and rub with your hands, all the while making it stronger, more intense and concentrated. Physically take your hands and sense yourself creating a ball of light. The more intention and desire you put into it, the more you can sense the energy building to higher and higher levels.

In your mind, envision what dream goal for love you want this energy sent toward. See the image as clearly as you can before you pulse the energy toward the goal. Physically, you can see it as a baseball being hurled toward the success of this goal, and when it's successful, it's like hitting a home run. Suddenly, all your dreams start coming true, and you feel like you are on top of the world with your energy field focused and expanded. Continue sending this brilliant white light toward your love goal for a few minutes.

When you are done with the ritual, honor your divine ancestors and dream helpers by saying:

Thank you, divine ancestors and dream helpers. May you ever thrive and guide me.

Acknowledge the elements by saying:

I thank the elements for their guidance, protection, and assistance.

In your mind's eye, imagine pulling up the circle of light you drew with your crystal. Imagine stepping out of the sphere of white light and having it vaporize into the air around you. Allow the candle to safely burn down. If you prefer, snuff it out, and then relight it the next day and burn it safely down.

Dream Meditation for Love

The first part of this meditation is a variation of a technique given by Malcolm Godwin in his excellent book, *The Lucid Dreamer*. It stems from the traditional idea of counting sheep before you go to sleep, but in this case they are dream sheep intended to help you become lucid in your dreams.

Begin by breathing in and filling your lungs full of air. As you hold it for a moment, the air in your lungs transforms into white light and spreads throughout your body. Exhale, and as you do so, imagine a pure white dream sheep leaping over a low fence. Imagine as much detail about the sheep as you can from the color of its eyes and shape of its face to the size of its body and the way its hind legs propel it over the fence. Say to yourself, "One dream sheep, I am dreaming," before taking another deep breath and repeating the whole process again with a second dream sheep.

Do this exercise several more times, becoming more and more conscious of the details of your dream sheep. Remember to count each one and remind yourself that you are dreaming and that these are dream sheep. Whenever or wherever you see these sheep, you will become conscious that you are dreaming because these are dream sheep.

Now that you are in a very relaxed but aware state of being, imagine a relationship or love-related problem you have been having either with a dream or in your empowerment plan. Begin by viewing the problem from every aspect and in as much detail as you can, much like you did your dream sheep. Try perceiving your problem in every possible way imaginable. Immerse yourself into it and become One with it. Open yourself up to all help and assistance from both the divine and your dream allies.

After immersing yourself in the problem, it's time to incubate it and let it sit for a while until something illuminating happens, such as an inspiring thought, waking vision, or dream. Be aware that sometimes it happens in all three ways as the separation is only in your perception.

For the rest of the meditation, go to one of your favorite places such as by the seashore, in the mountains, or wherever else you like to go. Imagine yourself relaxing and doing what you like to do when you are at your favorite place. Tell yourself that you are on a mini vacation, and let your mind go where it wants to go, free of any restraints or boundaries. You can stay there as long as you want.

Dream Prayer for Love

Before drifting to sleep, say the following prayer:

Divine energies of love,
Please help me to attain my dreams
By understanding how I connect together
With the whole of Oneness.

Moving into sleep, remind yourself:

When I see my dream sheep, I will become aware that I am dreaming, and I remember my dreams when I awaken.

When you wake up, record and write down in your dream empowerment journal any dreams you remember as well as any insights and impressions you might have regarding your dreams and empowerment process.

Oracle of Dreams for Love

The basic idea with oracles is they open you up to the synchronicity that happens all around you on a daily basis. This synchronicity can often give you insights into your dreams and, in turn, help you attain them.

Go to a large grocery or department store. Before walking through the door, formulate in your mind the problem or question you want to solve regarding your dream empowerment goals for love. Just before you walk through the door, say:

I empower this store as a divine dream oracle.

The moment you walk through the door, imagine you have entered an oracular world. Be especially aware and conscious of everything that happens around you and how it connects together both with itself and you and your question. You may hear pieces of conversation from people walking by and see someone you know or someone who looks like someone you know, as well as the images around the store and the names of items on the shelves.

Be open to information and insights coming in many forms. Like a giant web of light, your life and everything else is all connected together. Train yourself to be aware of these connections, and you begin to understand the greater picture of your life, and attaining your dream goals for empowerment is a result.

Before leaving the store, make a note of any insights, impressions, and questions you had while shopping. Transfer these notes into your dream empowerment journal along with your question and the date. Also determine any correlations between your insights and observations and your question that you formulated when you walked into the store.

Dream Affirmation for Love

Write the following affirmation in your dream empowerment journal before saying it aloud to yourself several times:

Today and every day, I manifest my dreams for love.

Write the affirmation on notes that you put around your living space. Also write it on a card and place it in your wallet, next to pictures of your loved ones. Continue repeating the affirmation several times a day for 28 days or more.

Health

Manifesting your dreams for health involves doing the things you listed in your health plan, including diet, exercise, and setting aside time for enjoyment. Whatever it is you need to do to become more healthy, take a step at a time and simply do it. This is the most direct method for attaining your dream empowerment goals for health and well-being.

The dream techniques in this section help you to clear out any fragments or remains of any "bad dreams" that you might still have hanging around, and help you achieve a deeper level of lucidity in your dreams and waking life.

Sacred Healing Dream Space

Add a clear quartz crystal and a smudge stick to your sacred healing dream space. The crystal can be the same one you used for previous rituals.

Light the smudge stick and hold the crystal over the smudge and allow the smoke to totally envelop the crystal, while saying:

Elemental power of fire, cleanse this crystal of all energy.

After extinguishing the hot coals of the smudge, empower the crystal by saying:

Empowering God and Goddess, please fill this quartz crystal with your healing dream energy.

Dream Ritual for Health

The purpose of this ritual is to help you clear out the energetic residue of a bad dream. You will need the quartz crystal and smudge stick from your sacred space and a bowl or plate to catch the burning ash of the lit smudge.

Light the smudge stick and when it begins to smoke, walk the parameters of your sacred ritual space, holding the bowl under the smudge to catch any hot ash. (*Note:* Open the windows and turn on the fan as the smudge may set off your fire alarms.) As you spread the cleansing smoke throughout your living space, chant:

Depart and be gone all harmful and unwanted energies. I ask this in the name of the Lord and Lady, Amen.

After you have finished cleansing your sacred ritual space for health, carefully extinguish the hot coal from the smudge, and imagine a sphere of bright white light encircling you and your space. Invite the elements in by saying:

Elements of earth, air, fire, water, and spirit, I respectfully invite you into my sacred ritual space for health.

Sit down somewhere comfortable in your ritual space, and hold the quartz crystal in your power hand, sensing your energy and the energy from the crystal as they begin to mingle and become One. That's the beautiful thing about crystals—they can harmonize and synchronize their energies with anything and anyone.

Next, remember a bad dream you had recently that you sense has some residue still hanging around. Even when you deal with the issues of a troublesome dream and you quit having the dream, sometimes the fragments can linger in your psyche.

Sense yourself collecting all these fragments and remains of this bad dream and filling the crystal in your hand with them, while saying:

Let all that remains of my dream be transferred into the crystal, until my body, mind, and spirit are free of the fragments of this dream.

Once you feel you have let all the residue of the bad dream go into the crystal, light the smudge stick again and carefully pass the crystal through the smoke several times while saying three times:

Element of fire, cleanse this crystal now.

Once again, carefully smudge your ritual space before putting the hot coal out. Thank the elements by saying:

Thank you, elemental energies, for your help in manifesting my dreams of health.

Visualize stepping out of the sphere of white light, and then imagine the sphere diffusing into the air in all directions around you.

Dream Meditation for Health

Breathe in and sense all your energy being drawn together into a bright ball, and then when you breathe out, sense this ball of energy expanding out in every direction as far as your imagination goes. Each time you breathe in, sense the ball of energy coming back together within you, and each time you breathe out, sense the energy expanding farther and farther outward into the infinite spaces of Oneness. Become the boundless spirit whose imagination knows no boundaries.

Go to that place where the boundary or separation between dream and waking ceases to exist, and there is an open and integrated interaction between the worlds. Like two rivers coming together at the fork and becoming one enormous river, once they come together, you can't tell one droplet of water from another because the synthesis is complete.

Imagine the events of your day as being part of a dream. When you awoke this morning, what you did was wake up into another dream. When you went to work, went shopping, interacted with your family, it was all part of the dream. What this means is that everything is a dream whether you are sleeping or awake. Remember that the next time you are sleeping and the images start getting strange and surreal—remind yourself that you are dreaming.

Now that the separation between dream and waking has erased, imagine having the ability to manifest anything you want just by envisioning it in your mind along with the plans and actions to make it happen. By giving your dream empowerment goals for health and well-being focus and direction, you can live the life that up to now has only been in your dreams. When this happens, you feel empowered in every aspect of your being.

Now take a deep breath in and out, and imagine being bathed in bright white light for a few minutes. When you are done, take another deep breath and slowly come back to the present time and place.

Dream Prayer for Health

Before drifting to sleep, say this prayer:

Divine keepers and guardians of health,
Please empower me with your energy
And protect me in waking and dream.
Please help me to manifest my dreams of health.
Thank you, divine keepers and guardians of health.

As a lucid reminder, repeat the following to yourself as you drift to sleep:

When I begin dreaming, a voice reminds me that I am dreaming, and I am aware that I am dreaming while I am dreaming.

Upon waking, record or write down in your dream empowerment journal the details of any dreams you remember, including any insights and impressions you might have had both in the dream and upon waking.

Oracle of Dreams for Health

Go to a restaurant at lunch or dinnertime. Select a restaurant where you know the food is good, or if you're feeling adventuresome, one that you have heard has good food but you have never been to before. Before entering the restaurant, formulate your health question in your mind and then say:

I empower this restaurant as a divine dream oracle.

As you walk through the door of the restaurant, become aware of everything around you: the smells, conversation, decor, and people. As you move through the restaurant, continually check in on all of your senses: the sounds, smells, tastes, talking, and how everything feels. Make a few notes of these things and any insights as you enjoy your meal.

Upon returning home, transfer your notes to your dream empowerment journal and add the date and question. As with dreams, it is important to describe the original experience at the restaurant as it happened in your brief notes and then add your in-depth evaluations and comments afterward.

Dream Affirmation for Health

Write the following dream affirmation for health in your dream empowerment journal, and then say it aloud to yourself several times:

Today and each day, I am manifesting my dream empowerment goals for health and well-being.

Also write the affirmation on notes and place them on the refrigerator and places where you eat and exercise. Read the affirmation several times a day for 28 days or until you attain your dream empowerment goals for health.

Abundance

In her book *Simple Abundance*, author Sarah Ban Breathnach writes, "Not every one of our desires can be immediately gratified. We've got to learn to wait patiently for our dreams to come true, especially on the path we've chosen. But while we wait, we need to prepare symbolically a place for our hopes and dreams." In addition to this, I would like to add that we need to honor our dreams by actually thinking the thoughts and taking the steps to make them come true.

The dream techniques in this section help you to honor your dream for abundance and give you suggestions for re-entering a dream. Sometimes certain dreams either end prematurely by your waking up, or through examination, you wish you had been more aware of what was going on around you in the dream. Dream re-entry is a method for moving back into a dream and getting more information.

Sacred Abundance Dream Space

Select something that symbolizes one of your dream empowerment goals for abundance. Empower this symbol by placing your hands around it and saying:

Divine energies of abundance, empower my dream symbol with your radiance.

Dream Ritual for Abundance

The purpose of this ritual is to honor your dream and take the steps to make it come true. You will need a piece of paper, a pen, and your symbol of abundance from your sacred abundance dream space.

Imagine a bright sphere of white light completely encircling you and your sacred space. Invite the elements into your ritual space by saying:

Elemental energies of earth, air, fire, water, and spirit, please enter into my sacred ritual space and empower it.

Using the pen and paper, write what your dream for abundance is in one sentence or phrase. Place the paper on your sacred abundance dream space and honor it by proclaiming:

I give thanks to the God and Goddess
For bestowing this dream on me.
I will carry it with me until it comes true,
With their divine guidance and manifesting power.

Next, draw the symbol of your dream for abundance in the four corners of the paper, moving from the upper left corner clockwise around the paper. Then say:

Let this dream symbolize my future
As it manifests in time;
Let this be my empowerment
That continues to unfold.

Your dreams often tell you things you need to do to make your life what you want it to be. The idea is to follow your highest dream, to achieve abundance as you perceive it, and, in the process, empower yourself.

Take a moment to visualize your dream of abundance coming true. See it, be it, and make it happen. Expect it, desire it, merge with the divine, and you can manifest any dream you can dream.

Next, begin swaying and moving around your sacred ritual space to honor your dream for abundance through dance. With every movement, feel yourself bringing your dream for abundance more into focus and part of your waking world. After building up the energy in your space through your dancing, spread your arms and fingers outward, sending the energy out to the universe with the intention of truly attaining your dream empowerment goals for abundance.

When you are done, return your symbol to your sacred abundance dream space where you will look at it often. Then fold the paper with your goal listed and the symbols in the corners five times. Each time you fold it, say:

My dream goal for abundance is in my hands.

Put the folded paper in your pocket or purse and carry it with you until you attain your dream empowerment goal for abundance. When you do, unfold the paper and return it to the earth.

Finish by thanking the divine and the elements. Say:

I thank the divine for the dream and the elementals for their help in manifesting it.

Visualize yourself stepping out of the sphere of white light, and imagine the sphere diffusing into the space around you.

Dream Meditation for Abundance

This meditation is adapted from a dream technique given by Robert Moss in his book *Conscious Dreaming*. The technique involves re-entering a dream from which you wish to gain more information. Re-entry into a dream gives you a chance to explore the dream at a deeper level of perception.

Put on a recording of continuous drumming, and begin tuning your body and energy in to the repetitive rhythms. Breathe in and out in time with the drums, which bring focus to every aspect of your being. Let the drumbeats become steps to another level of consciousness.

Envision in your mind the events of the dream, complete with all the details you remember. The more you bring the location into focus, the better your chances for dream re-entry. Slowly flow back into the dream, and start playing out the events as they happen in the dream.

You become lucid of the fact that you are reenacting your dream and nothing you are experiencing can hurt you in a waking sense. This is one of the wonderful benefits of learning to lucid dream. You can experience things within the realm of dream before shifting them into the waking world.

Sense yourself moving back into the dream you want to re-enter. Become aware of more of the details, such as names and places in the dream. As you enter the dream, you are lucid of the idea that you are dreaming. Move the sequence of events in the dream further in perceived time, looking for useful information and guidance as to where to progress in your dream empowerment.

Continue doing this for as long as necessary.

When you are done, take a deep breath, slowly open your eyes, and clap your hands three times to come back to the present time and place.

Dream Prayer for Abundance

Say this prayer before you go to sleep:

Divine energies of abundance,
Please help me to manifest my dream.

From the time I go to sleep
To the time I awaken,
Give me the courage to continue
On my journey to personal empowerment.
Thank you, divine energies of abundance.

When you wake up, record or write down everything you recall from your dreams.

Oracle of Dreams for Abundance

Go to a shopping mall or shopping center. Before walking through the entrance, formulate in your mind a question from one of your dreams or your empowerment plan. Focus all your awareness on it, and just before you walk into the mall, say:

I empower this shopping mall as a divine dream oracle.

Then the moment you walk through the entrance of the shopping mall, be aware of everything happening on a multisensory level. Be aware of the sounds, smells, conversation, people and things you see, and feelings and impressions you have. Make a note of these things. Experience each moment and how it connects to every other moment. Let your awareness be open to the subtle cues that happen around you.

Afterward, transfer your notes plus any impressions and insights into your dream empowerment journal. Determine whether any of your experiences at the mall gave you any suggestions or help as to your dream problem. Also determine whether any of the events seemed to relate to any of your dreams.

Oftentimes, waking events will trigger dream recall.

Dream Affirmation for Abundance

Write the following affirmation in your dream empowerment journal, and then say it aloud to yourself several times:

Today and every day, I do the things to honor my dream for abundance, and make it come true for myself.

Write this affirmation on notes and place them around your living and work space. Say this affirmation several times a day for 28 days or more for best results.

Chapter Eleven

Enjoying the Rewards of Dream Empowerment

As you reach the stage in your dream empowerment process where your dream goals for empowerment have been attained, it is important to celebrate and enjoy your accomplishments. For a balanced life, play is as important as work, particularly with regards to love, health, and abundance. Enjoyment of your reward is a form of constructive play, and by thoroughly enjoying your successes, you empower yourself even more, giving you the energy to attain your future goals.

The idea in this chapter is to have fun, enjoy yourself, and take a well-deserved holiday, a vacation in your dreams. Now that you have become more lucid in your dreams, you can take the vacation of your dreams. The dream techniques in each of the following sections give direction and focus to your adventures, but where you go and what you do is entirely up to you.

Keep in mind that you are celebrating your achievement of attaining one or more of your dream goals, and in doing so you have learned techniques that help you to manifest your future dream goals. You have been successful, and now you can build upon this success and create more positive avenues in your life.

Hopefully, by now you are a lucid dreamer and have begun to perceive your dreams in many meaningful ways. Now that you have opened the dream door to the infinite reaches of dreamtime, you can also observe, direct, and participate in your dreams in such a way as to help you actually live the life you have always dreamed possible. You also now know that you have the imagination and abilities to make your dreams come true!

Love

For your dream vacation celebrating the love and relationships in your life, go somewhere you have always wanted to go. Take your primary partner or a good friend and go somewhere special to celebrate your success for a couple of hours, the day, or a week or two, somewhere that signifies love and close friendships to you.

Many times in life because of the obligations you make with work, family, friends, and anyone else who wants some of your time and effort, it seems you can never get away for a vacation. To help you feel more rested and refreshed, even if you can't take time off now, you can take a night off and go on vacation. Your dream vacation can last as long as you like as you can alter time in your dreams. This dream vacation in your dreams acts as the first step to manifesting an actual physical vacation in your waking life.

The idea is to keep dreaming and move on with your life. Every time you achieve a goal and make another dream come true, reward yourself. You deserve it, as you have successfully accomplished what you set out to do. This is the essence of empowerment.

Sacred Love Dream Space

Add a bouquet of fresh flowers in a vase filled with water to your sacred love dream altar. Hold the vase of flowers in your hands, and say three times:

Bless these beautiful and divine flowers.

Also select a couple of items that you would like to take on your dream vacation celebrating love such as a beach towel, your car keys, your sunglasses, a travel brochure, or your passport. Place these items on your sacred love dream space.

Next, empower the dream vacation items by placing your hands over the items, palms down, and saying:

Loving and divine ones, bless these dream vacation items with your divine power.

Dream Ritual for Love

The purpose of this ritual is to give thanks to the divine ones of love and your dream helpers. You will need the bouquet of fresh flowers in the vase from your sacred love dream altar.

Imagine a sphere of bright white light completely encircling you and your sacred ritual space. Welcome the elemental energies into your ritual by saying:

Elemental energies of earth, wind, fire, water, and spirit,
Please come into my sacred ritual space now. I welcome you.

Now take the flowers, which express your thanks, and hold the bouquet up between your hands and say:

Divine ones of love and my dream helpers,
With your guidance, protection, and blessings,
I have successfully attained my dream goals for love
And now I thank you with all my heart.

Place the flowers in the vase filled with water on your sacred love dream altar next to your dream vacation items. Spend at least 15 minutes focusing on the flowers as you imagine sending your heartfelt thanks to the divine ones and your dream helpers.

When you are done, thank the divine and the elements by saying:

I thank the divine and the elements for empowering this ritual with their helpful energies.

In your mind's eye, visualize stepping out of the sphere of white light, and imagine the sphere diffusing into the air around you into Oneness. Keep the flowers on your dream love altar until they are spent. Then as you return them to the earth, say three times:

Thank you, divine ones and dream helpers, with all my heart.

Dream Meditation for Love

Begin by focusing your attention on your dream vacation items. Make a mental note of each of them in your mind as you pick up each of these items, one at a time, and hold it in your hands for a few moments. As you hold each of the items, take a deep breath in through your mouth, focus on your dream vacation in your mind's eye as you still your breath for a few seconds, and then as you pulse your breath sharply out your nose, imagine planting the image of your dream vacation in the item in your hands. Repeat this process three times for each item. Then put the dream vacation items back on the altar.

Next, turn on some soft meditative music that reminds you of your dream vacation destination, dim the lights, and recline comfortably. Close your eyes, and breathe in deeply. Still your breath for a few moments, and then exhale, sensing all of your tensions and troubles being blown away with your outgoing breath. Breathe in a second time, and as you hold it for a moment, focus on the tension in your neck and shoulders. Now as you release your breath, feel all of the tension being swept away with your exhale. Take in a third breath, and as you hold it, imagine white light coming in and revitalizing every cell in your body. When you exhale, you feel relaxed and aware, ready for adventure.

In your mind's eye, imagine getting all the things together that you want to take on your dream vacation celebrating love. Unlike getting ready for waking vacation, on dream vacations you don't have to worry about forgetting anything, such as tickets or money or clothes, because it's all a dream. Everything has already been taken care of, and all you have to do is enjoy the experience.

While you are getting everything ready for your dream vacation, remember to include the items you put on your sacred love dream space. When you see them in your dream, you will know you are dreaming and your lucid dream vacation will truly begin.

In your mind's eye, imagine putting all the things you want to take into your dream bag, which is a little like Felix the Cat's magical bag in the popular vintage television cartoon in that it can hold anything and everything. If you are going with someone, be sure to imagine picking her or him up before you start your dream vacation.

Again breathe in deeply, hold it for a moment, and then exhale, imagining yourself riding the breeze to wherever you want to go. No tickets, no standing in line, no delayed departure time; only pure relaxation and enjoyment, like a vacation should be. Knowing this in advance, you should easily be able to enjoy your dream vacation celebrating love.

Continue enjoying your vacation for several minutes, and if you like, go directly into sleep and dream. Or if you want to say the prayer after the meditation before you drift to sleep, take a deep breath in and out, begin moving your toes and fingers, slowly open your eyes, and come back to the present time and place for prayer.

Dream Prayer for Love

Say this prayer before you go to sleep, either before or after the Dream Meditation for Love:

Divine mother of love,
Divine father of peace,
Let me know both your faces,
So that my life will always be peaceful and loving.
Thank you, divine mother and father,
For your continued help and guidance.

As you are moving into sleep, remind yourself over and over again:

When I see my dream vacation items, I know I am dreaming and I go lucid and have a joyful dream vacation.

After you wake up, record or write into your dream empowerment journal everything you remember from your dream, your dream vacation experience, as well as any impressions and insights.

Oracle of Dreams for Love

Movies make fascinating dream oracles because dreams are essentially mini-movies that play out in your mind each time you go to sleep. In both movies and dreams, anything can happen even if it defies the physical laws of science. And nothing that happens is particularly real, except to you, the viewer, as you perceive it as you watch the events and take in their meaning.

For this oracle, treat yourself and go see a movie you have wanted to see, one having to do with romance and relationships. Remember, you are going in order to have an enjoyable experience, but at the same time, dream empowerment is an ongoing process. This means that you should always keep your awareness in a heightened state. Use as many multi-sensory cues as you can in order to perceive and be aware of the synchronicity that happens continually all around you.

As you walk into the movie theater, say to yourself:

I empower this movie as a divine dream oracle.

Watch the movie carefully. Focus your awareness on it, and jot down anything that really catches your attention. After the movie, write down in your dream empowerment journal those scenes, lines, events, or characters that caught your attention. Also make a note of any thoughts, observations, and impressions you had while watching the movie. Does the title of the movie or any of the events in the movie remind you of anything in your dreams? What were you thinking when the movie ended and the credits began to show? What does this tell you about how you perceive empowerment and your dreams? Be sure to date your entry.

Dream Affirmation for Love

Write this affirmation in your dream empowerment journal, and then say it aloud to yourself several times:

Today and every day, I am greatly empowered by my success in attaining my dream goals for love in every way. I joyfully celebrate love and enjoy life.

Write this affirmation on note pages that you attach to places such as your front and back doors, so you see and read the affirming message each time you enter and exit your home. Write your dream affirmation for love on the calendar page each morning for the next 28 days or more, repeating it aloud each time you write it.

Health

To reward yourself for attaining your dream goals for health, you will be creating a healthy and pleasant place and then going there in dream. As you experience this place that you create in dream and realize you are dreaming, you will know that you are a full-fledged lucid dreamer, complete with dream wings that enable you to fly to anywhere and any time you like in your dreams.

Sacred Healing Dream Space

Place a book that has helped you on your healing journey such as this one on your sacred healing dream altar along with a white candle. Empower the book by holding it in your hands, merging with Oneness, and saying:

Sacred healing energies, please fill this book with lucid dreaming power.

Next, hold the candle in your hands, merge with Oneness, and say:

Sacred healing energies, please fill this candle with lucid dreaming power.

Dream Ritual for Health

The purpose of this ritual is to create a healing place that you can go to in your dreams and enjoy as a reward for successfully attaining one or more of your dream empowerment goals for health. You will need the book and candle from your sacred healing dream altar, your dream empowerment journal, and a book of matches or a lighter.

Imagine a sphere of bright white light encircling you and your sacred ritual space. Invite the elements into your space by saying:

Elemental energies of earth, wind, fire, earth, and spirit, please honor my sacred ritual with your presence. I welcome you now.

Put the candle in its holder and light it. Dedicate the candle to divine health and well-being by saying:

I dedicate this candle to divine health and well-being.

Next, on one of the pages of your dream empowerment journal, write out the things that your perfect health place would have, such as mineral springs, a waterfall, crystal healing rooms, expert massage therapists, healthy cuisine, and a private lake or pool for swimming. Let your dreams run wild, and list as briefly or in as much detail as you want all the things you would like to experience in your dream health place. The only requirement is that you set up a sacred healing dream space that is an exact replica of the one you have set up in your bedroom. Other than that, everything else can be of your own choosing.

After you have finished writing out all the things that you want in your dream health place, place your dream empowerment journal on your sacred healing dream space a safe distance in front of the lit candle. Ask for the help of the elements and energies of divine health in creating your dream health place by merging with Oneness and saying:

Elementals and divine energies of health,
Please help me to create my dream health place.

Gaze into the candle and create your dream health place in your mind's eye. Starting with your sacred healing dream space, visualize with as much detail as you can all the aspects of this place coming into being. Do this for several minutes until the place is firmly planted in your mind. Now call out:

Elementals and divine energies of health,
As I dream I go to my dream health place.
Let it be so!

When you are finished, thank the elements and divine energies of health by saying:

Elemental and divine energies of health, thank you for your help and blessing in this ritual.

Visualize stepping out of the sphere of white light that you stepped into at the beginning of the ritual, and imagine the light dissolving into Oneness.

Allow the candle to safely burn down, or snuff it out and burn it down all the way the next day.

Dream Meditation for Health

You can say the dream prayer for health either before or after this meditation. If you choose to say it before, you can go immediately into sleep from the meditation without coming back to the present time and place.

1-2-3, breathe in. What do you see in your mind's eye? 1-2-3, you are holding your breath and building up power. 1-2-3, exhale and envision that power being directed at what you see in your mind.

1-2-3, breath in again, but this time see your dreams for health and well-being in your mind. 1-2-3, hold your breath and expand your power. 1-2-3, exhale and move that power and energy toward your dreams and desires, seeing them happen and come to fruition in your mind.

As you imagine attaining your dreams, sense a wave of relaxing relief move over your body. With one more relaxed breath, breathe in while you visualize everything that is bothering you right now; hold it for a moment, and then sense your worries moving out of you with your breath. For now, let go of it all, as you get ready to go to your special dream health place. If you find you need it later, you can always come back to claim it after your healing dream vacation.

As you are getting your things ready, you begin to map out in your mind all the areas of your dream health place. Start with your sacred healing dream space and imagine all the things on it, including the white candle and book on healing that you recently added.

Moving onward from your sacred space, imagine going to the other spots that you wrote out in your dream empowerment journal. Go to each area and map it out in your mind. The amount of detail you add to your mental map is up to you.

You are now ready to go on an adventure to your dream health place. All your things are together, and your way has been set. You will be traveling by Trans-Dream Airways, and you will be your own dream pilot.

Remember that when you get to your dream health place and see your sacred healing dream space, in particular the white candle and book on healing, you will become aware and know that you are dreaming and that your lucid health vacation has begun. Enjoy yourself!

Dream Prayer for Health

Say this prayer before you go to sleep:

Divine healing spirits,
Please empower my dreams with your energy,
So that they are illuminated with your blessed presence,
And help my positive dream adventures of good health
Transform my waking life into one of well-being.
Thank you, divine healing spirits,
By earth, air, fire, water, and spirit. Amen.

Give yourself this reminder as the last thought before drifting into sleep:

As I see the white candle and book on healing in my dreams, I know I am lucid dreaming and I go to my dream health place.

Oracle of Dreams for Health

Read a book you have wanted to read that in some way relates to your health. Doing things you want and need to do is one of the ways of getting yourself healthier, and books can provide considerable assistance on several levels. They can bring you everything from entertainment and intrigue to information and insights about your own life.

Begin by holding the book in your hands, merging with Oneness, and saying:

I empower this book as a divine healing oracle.

Next, in your mind formulate a health question or something that has been bothering you. Now open the book and begin reading. Enjoy the book while at the same time looking for connection points and synchronicity to what has been happening in life regarding your health, both in waking and dream. Take the time to read the book, and really understand what the author is saying. How does it pertain to what you are doing in terms of health? In what ways do the author's experiences sound similar to yours?

If you read quickly, then you might want to wait until you have finished the book to write down your ideas or impressions in your dream empowerment journal as well as the date and your question or problem. If you like to read at a more leisurely pace, keep your journal close by so you can write down any insights as they occur to you.

Dream Affirmation for Health

Write this affirmation in your dream empowerment journal, and then say it aloud several times each day:

Today and every day, I am greatly empowered by my success in attaining my dream goals for health in every way. I joyfully celebrate my well-being and good health.

Write this affirmation on notes and put them on your bathroom mirror so you see it each time before you go to sleep and each time when you wake up. Every time you see the note displaying the affirmation, read it aloud. Do this for 28 days or more for best results.

Abundance

The path to abundance is forever changing, much like the staircases at Hogwart's School of Magic in J. K. Rowling's extraordinary *Harry Potter* books. As your dreams change, so do your expectations, goals, and plans. That's all part of being an evolving human being.

Change is an essential part of any dynamic system. Otherwise, things would remain static. The perceived passage of time happens when individual images are propelled forward. The individual images, when flashed like a deck of cards being shuffled, produce movement. This movement is perceived as time, moving from point "A" to point "B," and so on down the list. When dynamic images move through your perception in sequence, then subsequently your perception evaluates in terms of sequence, which is the essence of time. Through these sequences, you attain your goals, which in turn propels you forward in time.

Sacred Abundance Dream Space

Add to your sacred abundance dream altar a gold-colored candle, a vial of lavender oil, and something that symbolizes a dream portal. Make it a round metal object, such as a ring, bracelet, or necklace you wear, a round key chain, a small metal wheel, or one of those metal rings that you catch as you ride the merry-go-round.

Empower your future dream portal by saying:

Divine powers that be, please empower this dream portal with your abundant energies.

Next, hold the candle between your hands and say:

Divine powers that be, please empower this golden dream candle with your abundant energies.

Now, roll the vial gently between your palms until it warms up and then say:

Divine powers that be, please empower this lavender dream oil with your abundant energies.

Dream Ritual for Abundance

The purpose of this ritual is to create a dream portal that you can step through in your dreams. You will need the circular object that represents your dream portal, gold-colored candle, and lavender oil from your sacred abundance dream altar.

Imagine a sphere of bright white light encircling you and your sacred ritual space. Invite the elements into your ritual by saying:

Elemental powers of earth, air, fire, water, and spirit,
Please honor my sacred ritual space with your presence.

Next, rub a thin film of lavender oil on the candle. Then anoint yourself with the oil on the wrists, ankles, throat, and third eye. Wipe any remaining oil from your hands and light the candle, dedicating it to the divine energies of your preference.

Rub a few drops of the lavender oil on your circular object. If the item is fragile, just put a drop or two of the oil on the strongest part so you won't damage the item. Hold the anointed circular object between your hands and say three times:

Divine powers of abundance and plenty,
Please fill this object with your helpful energies.

Set the circular object in front of you on the altar, and through your breath and intention, begin building the field of bright golden energy that surrounds it. Use your eyes to bring focus to your thoughts as you continue to build up the golden energy field around the object. Feel it! Sense it! Be it!

Once you have built up the energy, start directing your breath and intention toward creating a dream portal with the object. You are creating an energetic vortex that you can use any time in your dreams to go any place and to any time you want.

Next, call on the divine powers of abundance to fill your dream portal. Hold the object in your power hand and say:

Divine powers of abundance, please empower this dream portal,
So that I can use it in my dreams
To go any place and to any time I desire.

Now hold up your dream portal (the circular object) so that it is illuminated in the candlelight. Focus your awareness on every detail of the object. See it with your eyes; then close your eyes and see it in your mind's eye. Do this several times so that when you see your dream portal in your dreams, you will be aware that you are dreaming and know that you can use your dream portal to go any place and any time you want in your dreams.

When you are done, thank the divine and the elements by saying:

Elemental energies of earth, air, fire, water, and divine spirit, thank you for honoring my sacred ritual space and for your blessings.

Imagine stepping out of the sphere of white light you imagined at the beginning of the ritual, and visualize the sphere diffusing into the air around you into Oneness. Allow the candle to safely burn down, or if you prefer, snuff it out and relight it the next day and let it burn completely down. Hold your dream portal in your left hand as you meditate, pray, and dream to access its power. Continue doing so until you successfully access your dream portal.

Dream Meditation for Abundance

Sit or recline comfortably. Roll the fingers of your power hand into a ball around your dream portal object from the previous ritual. Holding your hand in that position for a few moments, imagine in your mind's eye one of your dream empowerment goals for abundance. Imagine the ball of energy building up in your hands, and then quickly extend your fingers, while visualizing yourself directing the built-up energy out toward your dream goal for abundance. Do this several more times, each time building up the energy, focusing on your goal, and then releasing the energy in your hand toward it.

Now imagine your dream portal in your mind. You've just been given the keys to go wherever you want, absolutely any place you desire. This also includes any time period—past, present, and future. At this point the question becomes, where would you like to go this time?

Pick a time and place that you would like to go. Fix it in your mind, and then in a flash the dream portal transports you there, where you experience the world in its completeness with as much detail as you desire. You can use your dream portal to move you any place and any time you want, just by energetically moving through it.

Realize you can do this whenever you wish. When you see your dream portal in your dream, you will be aware that you are dreaming and know that you can use your dream portal to go any place and any time in your dreams.

When you are done meditating, take a deep breath, move your toes and fingers, and return your awareness to the present time and place.

Dream Prayer for Abundance

Just before you go to sleep, say this prayer:

Divine ones and dream helpers,
With this portal of dreams
Please show me the places and times
That will help me live my dreams for abundance
In both dream and waking life.
Thank you, my dream friends, blessings always.

As you drift to sleep, give yourself the suggestion:

As I see my dream portal in my dreams, I know I am lucid dreaming and can go to any place and any time I desire.

Upon awakening, record or write in your dream empowerment journal everything you remember about your dreams. Make a special note of any places or times you visited through your dream portal.

Oracle of Dreams for Abundance

This simple oracle uses the change in your pocket, coin purse, or wallet. Begin by taking out the change from your pocket or purse and holding it in your hands. Merge with Oneness, and say:

I empower these coins as a divine dream oracle.

Think of a specific question regarding your dreams for abundance. Focus all your attention on the question for a minute or two, and then put the coins on your dream altar for abundance.

Begin to examine the coins. First, notice the years of the coins and write them down in your journal under the question and date. What was happening in your life during these years? Make a note of any of the years that relate specifically to your question regarding your dreams for abundance.

Next, add up the coins and reduce the amount to the smallest number. For example, if the coins in your pocket or purse add up to $3.34, add 3 + 3 + 4 = 10, then 10 = 1 + 0 = 1. Refer to the Dream Number Chart in Chapter Seven for the significance of this number. Write down the number and it's meaning under the year numbers you noted in your dream empowerment journal. How does the meaning relate to your question? Also, make a note of the impressions or insights you have with regard to the years on the coins or the number they added up to.

Dream Affirmation for Abundance

Write this affirmation for abundance in your dream empowerment journal. Read it over and say it aloud or to yourself several times a day:

Today and every day, I am greatly empowered by my success in attaining my dream goals for abundance in every way. I joyfully celebrate my abundance and plenty.

Write the affirmation on notes and put them around where you sleep as reminders of your empowerment and success. For at least 28 days, repeat the affirmation several times a day until the affirming message becomes a part of your consciousness.

Chapter Twelve

Reviewing Your Dream Goals

In your life, the aspects of love, health, and abundance are naturally integrated into One. Nothing stands alone, but instead is an interconnected part of the web of the whole commonly known as Oneness. Just as reflected in your life, all parts of Oneness affect all the other parts. Everything relates to everything else. From the stillness, you learn to walk. From the silence, you learn to talk. From the emptiness, you learn to fill the void. From your dreams, you learn to live life to its fullest.

When the energies and prayers of people come together and ask for divine guidance, it's like a signal to the divine superheroes and elemental energies to help balance things back up, a balance that we come to rely on and expect. Oftentimes this is the main thing that keeps us sane and moving forward in life—we know that as we proceed in our personal journey, there comes a time when we move beyond the point where we struggle with our life to one where life becomes a true reflection of who we are.

Author and advocate of dreams Anaïs Nin said that "Dreams pass into the reality of action. From the action stems the dream again: and this interdependence produces the highest form of living." This reflects the proverbial egg and chicken cycle—the egg produces the chicken which in turn produces the egg. It's a continuous cycle, ever-beginning and ever-ending, which is a circle within a circle. As you move through the small circle, you are also moving through a larger circle, and then on an expanded level, an even larger circle. This spiral eventually circles to the divine.

In terms of your dream empowerment, your dream spirals into your thoughts, which coalesce into your dream empowerment goals. Your goals spiral into an active plan, which spirals into the steps of your plan. By taking the actual steps in dream and in waking that you list in your dream, your efforts eventually spiral into the attainment of your dream empowerment goals. This success fuels future empowerment.

Many times plans change, so you need to remain flexible. Keep in mind that what you dream of at 16 might be quite different than what you dream of at 60. Be willing to adapt your plans and flow with the times and stages of your life.

Realistically, once you follow through with your plans and take the steps, you will most likely be successful in reaching your dream goals. And then through your empowering experiences, you create new dreams. This begins the entire process over again. It's like a many-layered circle consisting of a dream within a dream, within a dream, within a dream, and so on.

Because the empowerment process is constantly dynamic, it continually evolves in ways that, with focus and effort, can help you realize your full potential and live your dreams. Much like your dreams themselves, the empowerment process is a coherent micro- and macro-process that evolves each time you dream and then awaken.

On a micro level, you dream your dreams and this process creates your personal reality. On a macro level, the creatures of the world all dream their dreams, and this coalesces into One and creates the world on a global level. To expand this idea a step further, the energies of the universe all dream their dreams, which creates the universe on a universal level, and so on. And all dreams affect all other dreams, both micro and macro.

As you continue to evolve personally and globally, once you have achieved your first dream goals for empowerment, it's time to create new goals and begin working on them. In this way, the empowerment process encourages your natural evolution.

The dream techniques in this chapter are blended together into One. This is done as a reminder that the aspects of love, health, and abundance are separate as a means of practical perception and learning, but ultimately everything becomes integrated into one and reflects who you are as a complete human being.

As you begin to comprehend your intimate connection with Oneness, you will begin to understand and especially notice the many levels of synchronicity that continually occur. That's when you will know that your every breath, thought, action, feeling, and dream is sacred and divine—that the universe is truly at your fingertips, both in dream and in waking. As you dream it, so your life becomes. So go ahead and dare to dream your empowering dreams of love, good health, and abundance and enrich your life every night and every day.

Sacred Dream Space for Love, Health, and Abundance

Create positive change with the natural power of color by adding pleasing hues to your sacred dream space for love, health, and abundance. Do so by painting and decorating your sacred dream space for love, good health, and abundance in specific colors that promote certain types of dreams. Also, wear sleepwear in these dream-promoting colors. Be sure the colors you choose are colors that you like, as they will be influencing you in waking and in dream.

To encourage dreams of love, decorate your sacred space and altar in and wear white, pink, rose, red, lavender, purple, or violet, or pleasing combinations of these colors. To encourage dreams of healing and well-being, decorate your sacred space and your altar in and wear blue, green, blue-green, turquoise, white, or earthy brown. To encourage dreams of abundance and plenty, decorate your sacred space and altar in and wear gold, green, orange, or silver.

As you decorate—for example, make your bed, paint the walls, add colorful posters and pictures as well as colorful textures here and there—chant these words over and over:

May this space be filled with love, good health, and abundance, today and every day.

If you like, you can also dedicate your colorful decorations to the divine presence(s) of your choice to add divine energy to your sacred space.

Dream Ritual for Love, Health, and Abundance

The purpose of this ritual is to reflect upon your dreams and consider future dream goals. You will need your dream empowerment journal, three blank pieces of notebook paper, and a pen.

Imagine a sphere of bright white light enveloping your sacred ritual space. Invite the elemental energies into your space by saying:

Elemental energies of earth, air, fire, water, and spirit,
Please honor my sacred ritual space with your presence now.

Start by writing "Love" on the top of one of the notebook pages, "Health" on the top of another, and "Abundance" on the top of the third sheet.

Now sit back for a few minutes and take a few deep breaths. Next, imagine a bright, white luminous star in your third eye. You can do this with your eyes closed or open. Once you see the star clearly in your third eye, open your dream empowerment journal and begin reading through the dreams you have written down while moving through your dream empowerment process. As you read, be aware of who you are in your dreams in terms of love, health, and abundance. Also, notice how your dream self changed while you were going through the various dream techniques. Take a few moments now and imagine the bright white star in your third eye growing larger and brighter. Then with new insight, write any observations, impressions, or messages in your dreams regarding love, health, and abundance on the separate pieces of paper.

After you are done going through your dream empowerment journal, then focus on the bright white star in your third eye for a moment or two, and call the divine into your sacred ritual space by saying:

Divine powers of love, health, and abundance,
Please empower my ritual space with your presence now.

Now place the three notebook pages side by side where you can easily view them together. Begin looking at how these three aspects of your life—love, health, and abundance—integrate to form the whole of who you are. Also look at how all of the aspects connect together into One and influence who you are, both in dream and in waking.

Again, focus your awareness on the bright white star in your third eye for a few moments, and then note in your journal your impressions and reflections that you have regarding not only who you are in dream but also how this reflects who you perceive your waking self to be. Also, write who you truly want to be, who you dream of being.

Focus on the bright white star in your third eye. Imagine connecting the three aspects of your life—love, health, and abundance—together into one by imagining a bright white beam of light moving out from the luminous star in your third eye and connecting the three lists in front of you into a bright, clockwise-spinning spiral of light. Then say three times:

Love, health, and abundance are One
Dream and waking are One.
We are One.

Now imagine continuing on your journey to personal empowerment. Reflect on some of the things you have been thinking about in terms of new dream empowerment goals. List a few of these on the sheet in front of you. Imagine the bright white star growing brighter in your third eye. In the light, imagine yourself attaining your dreams. Enjoy the experience for at least 15 minutes.

When you are done, thank the divine powers by saying:

Divine powers of love, health, and abundance,
Thank you for your help and blessings.

Imagine stepping out of the sphere of white light, and then visualize the sphere diffusing into the air around you into Oneness.

Dream Meditation for Love, Health, and Abundance

Turn on some meditative music and recline comfortably. Uncross your hands and legs. Begin to breathe in and out, and as you do, imagine a halo of white light that starts swirling at the top of your head. With each breath you take, the halo spreads down from your head to your neck, then down to your shoulders and arms. Soon the halo of white light has continued its way down your body to your stomach and waist and down your legs to your knees, ankles, and feet. Once the halo has reached your feet, you sense an energetic glow, revitalizing you from head to toe.

Using the information you gained from the previous ritual, formulate in your mind three reflective questions relating to your dream empowerment process—one about love, one about health, and one about abundance.

Once you have formulated your questions, then it's time to choose three dream teachers to come into your dreams so that you can ask them your questions in the hope that they can give you some insights as to the solution. In terms of love, you could invite the goddess Venus into your dreams, for health you might choose Edgar Cayce, and for abundance perhaps Buddha. It all depends on the nature of your question. Your dream teachers can be living, dead, otherworldly, or divine. Choose whomever you think and feel will provide the most helpful insights into your question.

Now, in your mind's eye imagine standing in front of a large full-length mirror. Personalize the mirror by fashioning it in an unusual way, perhaps covering it with gemstones, acorns, and sea shells or by coloring the mirror frame with bold colors or lush fabrics. If you like, the mirror might even be a living mirror that talks and moves.

After you have personalized the mirror, imagine staring into it. As you do, you see your innermost desires pictured before you in the mirror's reflection. These images are so real that you can reach out and touch them as they are mirrored before you. Imagine doing just that now. The longer you focus on the images, the more real they become, until you can sense them on every level—sight, smell, taste, touch, sound, and intuitively. Now imagine the images moving out of the mirror into your daily life, making them "real" to your waking perception. At this point, you understand that you can create the life you want just by imagining it in the mirror and transferring the image over into the waking world.

Take a deep breath, imagining the swirling halo of white light flowing out of the mirror and completely surrounding you. Breathe in the white light, filling yourself with positive energies of love, good health, and abundance. Breathe in deeply once again and exhale completely. Begin gently moving your hands and feet. Slowly open your eyes and come back to the present time and place.

Dream Prayer for Love, Health, and Abundance

As you say this prayer, imagine a brilliant white luminous star in your third eye. Go ahead and personalize the prayer by changing it in any way to better suit your needs and spiritual preferences:

Great cosmic spirit, please hear my prayer.
Thank you for your sacred gifts.
Thank you, divine one, for your love.
Thank you, divine one, for your healing power.
Thank you, divine one, for your generosity.
Thank you for helping me dream my dreams.
Thank you for helping me now live my dreams.
Thank you for your guidance and blessings.

As you drift to sleep, imagine a relaxing, luminous white star softly lighting up your third eye, and repeat over and over:

I live my dreams of love, good health, and abundance. Dream and waking merge into One.

When you wake up, record or write down everything you recall. Before you do, take a deep breath and imagine the bright, luminous white star in your third eye. Doing so often helps clarify your dream recall. Continue imagining the star as you record or write down what you remember from your dream. Make the white star brighter and brighter as you note any dream insights, impressions, or especially vivid elements.

Oracle of Dreams for Love, Health, and Abundance

Everything, whether animate or inanimate, is a part of Oneness and can be used as a divine oracle. The best way to become aware of the daily oracles in your waking life is to pay attention to signs, symbols, words, songs, images, and so forth during the day, and also during your dreams. For example, make an effort to be more aware of the oracular messages that may come through your television or radio, in conversations, in the names of people, pets, places, things, in names of stores, and in messages from dream helpers or in lucid dreams—everything connects into One.

As you go through the day, be aware that everything that happens to you is, in a sense, an oracle that connects your life with the outer world, often in synchronistic ways. For example, notice subtle cues in the form of repetition of things, such as if images and references of wolves keep popping up in dream and waking, then there is often something more going on and you should look deeper. You could do a little research and find out more about wolves and then take some time to reflect on what this means in your life.

By becoming more aware of the oracular power in everyday life and things, you also expand your sense of reality, both in waking and in dream. This ultimately leads to expanded personal creativity, abundance, and more satisfying relationships.

Dream Affirmation for Love, Health, and Abundance

Write the following affirmation in your dream empowerment journal:

Today and every day, I realize my dreams for love, good health, and abundance, and I am empowered and enriched in every way.

Each time you repeat the affirming phrase either aloud or to yourself, imagine the bright white star in your third eye. Also tap into the powers of the energy centers or chakras in your body by imagining the star of light in your other six primary chakras, in colors which correspond with those specific chakras. They are as follows:

- White: Crown Chakra (7th)
- Violet: Third Eye (6th)
- Blue: Throat Chakra (5th)
- Green or Rose: Heart Chakra (4th)
- Gold: Solar Plexus (3rd)
- Orange: Sacral Chakra (2nd)
- Red: Root Chakra (1st)

Be sure to write the affirmation on notes and put them around your home and workplace where you will frequently see and read them—for example, on the refrigerator, microwave oven, television, computer tower, mirrors, and doors. In addition, write the affirmation on your business card and pull it out now and again to read the affirming phrase. Repeat this process several times a day for at least 28 days for the most empowering and illuminating results.

Appendix A

Dream Interpretation Symbols

The following list of symbols is provided only as a guideline. Keep in mind that definitions change depending on the time, situation, dream, and person, so remember to apply these meanings accordingly.

altar Symbol of the divine, connection with divine, a place of honoring the spirit and your inner self, a place of quiet, prayers, a sacred space, your spiritual self, altered states of consciousness.

amulet Protection, healing, talisman, dream helper, dream messages.

angels Divine messenger, symbol of love, spiritual messages of importance, divine blessings and guidance, divine healing and protection, your guardian angel is a special companion and protector, possible alien contact when the angel is not humanlike.

bell Traditional Feng Shui cure, a feminine symbol of the Goddess, rung during ritual to create a positive vibration or frequency.

bowl Corresponds to the north direction and the earth element. The universal purifier. A symbol of the goddess, the bowl represents the womb.

bridge Transition, change, changing consciousness, birth, death, initiation, moving between worlds, connecting two ideas together, bridging the gap between people and ideas, taking risks, a gateway to the divine, finally getting over that bridge that previously eluded you.

butterfly Dream helpers, transformation, metamorphosis, embracing your dreams, moving to new places, freedom. The butterfly often represents complete personal change. They are also divine messengers.

castle Protected in your home, state of your family, abundance, plenty, attaining your dreams, ancestral dreams, the dream world, spiritual temple, spiritual sanctuary, magical fortress.

cat Developing sensuality and sensory abilities, extrasensory abilities, developing poise and agility, transformation, meditation, lucid dreaming, cunning, stealth, keeping secrets, unconditional love, companionship.

cave Hidden mysteries, protection, symbol of feminine power, subconscious mind, cave-ins, ancient wisdom, spiritual retreat, treasure, spiritual wealth, the power of divination, the womb of the Earth mother, dream incubation.

children Signify the inner child, play, happiness, innocence, childhood memories, parental issues either as a child or parent. Imagination, carefree spirit, a need to relax and play, childhood talents and dreams, parts of yourself that you left behind when you were a child.

circle Symbol of the Goddess, full circle, coming around again, eternity, ancestral connection, higher realms of consciousness, protection, boundary group, a sacred geometric doorway to other realms of consciousness.

clock Timing, your relationship to time, on time, out of time, short of time, in time, the ticking of your life. Alarm clock could be a personal awakening, wasting time, using time more wisely.

clouds Flying, no worries, dream messages, spiritual understanding, inspiration and imagination, inner harmony, different types of clouds mean different things—such as storm clouds, lightening-illumination.

clover Beauty, healing, fortune, fertility, good luck, visions, protection, love, fidelity, success.

coins Abundance, money, old coins mean history, date on the coin, change. Finding the coins could mean finding fortune, coining a phrase. A coin is two-sided, which may indicate you need to flip your life over and look at the other side of things.

computer Communication, ideas, knowledge, automation, work, answers, play, games, global awareness, technology, mind, memory, a need to update your files.

crystals and gemstones Agate (grounding and balancing your dreams, self-confidence), Amber (tree power and wisdom, communication with energies of the trees, healing and protective dreams), Amethyst (divine communication, wisdom, banishing nightmares, dream protection), Citrine (dream messages, lucid dreaming), Clear Quartz (divine guidance, healing dreams, ancestral dreams), Diamond (divine inspiration, personal strength and clarity), Emerald (ancestral dreams, elemental communication), Jade (dream protection, lucid dreaming, abundance), Lapis (shape-shifting dreams, animal dream helpers, psychic ability), Malachite (shape-shifting dreams, healing, abundance), Moonstone (lunar power, feminine wisdom, divination, healing and inspiring dreams), Rose Quartz (love, romance, dream creativity, divine love), Ruby (personal power and dream protection, divine inspiration and passion), Sapphire (dream protection, creative dreams, stimulates lucid dreams), Topaz (spiritual dreams, intuitive dreams), Turquoise (dream wisdom, dream communication with your ancestors, devas, star beings, and elementals).

cup Symbol of water and the west, the chalice or cup holds water or wine, the loving cup of the Goddess is a sacred vessel of femininity.

dog Developing loyalty and unconditional love, both to yourself and others, healing, protection of goals and possessions, friendship, companionship, heightened senses, tracking ability, intuition, developing instinctual awareness and personal integrity, faithfulness.

dolphin Using energy wisely, finding joy, love, and playfulness in daily life, using your breathing to access altered states of consciousness, developing natural intelligence and grace, eloquence, lucid dreaming abilities, accessing dream time and other dimensions of awareness.

door Open door would represent new opportunities. Locked door might mean opportunities momentarily locked away, transition, moving from one space to another, altered states of consciousness, new knowledge.

dragonfly Moving beyond your present awareness, lifting the veils of perception, multidimensional travel, lucid dreaming, transmigration, developing dreaming abilities, transformation, metamorphosis, change.

driving Movement of ideas, new information, transition, new dream landscapes. How hard are you driving yourself? Are you driving the car? What is your destination? Other people's goals if you aren't driving? Driving your car represents you. Are you driving to something or driving away from something?

drum A bridge to the spirit or dream world and altered states of consciousness, a tool of vibration and sound that is associated with the air and earth elements. Do you need to drum something up in your life?

eagle Divine connection, inspiration, courage, wisdom, insight, creative power, messages and gifts from a spirit, power and sheer will applied toward positive patterns, learning how to unleash your imagination, developing keen powers of observation, solar power, seeing the larger picture.

egg Dreaming of eggs signifies abundant wealth, and an egg with a double yolk is a powerful sign of good fortune. If the egg is cracked, there are new discoveries on the way. If the egg is cooked, it may mean sustenance. If the egg is boiled, it may indicate you are being too rigid about something, or represent whatever hard-boiled eggs mean to you; for example, picnics or Easter eggs.

elephant Strength, prosperity, wisdom, happiness, removing any obstacles in your life, utilizing all educational opportunities. The Zulus of Africa say the elephant brings happiness into the home.

falcon Swiftness, power, insight, developing psychic ability and alchemical mastery, learning to ask the correct questions, divine guidance, multidimensional awareness and travel.

feet Mobility, connection with the earth, grounded, taking the steps for achieving your goals, understanding your life, your support, lucid dreaming, your foundation, your direction in life.

flowers Blooming flowers signify abundance and happiness, seeing the beauty in your life, relationships, and work. A big colorful bouquet or smelling fragrant flowers indicates joy. Flowers in general signify dream messages from the nature spirits. African Violet (protection, pure love, renewal), Azalea (love, romance, healing, well-being, balance), Camellia (abundance, wealth, beauty, harmony, peace), Chamomile (peace, tranquility, harmony, success, abundance, empowerment, healing), Chrysanthemum (friendship, engagement, love, romance, protection), Daffodil (happiness, fertility, good luck, joy, beginnings), Daisy (divine blessings, romance, love, passion, happiness, and good health), Gardenia (harmony, spiritual love, healing, love), Honeysuckle (love, romance, attraction, prosperity, wealth, protection, happy marriage, fertility), Hyacinth (perfection, protection, joy, success, pleasure), Iris (purity, wisdom, protection, rebirth), Jasmine (lucky in love, abundance, romance, sexuality), Lavender (healing, well-being, peace, harmony, love), Marigold (abundance, nature spirit dream helpers), Orchid (love, passion, spiritual inspiration), Rose (love, romance, passion, commitment, marriage, joy, feminine power), Sunflower (abundance, prosperity, wealth, riches, harvest, knowledge, success, solar power).

flying Going beyond the bounds of ordinary reality, moving between worlds, seeing the larger picture, moving into a higher consciousness, success, liberty, abundance, independence, out-of-body experiences, lucid dreaming, rising above conflict, creativity, imagination.

fruit Blackberry (dream protection, healing dreams, personal awakening, wealth), Apple (love, healing, happiness, immortality, spiritual messages, fertility), Apricot (love, inspiration, partnership, friendship, joy), Banana (fertility, abundance, creativity, healing, harmony), Cherry (love, romance, friendship, divination), Fig (love, romance, passion, fertility, divination), Grape (cooperation, healing, clarity, fertility, love, romance, passion), Lemon (friendship, harmony, healing, blessing, purification, clarity), Orange (friendship, romance, love, fertility, wealth, abundance, riches, divination, prosperity), Peach (healing, love, romance, fertility, longevity, abundance, success, beauty, cooperation), Pear (sexuality, fertility, love, romance, abundance, wealth, riches), Pomegranate (success, prosperity, abundance, good fortune, healing, fertility, divination), Strawberry (love, romance, passion, sexuality, attraction, good luck, joy, happiness, playfulness).

garden What you are cultivating in life, seeds, creative dreams, imagination, hopeful harvest, symbol of nourishment and life, food, personal patterns, mother, earth, abundance, Goddess, life, creation.

Goddesses Female aspects of yourself, divine love, divine dream messages. Check out the specific Goddess and see what her qualities are—do you want to integrate these qualities into your life?

Gods Masculine aspects of yourself, divine love, divine dream messengers, research particular Gods that you dream about.

gold Solar power, symbol of successful goal completion, signifies light and inner peace, treasure, abundance, riches, great wealth, loving cup, golden gems of wisdom, security, protection.

hands Lucid dreaming, manipulation, getting a grasp of things, things you can't get hold of, creation, manifesting, reaching out to new ideas and people.

honey Prosperity, love, romance, passion, harmony, peace. Symbol of the Goddess and the sacred prophetic power of bees. Does your life need sweetening up? Are you facing a sticky situation?

horse Learning how to use power correctly, divine inspiration and creativity, taking authoritative action and standing tall, warning of possible danger, developing inner awareness, quickness of thought. The horse can carry you fast and far through the dream world.

house Symbol for spiritual, mental, and physical self. The condition of your home reflects the condition of your life. Different rooms signify different parts of your life. Represents your roots, security, and personal structure. Rooms represent different aspects of your consciousness; for example, library, study, nursery.

incense burner or censer Representing the fire and air elements, your messages are carried in the incense smoke to the divine. Is there something you need to smoke out in your life?

leopard Honoring your choices, divine inspiration, wise decisions, stalking your opponent, shamanic power, altered states of awareness, shape shifting, using power in positive ways.

lion Strength, building personal power, working cooperatively, the ability to relax, protection, power, prowess, working together as a family.

mirror Reflection of yourself, divination, imagination, inspiration, memories, opposites, portal, your double self, the unity of opposites, protection, other realms of awareness.

money Dream images of abundance and prosperity are good luck signs. Finding money in your dreams often indicates new opportunities and changes for the better both personally and professionally. An inheritance in your dream may indicate that you will receive a legacy or boon. Gold, metals, coins, jewelry, and medals often symbolize financial gain.

moon Feminine energy, Goddess, subconscious mind, memories, lucid dreaming, divine guidance, divine healing, divine light, lunar power, dream messages, romance and inspiration.

movie What's the movie about? Represents lucid dreaming, hopes, dreams, desires, psyche, subconscious, a view of your life—past, present, and future, acting out your life, directing your life.

moving to a different home Transition, transformation, leaving the past behind, new surroundings, warning, unsettled issues, some action you need to take, changing states of consciousness.

music Divine messages, healing, inner harmony and alignment. Depending on the type of music, it reflects your moods and state of consciousness. If there are words, what do the words say? Relaxation, completion, tuning in to your feelings and emotions.

numbers Phone numbers, birth dates, important dates, dates in history, past lives. Check the number with the dream and what's happening in your life right now. What's your lucky number? Does someone have your number?

nuts Almond (abundance, fertility), Brazil Nut (love, wealth, attaining goals), Cashew (good luck, success, fortune, abundance), Pecan (abundance, success, prosperity), Walnut (good luck, fortune). Are you feeling nutty or going nuts?

owl Learning discernment, knowing the difference between truth and deception, transformation, trusting your insights and first impressions of people, feminine power, developing your intuitive skills, attuning to lunar cycles, moon magic, sacred symbol of the Goddess.

parrot Longevity, developing personal skills by mimicking and imitating others, apprenticeship, practicing and refining dreaming skills.

pets Whether living or deceased pets, the ones in your dreams are almost always dream messengers or helpers of some kind. Also indicates lucid dreaming, dream protection, old memories, past lives, divine healing.

portal Vortex between worlds, divine communication, a view into another world, new ideas, new people, moving to new locations.

rabbit Fertility and birth, good luck, fearless and quick action, learning how to listen to your inner voice, hiding secrets, conceiving ideas, living by your wits, agility. The rabbit's foot is carried for fertility.

rainbow Success, attainment, imagination, dream messages from nature spirits, divine and lucid dreaming, sign of blessings, a sign that you are going in the best direction possible, divine guidance, hope, joy, happiness, personal realization, protection, healing powers of the chakras.

ring Dream portal, unity, marriage, commitment, love, personal power, strength of love, friendship, creativity, taking life in hand, symbol of divine unity, Oneness.

ritual Cycles in life, communication with the divine, habits, pomp and circumstance, lucid dreaming, patterns, prayers and blessings, set order of things, elemental energies, magical experiences, initiation.

salt Protection, purification, cleansing, nothing will grow when it is covered with salt.

school/classroom Knowledge, teaching, authority, order, schools of thought, education, expanding your consciousness.

sea shell Escaping into a shell, breaking out of old patterns, memories, feminine intuition, the power of the ocean.

shaman Ancient wisdom, divine knowledge, power of the nature spirits, lucid dreaming, dream messages, magical happenings, altered states of consciousness, out-of-body experiences, shape shifting, rebirth, death of the old self, healing, ancestor dreams.

stars Symbols of divine light, divine blessings, divine protection, divine healing, heritage, illumination, altered states of consciousness, the five elements, ancestral dreams.

swimming Can represent sexual dreams, spiritual activity, Oneness, coherence, relaxation, the water element, fluidity, staying afloat in times of turmoil, a sign you should take up swimming for your own well-being. If you don't swim, a need to learn new things, or you may be in over your head.

table A symbol of the Goddess, a well-set table with shining silverware, crystal stem glasses, fine china, fine table lines, and more represents sustenance, enrichment, wealth.

teacher Inner and outer messages, knowledge, finding answers, learning new things, divine guidance and healing.

television Being tuned in, receiving messages, being aware of what's on the screen, switching channels, focusing on specific issues in your life, turning on and turning off aspects of yourself, changing your view of things, memories, past lives, divination.

temple Portal between the divine and Earth, inner sanctuary, inner healing, creativity, imagination, learning, your physical body, health.

time Dawn (a time of renewal, rebirth, new ideas dawning, communication with nature spirits), Morning (awakenings, beginnings), Noon (solar power, strength), Afternoon (harvest, fruition of dream empowerment goals), Dusk (solar and lunar energies conjoin and the portals to the dream world, open and divine communication), Night (lunar and stellar power, hidden or cloaked aspects), Midnight (magical time for change and influencing your goals).

trees Stately and tall, with some much older than even our ancestors, trees represent earthly wisdom and the power of Mother Earth. Bay (purification, cleansing, divination, ancestral wisdom), Beech (hopes, wishes, scholarship, literary abilities, creativity, inspiration), Birch (protection, purification, birth, new beginnings, new opportunities), Cedar (wealth, riches, abundance, harmony, healing, strength, clarity, purification), Cypress (longevity, healing, strength), Dogwood (abundance, fortune, beauty, hopes, protection), Elm (friendship, romance, love, well-being), Eucalyptus (healing, protection, cleansing, ancestral dreams), Hawthorn (fertility, joy, happiness), Hazel (fertility, protection, magical dreams), Maple (protection, love, longevity, good luck, abundance, fortune, riches), Oak (success, prosperity, abundance, wealth, riches, protection, nourishment, good luck, personal power), Pine (protection, healing, fertility, rebirth, wealth, abundance, purification), Willow (flexibility, adaptability, divination, healing, inspiration, wisdom).

unicorn Acknowledging beauty, love, and friendship, learning the gentle side of life, developing magical and psychic abilities, occult wisdom, multidimensional travel and awareness.

wand An extension of your arm and hand, associated with the east and the air element, you can bridge the dream world and direct energies in specific patterns with a wand. Is it your wand or someone else's?

water Bodies of water and the bathtub, flow, fluid, reflection, relaxation, resonance, aspects of the moon and Goddess, tides; muddy water—things being stirred up; rivers—spiritual flow, the waters of life; pure water—clarity of thought and dreams; puddles—left-over emotions.

waterfall Symbol of overflowing love, plenty in life, personal healing, refreshing, revitalization, emotions flowing, represents beauty, natural power.

well Source of the divine, hidden knowledge, symbol of the Goddess, feminine wisdom, the well of the world, the water of life, childbirth, creative inspiration.

wheel Cycles, seasons, movement, change, wheel of life, wheel of fortune, getting to the hub of things, getting things rolling.

window Perception, new views, point of view, insights. What's happening with the window? Stained glass indicates spiritual messages. Dirty windows may represent the need to cleanse your perception so you can see the whole picture.

wolf Developing your sense of smell, inner and primal knowing, loyalty to family, steadfastness, guidance in dreams, discovering new ways of doing things, endurance, lucid dreaming, dream protection, shape shifting, shamanic ability, ancestral messages, moving beyond socially accepted constraints.

Appendix B

Bibliography

Ackroyd, Eric. *A Dictionary of Dream Symbols*. London: Blandford, 1993.

Barasch, Marc Ian. *Healing Dreams*. New York: Riverhead Books, 2000.

Benson, Herbert, and Miriam Klipper. *The Relaxation Response*. New York: Avon, 1976.

Bluestone, Sarvananda. *How to Read Signs and Omens in Everyday Life*. Rochester, VT: Destiny Books, 2002.

Bowater, Margaret M. *Dreams and Visions*. Freedom, CA: The Crossing Press, 1999.

Buhlman, William. *The Secret of the Soul*. New York: HarperSanFrancisco, 2001.

Canfield, Jack, Mark Victor Hansen, and Les Hewitt. *The Power of Focus*. Deerfield Beach, FL: Health Communications, Inc., 2000.

Chaline, Eric. *Tai Chi for Body, Mind, and Spirit*. New York: Sterling Publishing Company, 1998.

Chopra, Deepak. *Whispers of Healing*. Los Angeles: The Relaxation Company, 2002.

———. *Whispers of Spirit*. Los Angeles: The Relaxation Company, 2002.

Coghill, Roger. *The Healing Energies of Light*. Boston, MA: Journey Editions, 2000.

Crosse, Joanna. *Encyclopedia of Mind, Body, Spirit, and Earth*. Boston, MA: Element, 1998.

Dahl, David Rains. *The Blue Deer and Other Dreamtales*. Santa Barbara, CA: Capra Press, 1998.

Davich, Victor. *The Best Guide to Meditation*. Los Angeles: Renaissance Books, 1998.

Delaney, Gayle, Ph.D. *Living Your Dreams*. San Francisco, CA: HarperSanFrancisco, 1979.

Devereux, Paul, and Charla Devereux. *The Lucid Dreaming Kit*. Boston, MA: Journey Editions, 1998.

Douglas, Ray. *Dreams and the Inner Self*. London: Blandford, 1999.

Emery, Marcia. *Power Hunch!* Hillsboro, OR: Beyond Words Publishing, 2001.

Feuerstein, Georg. *Lucid Waking*. Rochester, VT: Inner Traditions International, 1997.

Fink, Georg. *Dream Symbols from A to Z*. New York: Sterling Publishing Company, Inc., 1999.

Garfield, Patricia. *Creative Dreaming*. New York: Simon & Schuster, 1974.

———. *The Dream Messenger*. New York: Simon & Schuster, 1997.

Godwin, Malcolm. *The Lucid Dreamer*. New York: Simon & Schuster, 1994.

Grant, Russell. *The Illustrated Dream Dictionary*. New York: Sterling Publishing Company, 1996.

Harary, Keith, and Pamela Weintraub. *Have an Out of Body Experience in 30 Days*. Aquarian Press, 1990.

Harrison, Yvonne. *Sleep Talking*. London: Blandford, 1999.

Hay, Louise. *You Can Heal Your Life*. Carson, CA: Hay House, 1984.

Jung, Carl G. *The Archetypes of the Collective Unconscious*. Princeton, NJ: Princeton University Press, 1990.

Kabat-Zinn, Jon. *Wherever You Go, There You Are*. New York: Hyperion, 1994.

Klein, Bob. *Movements of Magic*. North Hollywood, CA: Newcastle Publishing Company, 1984.

Knight, Sirona. *Celtic Traditions*. New York: Citadel Press, 2000.

———. *Dream Magic*. San Francisco: HarperSanFrancisco, 2000.

———. *Exploring Celtic Druidism*. Franklin Lakes, NJ: New Page Books, 2001.

———. *Empowering Your Life with Wicca*. Indianapolis: Alpha Books, 2003.

———. *Faery Magick*. Franklin Lakes, NJ: New Page Books, 2002.

———. *Goddess Bless!* Boston, MA: Red Wheel, 2002.

———. *Love, Sex, and Magic*. New York: Citadel Press, 1999.

———. *The Pocket Guide to Celtic Spirituality*. Freedom, CA: Crossing Press, 1998.

———. *The Pocket Guide to Crystals and Gemstones*. Freedom, CA: Crossing Press, 1998.

———. *The Book of Reincarnation*. Hauppauge, NY: Barron's, 2002.

Knight, Sirona, et al. *The Shapeshifter Tarot*. St. Paul, MN: Llewellyn Publications, 1998.

Krippner, Stanley, ed. *Dreamtime and Dreamwork*. Los Angeles: Jeremy Tarcher, 1990.

LaBerge, Stephen. *Lucid Dreaming*. New York: Ballantine Books, 1986.

Lambert, Mary. *Color Harmony for Better Living*. New York: Sterling Publishing Company, 2002.

Leach, Maria, ed. *Standard Dictionary of Folklore, Mythology, and Legend*. New York: Funk & Wagnall's Company, 1950.

Linn, Denise. *The Secret Language of Signs*. New York: Ballantine Book, 1996.

Long, Jim. *Making Herbal Dream Pillows*. Pownal, VT: Storey Books, 1998.

Melbourne, David F., and Keith Hearne. *Dream Interpretation*. London: Blandford, 1997.

Mellick, Jill. *The Natural Artistry of Dreams*. Berkeley, CA: Conari Press, 1996.

Miller, Gustavus Hindman. *10,000 Dreams Interpreted*. New York: Rand McNally & Company, 1986.

Mindell, Arnold. *River's Way*. New York: Penguin Books, 1985.

Moon, Janell. *Stirring the Waters*. Boston, MA: Journey Editions, 2001.

Oman, Maggie, ed. *Prayers for Healing*. Berkeley, CA: Conari Press, 1997.

Perkins, John. *The Stress-Free Habit*. Rochester, VT: Healing Arts Press, 1989.

Rector-Page, Linda. *Healthy Healing*. Sonona, CA: Healthy Healing Publications, 1992.

Reed, Henry. *Dream Incubation*. Journal of Humanistic Psychology, Vol. 16, No. 4, 1976.

Sams, Jamie, and David Carson. *Medicine Cards*. Santa Fe, NM: Bear and Company, 1998.

Schiller, David, and Carol Schiller. *Aromatherapy Basics*. New York: Sterling Publishing Company, 1998.

Scully, Nicki. *Power Animal Meditations*. Rochester, VT: Bear & Company, 2001.

Shapiro, Debbie. *Your Body Speaks Your Mind*. Freedom, CA: Crossing Press, 1997.

Shapiro, Debbie, and Eddie Shapiro. *Peace Within the Stillness*. Freedom, CA: Crossing Press, 1998.

Shumsky, Susan. *Exploring Meditation*. Franklin Lakes, NJ: New Page Books, 2002.

Siblerud, Robert. *The Science of the Soul*. Wellington, CO: Sacred Science Publications, 2000.

Simpson, Liz. *The Healing Energies of Earth*. Boston, MA: Journey Editions, 2000.

Skafte, Dianne. *Listening to the Oracle.* New York: HarperSanFrancisco, 1997.

Tanner, Wilda. *The Mystical Magical Marvelous World of Dreams.* Tehlequah, OK: Sparrow Hawk Press, 1988.

Tart, Charles. *Altered States of Consciousness.* New York: John Wiley, 1969.

Taub, Edward. *Seven Steps to Self-Healing.* New York: DK Publishing, Inc., 1996.

Telesco, Patricia. *FutureTelling.* Freedom, CA: Crossing Press, 1998.

Tolle, Eckhart. *Practicing the Power of Now.* Novato, CA: New World Library, 1999.

Ullman, Montague, Stanley Krippner, and Alan Vaughan. *Dream Telepathy.* Jefferson, NC: McFarland, 1989.

Van De Castle, Robert. *Our Dreaming Mind.* London: Aquarian Press, 1994.

Vollmar, Klaus. *The Little Giant Encyclopedia of Dream Symbols.* New York: Sterling Publishing Company, Inc., 1997.

Wesselman, Hank. *Medicinemaker: Mystic Encounter on the Shaman's Path.* New York: Bantam Books, 1998.

Winsor, Janice. *Opening the Dream Door.* Carmel, CA: Merrill-West Publishing, 1998.

Worwood, Valerie. *The Complete Book of Essential Oils and Aromatherapy.* New York: New World Library, 1995.

Index

G

H

I–J

K–L

M–N

O

P–Q

R

T–U–V

W–X–Y–Z